ORDER FROM CHAOS

Responding to traumatic events

Marion Gibson

Consultant editor: Jo Campling

Third edition

BASW

BRITISH ASSOCIATION
OF SOCIAL WORKERS

First published in 1991 by Venture Press, 16 Kent Street, Birmingham B5 6RD

This paperback edition published in Great Britain in January 2006 by

The Policy Press
University of Bristol
Fourth Floor
Beacon House
Queen's Road
Bristol BS8 1QU
UK

Tel +44 (0)117 331 4054
Fax +44 (0)117 331 4093
e-mail tpp-info@bristol.ac.uk
www.policypress.org.uk

© Marion Gibson 2006

British Library Cataloguing in Publication Data
A catalogue record for this book is available from the British Library.

Library of Congress Cataloging-in-Publication Data
A catalog record for this book has been requested.

ISBN-10 1 86134 697 2 paperback
ISBN-13 978 1 86134 697 1

A hardcover version of this book is also available.

Cover design by Qube Design Associates, Bristol.
Printed and bound in Great Britain by Hobbs the Printers, Southampton.

Dedicated to the past, the present and the future…

THE PAST

To the memory of my husband Tom,
who taught me to live one day at a time,
and to live each day as if it was my last.

THE PRESENT

To Paul and Gayle,
who provide me with constant love and support.

THE FUTURE

To my precious grandsons Leon and Max,
who are the future,
with my hope that they will grow up in a more peaceful world,
and see the challenges of life as opportunities.

Contents

List of tables and figures

Tables

Figures

Foreword

The trouble with disasters is that they are just too big. Whether person-made or due to 'Acts of God', we are all dwarfed by them. Suddenly, without hindrance, the ordered course of our existence is laid to waste, a great swathe is cut through places, people and the communities they serve.

The effects spread out like ripples far beyond the point of impact. Victims, injured, survivors, bereaved families, onlookers, friends and neighbours, helpers and professional caregivers, and whole communities are caught up in the turmoil of events whose effects will be felt by generations yet unborn. Disasters are the stuff of history and nightmares. Life, in their vicinity, will never be the same again.

Faced with the massive human misery that is the inevitable consequence of a disaster, we can be forgiven if we recoil. However much we care, there is so little we can do that we are tempted to do nothing at all; we back away shocked and appalled. How can we possibly cope with all the chaos that has been unleashed?

Disasters cause some to lose and others to use their heads. One is reminded of the notice which was distributed in London during the *blitzkrieg* – 'If an incendiary bomb falls near you, don't lose your head, put it in a bucket and cover it with sand.' Marion Gibson has provided us with a bucket of sand with which we can dampen down the flames of disaster. Thus armed, we have less need to panic or to hide.

The book enables us to 'partialise' the chaos into bite-sized chunks that ordinary mortals can digest. With a knowledge that is based on personal experience, common sense and wide reading, Marion Gibson outlines the plans, the training and the techniques that can be used by members of the caring professions and by volunteer counsellors to bring order out of chaos, and to increase the probability that the changes that are inevitable in the aftermath, instead of adding to the damage, will lead to personal, social and spiritual growth. She accomplishes this in a matter-of-fact way that plays down rather than inflates the sentiment, the drama, which attracts journalists, onlookers and many helpers to a disaster area and can easily produce an unbalanced and emotion-driven response.

The concepts of helping following a major disaster are integrated into a discussion on the everyday personal disasters faced by many people. This discussion widens the appeal of the book and brings home its relevance to the common disasters that receive less public attention than the larger-scale but rarer ones.

Since the second edition of this book was published, the author has added to her knowledge of disasters, the result of her work in the wake of 9/11, the Boxing Day tsunami in the Indian Ocean and, most recent, the terrorist bombs in London on 7 July 2005. These experiences have enabled her research into the training needs of responders to develop a modular programme, which can be adapted for professional groups, voluntary organisations, emergency services, management and family members of those who may be traumatised by their work.

Colin Murray Parkes, MD FRCPsych.

Preface

Ted

Ted, the elderly man sitting in the corner of the day room in the geriatric unit, stared at the television. The early afternoon programme was a cowboy film. The patients, who were able to follow the story, cheered as the cavalry rushed to the aid of those trapped in the besieged fort. The battle raged and then there was a loud explosion. At this point, Ted became agitated and curled up into the foetal position covering his head with his hands and moaning in a distressed way. Any attempts to comfort him were roughly rebuffed as an intrusion into his distressed world. Further approaches made his rejection more forceful and he hit out. He was helped to his bed and given sedation to calm his agitation. His eyes appeared to express intense fear as he scanned his frightening world, a world to which he had been transported by the sound of the explosion. One of his fellow patients watched with a mixture of curiosity and sympathy, and commented 'shellshock'.

Ted's tortured face relaxed with the sedation, and his eyes became less furtive. What visions of the hell had he recaptured from his war experiences as a young soldier? The film had prompted his journey back to his memories through the stimuli of sound. How many years had it been since he had stood on the fields of France and watched his friends being blown to pieces by the impact of a bomb? How many times had reminders of such events caused him to relive his nightmares? Ted came from an era where such reactions were common in returning soldiers, and accepted by family and friends as an inevitable consequence of their experiences.

Michael

In 1979, in the Royal Victoria Hospital, Belfast, a young man was transferred into the orthopaedic ward from the intensive care unit. Six days earlier, he had been caught by a terrorist bomb as he walked into the bus station. As the weeks went by, his multiple fractures began to heal and he began to walk again as the result of a painful rehabilitation process. He remained reluctant to talk about his experiences. It was as if he needed to reserve all his strength to make his body whole again. He wanted to remain brave for his wife and young children.

Following his discharge, I arranged to visit him at home. The couple appeared enthusiastic about this visit. They explained that the 'homecoming' had been more difficult than they had imagined. When Michael's wife left the room, he quietly began to tell of his current mental distress, which had developed since he had left the safety of the hospital 'cocoon'. Michael said that his sleepless nights were haunted by his memories. The full psychological and physical impact of the explosion was now very acute as he considered his future as a disabled person.

Michael needed to talk of the day the bomb had shattered his life and that of his family. He recalled that he had been anxious to get home, as it was the day of his son's second birthday. He wanted to help his pregnant wife get ready for the party. Then the bomb exploded. As he recalled the events that followed in vivid detail, his body stiffened, he began to sweat and his eyes took on the frightened look that had been observed in Ted. His psychological pain was obvious. He described how intrusive and distressing his memories had become. His physical pain seemed to be diminished in the midst of his mental anguish. Michael was later diagnosed as having Post-Traumatic Stress Disorder (PTSD). Psychiatric intervention and social work support aided his psychological recovery, which had to be accomplished in parallel with his physical rehabilitation.

Mary

Mary was an experienced accident and emergency nurse. She found it difficult to explain why she had sought counselling help. She had been involved with many traumatic incidents over the years and she had always coped. Her voice became difficult to hear as she sobbed out details of her current distress. She had not been sleeping; she was haunted by the memories of a fatal accident that had involved a young baby. Her husband had become intolerant of her moods and her irritability with her children. He had told her to 'pull yourself together or get out of that job'. Both these solutions were unacceptable to her. If she could 'pull herself together', she would ... she had not chosen this hell. She loved her job, and had trained hard to get to her present level of competency. She needed support to discuss her reactions and develop strategies to combat the distress caused by the associated symptoms. Mary needed reassurance that it was the incident that was abnormal, not her. She remained at work throughout the counselling process. In time, Mary was able to integrate her memories of that fatal road crash into her life and future practice in such a way that they no longer presented a threat to her physical or psychosocial well-being. She became more relaxed at home as she developed ways of coping with the psychosocial impact of her work.

Arthur

Arthur was a driving instructor with a bus company. Several weeks prior to his appointment, he had witnessed a sectarian murder. He had been determined to return to work as soon as possible after the incident and with the support of his manager had returned within two days. Although he had continued with his usual work schedule, trainee drivers and colleagues had reported that he was 'detached and quiet, not able to concentrate and irritable at times'. Arthur had been prescribed medication to alleviate his sleep disturbance and intrusive dreams. When Arthur's manager had initiated the referral to Staffcare (an organisation which provides support and training to employers, and to employees who are experiencing stress), he had sought guidance on how he and his colleagues could provide Arthur with appropriate support through this difficult period.

Arthur presented as very apprehensive about counselling. He quickly established that he had attended the session 'to please the boss'. Arthur felt that he was letting himself and his company down by his inability 'to get back to normal'. He commented that he knew there was nothing anyone could do to help and that he felt his recovery was totally his own responsibility.

Arthur gradually began to talk of the incident and the true impact that it was having on his life. He described sleep disturbances, visual flashbacks, lack of concentration and inability to function as a father and a husband. He was aware that his reactions meant that he was withdrawing from social contact and becoming uncharacteristically introverted in his outlook and behaviour. He had increased his intake of alcohol considerably in an attempt to escape his thoughts. Support from his wife was rebuffed and her efforts to make him 'normal' again were making him angry.

Arthur became distressed as he talked about his wife and children who had always been the focus of his life. Tears began to flow and he apologised profusely for such a display 'of weakness'. He had never wept in the presence of anyone before, but he admitted that he had been weeping as he took many lonely walks since the incident. He then stated that there had been times when his fear of going mad, coupled with his unusual pattern of behaviour, had produced suicidal thoughts.

The outpouring of emotion exhausted his physical resources. A break was taken to allow him to reflect and recover some of his composure. While coffee was being prepared, I gave Arthur a copy of a leaflet, which outlined the normal response which may be experienced after a traumatic incident. At first he read it in a disinterested way as he slumped in the chair. Suddenly he sat up and said with enthusiasm:

> That's a description of me…it could have been written about me…Does this mean that other people can feel like I do?…Does this mean that I am not going mad?…Can I show this to my wife?…I was terrified to tell anyone how bad I was feeling in case they confirmed that I was going mad…

His reactions to the leaflet tumbled out as rapidly as his painful disclosures. He then became very angry: 'Why the hell didn't anyone tell me this before … why had I to suffer in silence so long?'

Shellshock, trauma reactions, Post-Traumatic Stress Disorder, are some of the words used to encompass a complicated constellation of symptoms which engulf many of those who have experienced severe trauma in their lives. The trauma can result from a personal incident, such as Arthur had experienced, or major disaster, which has a psychosocial impact on many lives, as in the case of Ted. As a result of such incidents, chaos is caused in both physical and psychological terms. The symptoms which may occur can intrude on all aspects of daily living.

The traumatic incidents that had affected Ted, Michael, Mary and Arthur were very different and spanned some 60 years. The common feature was the psychosocial impact of their traumatic memories. They could all be classed as 'victims' of experiences that they could not avoid. To become a 'survivor' of such events, each of them needed to understand their reactions and to be given support to develop appropriate coping strategies for the future. They had to seek ways of bringing order out of their cognitive chaos.

During the 60 years covered by the traumatic experiences identified, there has been growing research into such reactions. Unfortunately, this has not been matched by research into appropriate support for people who have been traumatised. The following chapters seek to add to this knowledge base in the hope that more people are not left 'to suffer in silence'.

Marion Gibson, October 2005

Acknowledgements

This book has been produced with the help and support of many colleagues from a variety of countries. This acknowledgement is to thank them all for their contributions. Some individuals are identified for their specialist skills which made the production of the book possible:

Jo Campling, Consultant Editor, for commissioning the original book in 1991 and for her continued trust in the author to produce and develop the subsequent editions.

Michele McMaster, Lecturer in Computing and Administration, for her infinite patience, encouragement and skills in converting the typed manuscript into production standards.

David McCabe, South and East Belfast Health and Social Services Trust, for his artistic talent in the production of the illustrative diagrams.

A special acknowledgement must be made to all those individuals affected by disaster who have trusted me to share their distress and whose courage has inspired me to continue in this work.

Notes on the author

Dr Marion Gibson PhD, MSSc, DipSW, CQSW and Advanced Dip in Psychological Trauma Management. Accredited Counsellor and Trainer

Marion Gibson started her career as a nurse. Following marriage she worked alongside her husband in community work in Liverpool and Belfast. This included work within traumatised communities during the 'Troubles' in Northern Ireland (NI). Following the premature death of her husband she trained as a social worker and has worked in both hospital and community settings. As part of her social work training she did a residential placement in a psychiatric hospital in Indianapolis (US) that was pioneering work with Vietnam veterans. This experience enhanced her interest in the psychosocial impact of trauma on people especially in the NI context. Trauma remained central to all her professional work and in 1989 she was one of the two social workers from NI sent to assist colleagues in the East Midlands area of England following the air disaster that involved many families from NI. Following this experience she was involved in the setting up of Crisis Support Teams in NI, and was a member of the national Disasters Working Party, which produced the report 'Disasters – planning for a caring response' in 1991. The first edition of 'Order from Chaos – responding to traumatic events' was published by Venture Press in 1991, with the second edition in 1998. She has also contributed to other books and published several journal articles on trauma related subjects.

Her special interest in the psychosocial impact of traumatic incidents on people has led to the opportunity of lecturing worldwide in such places as the Philippines, Poland, Africa, Australia, India, Singapore, Hong Kong, the USA and South America. In May 2005 Marion went to Belarus, at the invitation of the charity Leaves of Hope, to offer training to medical, nursing, social work and psychology staff involved in dealing with trauma, loss and grief inherent in the care of children with disabilities and the placement of abandoned babies.

Marion completed her doctorate in 2000 following extensive research into the impact on the personal and professional lives of ambulance personnel, social workers, nurses and clergy who helped those affected in the aftermath of the Kegworth air disaster and a terrorist bombing in NI. This research highlighted the pervasive nature of the psychological stress that can result, not only from providing a response to a major disaster, but also from repeated exposure to multiple smaller incidents. As a result of this research she designed a training programme to help organisations and staff to cope with the impact of trauma.

She was one of the two experts chosen to assist Sir Kenneth Bloomfield in his production of a report into the efficacy of the NI Criminal Injuries Compensation Scheme (2002), which involved many interviews with victims of terrorism. As a result of this work she was asked to become one of the members of the Compensation Advice Committee established by the Irish Government following the apology by the Taoiseach to those who as children had suffered abuse while in residential institutions under state supervision. This work involved research into the legal implications and interviewing many adult survivors to hear their experiences. The findings of this Committee led to the publication of the report 'Towards redress and recovery' (2002) and the establishing of the Redress Board to administer the compensation payments.

Marion Gibson is Consultant Director of Staffcare, which was established 12 years ago to assist organisations with 'their duty to care' for their employees in terms of their psychological well-being. Under contract, individual employees have access to a 24-hour freephone number to gain support, advice and access to confidential individual counselling. The service operates under the auspices of South and East Belfast Health and Social Services Trust in Northern Ireland but is totally self-funding. From small beginnings, Staffcare has now developed into an all-Ireland service that provides confidential counselling, critical incident stress management, training, consultancy and mediation services to 102 organisations in the statutory, private and voluntary sectors. This is achieved through a network of 206 qualified counsellors who respond to referrals in their own geographical area. Staffcare also undertakes project and consultancy work throughout Great Britain.

Marion was deployed to Thailand in February 2005, to work under the auspices of the British Red Cross in collaboration with the Foreign and Commonwealth Office, in the aftermath of the Asian tsunami. As a result of this work and of her pioneering work in this specialist field, her alma mater, Queens University of Belfast, honoured her with the 'Graduate of the Year 2005' award in June 2005 for promoting the ideals of the university in service to others within Ireland and beyond.

In her role as an accredited counsellor and trainer she has provided training for many diverse organisations from the universities, commercial organisations, voluntary organisations, security and emergency services and the International Christian Maritime Association to the health and local authority staff on the provision of a psychosocial response to any crisis situation. She was providing training in the headquarters of the London Resilience Team when the attacks by suicide bombers occurred on 7 July 2005. Theory was quickly changed into practice as support was provided to the team responsible for the initial response, the establishing of the support centre and the mortuary.

ONE

Order from chaos

Many words are used to refer to incidents that cause chaos in people's lives. Disaster, traumatic event, emergency, critical incident and crisis situation are but a few of the terms utilised. Common to all these terms is the fact that something has happened suddenly and, as a result, the ordered course of normal life has been changed.

This book was written in the aftermath of the greatest disaster that our world had experienced to date. (During the preparation of this book for publication, even the unimaginable statistics of the human tragedy recorded in the aftermath of the tsunami have been surpassed following the earthquake in Pakistan and Kashmir, with over 74,000 dead, 500,000 injured and 3.3 million people left homeless.) On 26 December 2004 at 7.58am (local Indonesian time), an earthquake began deep in the Indian Ocean creating a quake that was so powerful that it was recorded worldwide. The movement of the ocean bed created what geologists describe as a tsunami. The first wave, racing at a speed of 500mph, gathered water volume as it moved towards the land. The primary wave was followed by a second or return wave. Behind each primary wave lay a vicious trough, which was capable of sucking people and debris hit by the primary wave back out to sea. Subsequent waves brought further death and injury as this debris and human bodies were thrown back on to the land.

Figure 1.1 shows the geographical spread of the tsunami. The concept

Figure 1.1: Geographical spread of Asian tsunami

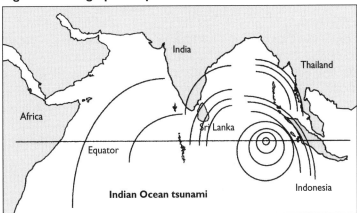

of the waves radiating from the epicentre reminds us of the numbers of people who were affected by this disaster. Within 20 minutes of the earthquake, the tsunami hit the low-lying market town of Band Aceh, Sumatra. Thousands of people died, all communications were destroyed and the area devastated. Within 80 minutes of the initial earthquake, the powerful waves swept into Thailand's coastal towns and local inhabitants and tourists lost their lives.

Witnesses in Sri Lanka were to describe how, 100 minutes later, they had noticed the noise of birds vacating the trees and flying inland. The sea appeared to rush away from the beaches exposing hundreds of yards of shingle beaches prior to the impact of the tsunami. The impact of the waves devastated coastal towns such as Gall. In spite of travelling hundreds of miles, the power of the tsunami was not diminished as it swept buildings from their foundations and toppled passenger trains off the tracks. The ruthless advance of the tsunami and the accompanying aftershock impact rushed towards the coastlines of India and the Maldives. Offshore islands in its path were particularly vulnerable, as some had been reduced to a few feet below sea level as a result of the initial movement of the seabed.

The loss of human life was so massive that the figures were impossible to record accurately, but it is estimated that over 300,000 died, many more thousands were injured, with millions rendered homeless and destitute. Early attempts at rescue and support appeared impotent against incalculable demands. Chaos predominated as survivors struggled to help each other and emergency services sought to save lives, to minimise further injuries and to control any potential for disease. Governments attempted to use devastated communication systems to assess need against an environment of total destruction in terms of all normal helping structures and the personnel involved. Chaos prevailed as individuals and organisational structures struggled to bring some order to the situation.

Chaos, according to the *Oxford English Dictionary*, is a state of confusion and disorder. These two words, 'confusion' and 'disorder', describe the psychological and practical problems experienced by people who have been subjected to a traumatic event. When we analyse what happens to people who are affected by a major disaster, these words are very applicable – there is confusion in their psychosocial reaction and disorder in their normal equilibrium of life. While the physical chaos caused by the disaster is observable, the level of human distress is often hidden following the initial outpouring of grief and distress. The physical injuries are also observable but many people, including those who seek to help, will carry invisible psychological scars as a result of their experiences.

In the period following a disaster, whether caused by a natural phenomenon such as a tsunami or person-made such as the terrorist attack on the United States on 11 September 2001, those affected are psychologically shocked and confused. They experience cognitive chaos as a result of information overload. This can result in feelings of numbness and a sense of unreality. Those who normally cope discover that they cannot cope and fear whether they will ever be able to cope again. They seek in the hours, days and weeks that follow to return to some order in their chaotic psychological state.

Life events such as the death of a family member, the diagnosis of a terminal or disabling illness, an assault or a road traffic accident can be described as a personal disaster or crisis, and those affected may also experience psychological confusion. When considering crisis situations in the workplace environment, such as a personal attack, sudden unemployment and the stress caused by bullying or harassment, psychological confusion can also occur here. The person affected has to cope with changed circumstances and to bring order out of their psychological reactions that will enable them to function adequately. It is important when assessing the level of confusion and disorder that results from a crisis that the situation is viewed from the perspective of the person affected and not from that of the observer. What constitutes a personal disaster for some people may be coped with routinely by others. The factors that make the difference between such reactions are complex and multiple and include previous life experiences, personality traits and the efficacy of social supports.

This book is about the psychosocial needs of those experiencing the results of a personal or major disaster that has caused chaos and disorder in their lives. The book aims to guide those who may be part of the helping process to make their interventions more effective by promoting a greater understanding of the psychological impact of trauma. The generic term 'responder' is used throughout the book to describe all those who are involved in the helping process. The use of the generic term does not diminish the role of the professional with specialist skills.

All responders and responding agencies need to be reminded of the needs of the whole person. Many organisations have emergency plans that are predominantly concerned with practical arrangements, as the psychosocial needs of people are not always recognised. There is a need to make plans for 'people provision' in all planned methods of intervention. After a disaster, buildings and communication networks

Figure 1.2: Time as a continuum associated with a crisis

have to be repaired and rebuilt but so does the psychological well-being of people.

The chapters of the book identify needs, provide theoretical perspectives, use case material and include prescriptive guidelines for responders. These guidelines may be adapted to meet the specific demands with which the responder is confronted.

Figure 1.2 above is used throughout the book to denote the passage of time. The timescale is not specific but the diagram may be used as a visual framework to give more clarity to various processes that take place. The line should be viewed as a continuum. The word 'crisis' is used to cover such terms as 'traumatic event', 'personal tragedy' or 'disaster'. The continuum can be used in relation to the people affected and also to the response provided by organisations.

The pre-crisis period

The pre-crisis period can mean hours or years but represents events that took place prior to the crisis. When dealing with a person who has experienced a personal disaster, consideration of this period will enable the responder to assess such dimensions as their life experience and social status in the home or work environment. Such knowledge will assist the responder in understanding the significance of the crisis for the person involved.

In the context of a major disaster, knowledge of pre-crisis events may be significant in the post-crisis reactions that will be experienced. Blame may be focused on whether warnings were given, or not given, and how organisations were, or were not, able to react in such circumstances. Various inquiry reports following the terrorist attacks on the Twin Towers of the World Trade Centre in New York and the Pentagon Building in Washington on 11 September 2001 (referred to as 9/11) gave a focus for the anger of those who had been bereaved or injured, when certain flaws were exposed in the pre-disaster intelligence collection (see case study 8, p 27).

Training, which includes the definition and development of inter-organisational roles, is an important consideration in the pre-crisis stage. Every effort should be made to promote understanding and collaborative planning between organisations required to work together at the time of a disaster. The quality of the post-crisis response is dependent on such preparatory work.

The immediate post-crisis period

This period can represent a period of hours or days after the event. These timescales cannot be specific. In the case of a major disaster, the immediate post-crisis stage represents the period of time from impact to when the emergency services gain control or leave the site. This is the period when the outcomes of the event are not known and when additional stress is caused by the lack of information. Information is difficult to access; uncertainty and rumour abound. Information may bring relief to some of the anxiety being experienced but it can also bring confirmation of the painful reality of the situation. It is during this period that those rescued are being classed as deceased or survivor. Some relatives become 'the bereaved' and may have to face the task of identifying the deceased.

From an organisational perspective, major incident plans are activated and procedures, which have been rehearsed, are enacted in the reality of the situation that presents. In the case of a personal disaster, this period can represent the time when family support is being organised. It can be a period of time when those most closely affected can feel very isolated, alone and frightened.

The short-term post-crisis period

This period may overlap with the immediate post-crisis period. In a major disaster, it is the period when the full facts of the event are emerging and the need for support is being identified. Management structures within the organisation involved in the response need to assess the need to 'stand down' the initial responders and plan for the longer-term response. In all types of crisis, provision of a basic practical nature may be the most appropriate at this stage.

The long-term post-crisis period

It is difficult in a major or personal disaster to define the period classed as the long-term post-crisis period. It is longer than the short-term period and can represent weeks, months or years. This period can represent the period of time when rehabilitation, in physical and psychological terms, takes place. The period of two years post-crisis has emerged as the most appropriate in terms of planning psychosocial support services following major disasters.

Disasters are not all negative in their outcome. People and communities may be changed by the event in a positive way so that the event for them is a period of growth. Out of the chaos a new order emerges. This process of growth is diagrammatically represented in Figure 1.3. The horror of the Asian tsunami (2004) was quickly the subject of media attention. The incomprehensible scale of the devastation almost stunned those not affected into a collective sense of impotence. Then organisations and communities began to gather practical help in the form of money or essential equipment to be sent to the affected areas. The financial assistance gathered by communities quickly became greater than support promised by governments. Diversity of political, ethnic and religious origins was forgotten in the face of such universal altruism. A similar response was often observed in Northern Ireland when the personal disaster of a sectarian murder took place. As a responder, one often anticipated a period of revenge seeking with associated reactions of anger and bitterness. More commonly, we encountered grieving relatives who cried out from

Figure 1.3: The trauma cycle: the opportunity for growth

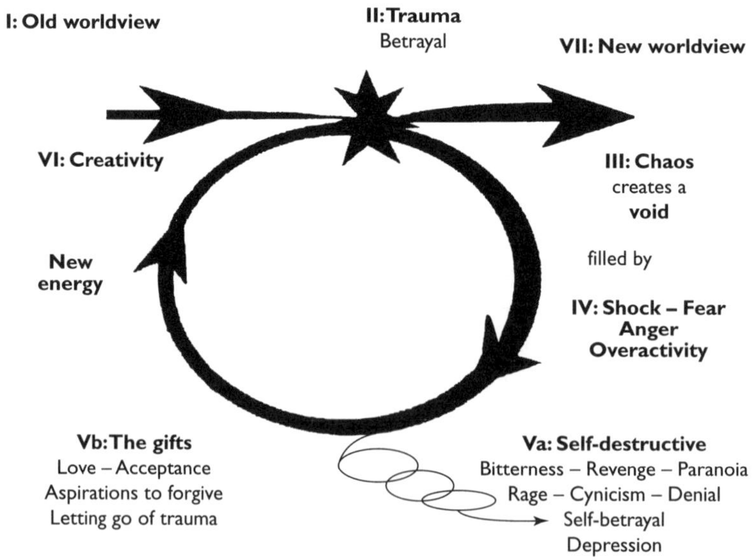

Source: Capewell (1996, p 3)

their personal pain to ask that no retaliation would be visited on another family who would then have to suffer similar pain and loss. The communion of acute pain often broke down the traditional barriers of mistrust and fear.

In Figure 1.3, Elizabeth Capewell identifies the process that occurs for individuals and organisations in the aftermath of a major disaster. It can also be used to describe the 'journey' that individuals have to take in their rehabilitation from the crisis that has affected their future. Pre-crisis in this model is seen as stage I. Things that were secure in the 'old world' have become insecure, coping mechanisms previously used successfully have become inadequate to meet new demands. The chaos is described as a 'void' that may be filled with shock, fear, anger and overactivity. Those going through the trauma cycle are then faced with self-destructive choices or working towards a creative outcome. Different terms may be used to describe these stages in other models, but this trauma cycle gives a sense of progress towards hope in the future. Creative learning can result from the destruction of disaster. For the responders, previous training and skills need to be adapted to meet new challenges. The lessons learned can be used in other areas of practice.

The families bereaved in the shooting tragedy at the Dunblane Primary School in Scotland (1996) found a purposeful outlet for their distress through the 'Snowdrop Campaign' to ban the possession of handguns. The desire to bring about change which may prevent a similar personal or community disaster, through legislative reform or changes in practice, can be a creative and positive outcome for those who experience feelings of helplessness at such times. This positive use of negative experiences can aid recovery and adaptation to changed futures.

This book outlines lessons learned by experience that can be used by responders and organisations in providing a caring response in the aftermath of traumatic events. It is the book that I would have needed when I was called on to respond to the Kegworth air disaster in 1989 (see case study 7, p 23). While my years of experience in responding to the needs of people facing trauma in their individual lives were relevant, this disaster presented special demands. The chaos of the situation produced feelings of inadequacy and incompetence as I struggled to cope with the volume and complexity of need presented. 'Getting on with the task', by adapting existing skills, brought a sense of order to the response. The creative learning gained from the experience of Kegworth and from trauma work in Northern Ireland was the basis for the creation of Staffcare. Staffcare is an organisation within South and East Belfast Health and Social Services Trust, which provides, under contract, a 24-hour confidential Careline, individual confidential counselling, critical incident stress management, mediation, consultancy and training to organisations throughout Ireland and Great Britain. The work of Staffcare is designed to assist organisations and their employees, who are experiencing the 'chaos' of stress, to regain 'order' in their organisational or personal psychosocial well-being. Staffcare is also an example of a positive creation built from the experience of responding to the chaos of traumatic incidents. The motto of Staffcare is 'There when you need us'.

Whether my work has involved strategic planning, training crisis response workers in a variety of geographical locations, providing support to those people injured and bereaved in the Asian tsunami or support to individuals facing stress in their lives, the concepts identified in this book have remained valid.

TWO

Disasters

In recent years we seem to have heard of many disasters. Advances in global media communication have resulted in almost instantaneous news of worldwide disasters. Television pictures of the school hostage situation in Beslan on 1 September 2004 entered our homes making us feel part of the anguish experienced by those who had to wait and watch. The subsequent shootings and the bomb explosion shocked and saddened all who could observe the destruction of buildings and so many lives. While technology improves communication, it was the failure of technology that caused the Chernobyl nuclear reactor accident (1986), which resulted in nuclear fallout on a wide geographical area. The impact of this type of incident may have long-term outcomes in terms of environmental damage or birth deformities caused by trans-generational gene damage. Failure of advanced technology can also be the cause of some of the transport tragedies. Even the planning of the major terrorist attacks on the United States on 11 September 2001, London on 7 July 2005 and the production of the terrorist bomb placed on the Pan Am flight that blew up over Lockerbie just before Christmas 1988 were the result of increased technical expertise as well as 'man's inhumanity to man' (in the words of Robert Burns).

Any statement concerning an increase in the occurrence of disasters must recognise that life in the 21st century provides more opportunities for technical or person-made disasters. The way that we use our world may contribute to environmental disasters in the future.

The word 'disaster' comes from the Latin word 'astrum' meaning star. From this we can see that disasters have long been thought of as 'ill-starred', denoting magical or luck elements that could be attributed to heavenly forces. Primitive human beings felt that disasters in their world were punishments from the gods. In this way, humans sought to make sense of and to rationalise traumatic events that were beyond their control.

There are many definitions of disaster to be found in the literature. The *Oxford English Dictionary* defines it as 'anything ruinous or distressing that befalls; a sudden or great misfortune or mishap; a calamity'. Beverley Raphael (1986) describes it as 'overwhelming events and circumstances that test the adaptational responses of community or individual beyond their capability, and lead, at least temporarily, to massive disruption of function for community or individual'. Raphael's definition reminds us of the concept of a personal disaster. While much of the research on the subject of disaster has centred on major incidents, this book seeks to include the dimension of personal disaster which can produce significant psychosocial reactions for the individual.

Disasters may occur suddenly or have a progressive onset as in the case of drought or famine. In the case of some major disasters, warnings of impending danger may have been issued by the authorities and ignored by the listener. Issuing warnings of hurricane Katrina to the population of the Mississippi area of the Gulf of Mexico resulted in mass evacuations from the area to designated places of safety. The warnings were not matched by the practical preparations made by the emergency services. This was evidenced in the scenes of chaos in the devastated city of New Orleans. It is noted that better practical plans were coupled to the warnings of hurricane Rita, which followed weeks after the devastation caused by Katrina. Hurricane warnings may allow the authorities to alert the population to take precautions. Inaccurate information contained in such warnings, however, can become the focus of great anger and post-disaster investigations. If warnings are issued too frequently about minor events, subsequent warnings about major dangers can be ignored.

Where time exists to prepare for the impact of a disaster, human beings are seen to react by wanting to ensure the safety of their family unit or group. Physical closeness and expressions of love and support become important. People may pray to their God for help to preserve themselves. If danger situations have to be faced, strangers can quickly become allies and such bonds often last after the event. This phenomenon is demonstrated when survivors form self-help groups to promote mutual support in the aftermath of a shared traumatic experience.

There are common features to many disasters but they are all unique in their own right. I believe that lessons learned in responding to one traumatic event can aid in the future response to a similar event. The core features that need to be considered are: the ripple effect; the types of individuals affected; and the type of incident.

The ripple effect

When you drop a pebble into a still pond of water the disturbed water ripples out from the point of impact. The wider the spread, the less pronounced the impact. This phenomenon also applies in the case of traumatic incidents. The site of the incident is only the epicentre of those affected, and many others are affected as the impact radiates out with those on the wider 'rings of reaction' being less affected. This concept can help responders to prioritise or triage need (see Figure 2.1, p 24).

The types of individuals affected

The recent report 'Working together to support individuals in an emergency or disaster' (2004) was organised and produced by the British Red Cross in collaboration with non-governmental organisations from the European Union and the European Economic Area (see www.redcross.org.uk). It listed the individuals affected as casualties, survivors, evacuees, relatives and friends, witnesses, emergency services and others responding. For the purposes of this book these are divided into three main categories:

- the bereaved;
- the injured and their relatives; and
- others traumatised, including the responders.

The bereaved

In the immediate post-crisis chaos, it may not be possible for the bereaved to be identified. In a workplace scenario where a manager has a fatal heart attack during the office coffee break, it will be his colleagues who respond and summon an ambulance. Some may even try to resuscitate him until the paramedics arrive. Shocked colleagues stand around aimlessly while they witness the futile attempts by the professionals. In such circumstances, the bereaved can be informed immediately. This is not a major disaster but, for the bereaved family and the colleagues who witnessed the death, it has the same potential to have a psychosocial impact on their lives. Following the Asian tsunami and the 9/11 terrorist attack, thousands were killed but, because of the particular circumstances in both these incidents, it was impossible to find or identify all the deceased. Lists of those missing were compiled from various sources but their category status soon became 'missing, feared dead' as the emergency services' rescue work turned into a recovery operation to collect the bodies or any identifiable remains. Such a situation causes added grief, and indeed legal complications, when no body is found and no death certificate can be issued. Searching can be prolonged and difficult. Responders in such situations must be tolerant and sensitive when dealing with the understandable reactions to this experience of trauma.

When I visited the United States in the wake of 9/11 (2001), I was involved in a workshop with responders who were dealing with the bereaved in New York, Washington and in the airlines involved. A chaplain working with fire fighters asked about the suitability of having a coffin present at a funeral ritual where no body had been found. Several participants felt that a coffin was necessary for the children, some of whom had friends who in similar situations had walked behind the coffin of their parent. My reaction to this question was based on experience of similar situations in Northern Ireland. I felt that children would be better hearing the truth of the situation as part of the total loss they were experiencing. My belief is that children can understand such painful truth if it is explained to them in age-appropriate terms and with loving support. Children need to hear the truth from those whom they trust. Any attempts to alter the reality will be found out in time. The whole truth could become a very painful reality when later in life a child finds out from a 'good' friend or playground confidant. Such a situation will leave the child wondering what other facts that were explained to them were also false. I recommended that where there was no body, the rituals could still include a photograph, a flag, a replica uniform and medals. This type of commemorative ceremony is most important for all concerned. Some of the bereaved may also want to delay any such ceremony because it represents the reality of the loss. Many such cases occurred for thousands of people in the aftermath of the Asian tsunami.

The core concept that is common to the majority of disasters is that they happen to ordinary people when they are doing ordinary things. People travelling to work, people at work, people on holiday, children at school, people enjoying a sporting event – people like you and me. Disasters serve to remind us of our own frailty and vulnerability. In major disasters, people may have to face death and destruction on a scale they have never contemplated before. Personal disasters may also cause major changes in basic family structure. The world becomes a less secure place. The unthinkable may have become a reality forcing a rethink on some basic facts about life itself.

Disasters cause disruption in our usual coping mechanisms that require major adaptations in our behaviour and strategies for living. If an individual responder or organisation is to design strategies for dealing with people in such events, it is necessary to remember that flexibility and sensitivity are essential. While core features seem to occur in disasters, the uniqueness of each situation makes the use of theory a matter of guidance rather than a set of procedures to be adhered to if a satisfactory outcome is to be achieved. Recovery, in a disaster situation, must be viewed with the same element of uniqueness as the event itself. Recovery represents a return to an acceptable level of psychological and physical equilibrium for those involved (see Chapter Six).

The injured and their relatives

In my experience, those who are physically injured appear to get more help and support from relatives, friends and the community than those who carry the invisible scars of psychological damage. A person with a broken leg, struggling to cope with their crutches, will find that people will assist by opening doors for them. If a person rushes towards a door in an agitated state and tries to get out quickly, no such help will be forthcoming. Few will understand that that person has suddenly been reminded of his confinement in a closed space during a fire that had ravaged through his home. The enactment is 'only in his mind'; he should not be acting in such a crazy manner. Anxiety about safety, hyper alertness to noise and an inability to enjoy social interaction are all part of the chaos associated with an acute trauma reaction (see Chapter Three).

Others traumatised

Witnesses who observe emergencies and disasters that affect others can also be traumatised. Their sense of relief that they were not bereaved or injured can be tinged with feelings of guilt. Those who were on annual leave when there was a bank raid in their place of work can be affected with similar feelings, but can also find themselves isolated by colleagues on their return to the bank. Colleagues who talk about their psychosocial reactions may finish their conversation with such comments as 'What would you know anyway? You were not there.'

Following a sectarian assassination attack in a betting shop in Belfast, the Crisis Response Team dealt with survivors and the bereaved in the nearby hospital, with one team being dispatched to the scene itself. An elderly man was seen sitting on a low wall cradling his head in his hands. When approached by one of the responders, the man explained that he had not been directly involved with the incident. He had been walking along the road towards the scene and, when he experienced the sights and sounds of the incident, he had slumped to the ground. This reaction was prompted by his memories of 17 years earlier: he had been in the nearby pub when an explosion had killed three people and he had scrambled out to safety. Reactions can be revived when similar sensory reminders exist. Responders are included in this category and it is important that their psychosocial needs are recognised by their organisations (see Chapter Eight).

Type of incident as an indicator of response required

In any discussion on models of intervention following an emergency or disaster, it is necessary to recognise that intervention will need to vary according to the type of event that has occurred: Berren et al (1980) propose a model whereby disasters can be classified according to five specific criteria:

1. degree of personal impact;
2. type of disaster;
3. potential for reoccurrence;
4. control over future impact; and
5. duration of the disaster.

They discuss the interaction of this five-factor typological classification as a model for determining appropriate intervention services. Their work is an aid to providing a conceptual framework within which we can use the varied literature and research that exist.

For the purpose of this book, the elements are identified to facilitate an operational response. A study of these elements will aid the process of pre-planning, as they should introduce the concept of the multiplicity of factors that could occur in any disaster. Table 2.1 is designed to aid the identification of the elements of cause, location and size.

Personal disaster

The addition of the dimension of 'personal' on this grid reminds us that each day people experience personal disasters. Many people are injured or suffer the onset of a life-threatening illness. To the parents of a child severely injured in a road traffic accident, this is a major disaster. The successful young sportsman who breaks his neck during a match will undergo a complete revision of his lifestyle. We can view these circumstances as a crisis of personal disaster proportions. A care worker in a residential home, who is attacked by a resident who has

Table 2.1: Elements in disaster

	Natural			Technical/person-made		
Personal						
	Small	Medium	Large	Small	Medium	Large
Local						
National						
International						

never been known to be violent, has also to adapt to a new demand on her caring skills. The young widow whose husband has died of cancer will experience the same sense of psychological and physical chaos as she seeks to find new ways to cope in her attempt to bring order from chaos. These people are experiencing a personal disaster where there may be less media attention and less society sympathy, because of the absence of media reminders of the events.

The definition of disaster for them is academic. Their need for help on an individual basis is very real. This need mirrors the needs identified for the larger number of people affected following a major disaster. The cause of personal disasters can also be classed as 'natural' or 'technical/person-made'.

Case study 1: death of a golfer (personal/natural/local)

The death of a golfer on the local golf course when he is struck by lightning is both natural and local in terms of our classification. The family can hope for local support in their bereavement. His name may appear as a national statistic of the storm but there will be little national focus on such an event.

Case study 2: road traffic accident involving death of a child (personal/person-made/local)

The death of a child on a busy road is a personal disaster for the immediate family circle. The death is reported in the local press and as a result a campaign for a pedestrian crossing is begun. The local community is united in its desire to change a situation. The parents find their support from the local general practitioner, church, school and neighbours.

Case study 3: home accident (personal/technical/local)

Three young boys are suffocated when they play hide and seek in a disused freezer that is on their parents' farm. This tragedy is personal and local but the nature of the accident is such that the national media carries the story. The coroner uses the inquest to alert the nation to the need for people to remove locks and lids from disused freezers if such a tragedy is to be avoided in the future.

Identification of the elements of disaster

Disasters can be divided into 'natural' and 'technical/person-made'. The term 'technical/person-made' is used to remind us of the human involvement that is usually present. Some writers have classified the different types as 'acts of God' or 'man-made'. These classifications return our thoughts to those of primitive human beings. Some examples:

Natural	*Technical/person-made*
Tsunami	Transport disasters
Earthquakes	Fire
Cyclones	Collapse of manufactured structures
Storms	Personal attacks
Forest fire	Chemical hazard
Lightning	Acts of terrorism/war

Natural disasters

Natural disasters occur when the powerful forces of nature in our world reach extremes. Earthquakes such as the Asian earthquake (October 2005) can be measured by the Richter scale. Technology has aided their anticipation but little can be done to prevent them, as was demonstrated in the Asian Ocean tsunami (2004). Calls for the urgent installation of an early warning system came shortly after the first waves had dissipated. The loss of over 300,000 lives, with many more thousands of people injured and some national economies shattered, stands as a solemn testimony to the awesome power of nature. We can only aim to limit its damage by making the construction of buildings more appropriate. The design and construction methods of the buildings were key features in the death of over 50,000 people in the Iranian earthquake of 1990.

The paths of cyclones and hurricanes can be predicted and some precautions taken by evacuating or securing buildings, but humans are virtually powerless in their path. It is not difficult to see how human beings previously described such events as the 'wrath of God'. The very structure of their world was shaken and they experienced terror that such power was possible.

The people involved may have been given warnings that can produce an initial sense of denial. This attitude is changed to shock when the warning becomes a reality. The impact of the reality can produce feelings of helplessness. The results of a disaster are usually calculated in terms of loss of life or the number of people injured. The loss of a home can result in a loss of identity through the loss of family memorabilia. People may be evacuated to places where they do not have their normal social networks of support to help them. In such circumstances, responders will initially need to provide practical support. Urgent evacuation from floods can have adverse results such as the abandonment of pets, people being without their usual medication, and the loss of personal effects and legal documents. The loss of 'roots' and community can have long-term effects, effects that are particularly traumatic for elderly people who may never regain the ability to re-establish 'roots' in a new area. These factors need to be considered in any intervention planned.

Natural/technical/person-made disasters

The categories of 'natural' and 'technical/person-made' are often intertwined. The floods that periodically sweep through Bangladesh are seen as the result of heavy rainfall and monsoon conditions. Yet we now know that they are the result of these natural factors and the destruction of the forests of Nepal. The cause of the disaster at Aberfan in Wales (1966) was initially deemed to be the rain, which had made the mountain of coal slag become unstable and engulf the local school. The subsequent enquiry into the event blamed the National Coal Board for the way in which the mound had been constructed and maintained.

The prolonged famine in Ethiopia was the result of both natural and person-made factors. The impact of the crop failure, due to adverse climate conditions, was exacerbated by the forced movement of people as a result of civil strife. Crops were not planted on time and the ones that grew were often left in the ground without people to harvest them. The person-made civil war, which also militates against the relief operations, compounds the psychosocial impact of the drought.

Technical/person-made disasters

Such disasters may result from an act of commission or omission by an individual. An act of commission is where an act is planned and executed to achieve a desired outcome. An act of omission is where the failure to perform an act can result in an unforeseen outcome. Where an individual plans to attack a nurse in an accident and emergency department in order to obtain drugs, this can be described as an act of commission. By failing to carry out a safety check, such as securing a load of produce on a container lorry, a serious accident may occur and this would be an act of omission. A technical failure in the design of the engines on the prestigious Concorde aircraft in 2000 allowed fragments of the damaged tyres to be sucked into the engines causing the fatal crash as it took off in Paris. These incidents are usually not deliberate but are the accidental consequence of an action or inaction.

War can be said to be an act of deliberate person-made disaster and certainly terrorism acts fit into this category. In such disasters, there is usually a person or a system to blame. The anger of those affected is usually centred on this perceived cause. This fact must be considered in the intervention that is planned. Nature or God can be collectively blamed for natural disasters but, in a technical/person-made disaster, the perpetrator may be accessible as a focus for anger and legal processes.

Case study 4: Hillsborough football stadium tragedy (1989) (person-made/local/national/small)

The need to consider the human dynamics of such disasters was clearly seen following the death of 95 Liverpool football fans on the terraces of Hillsborough ground at Sheffield, England (1989). An important match had attracted record crowds to the tightly packed spectator terraces that surrounded the stadium. The playing area was protected from overenthusiastic fans by a high wire fence, which was designed to prevent pitch invasions. This fence was the reason for so many dying and for the numerous injured when fans were crushed against the fence as the crowd surged forward. The media blamed the groundsman who had opened a gate to ease the crowd pressure. The police later became the focus for anger when their crowd management was proved to have been the cause. Yet it was the police who managed the casualty bureau and the mortuary where the bereaved had to cooperate with them, in spite of their growing anger.

Case study 5: bank raid (person-made/local/small)

This discussion on bank raids is equally appropriate when considering other incidents such as raids on a small shopkeeper, snatching money from a street trader or seizing drugs from a chemist's shop. These are all incidents where one or more persons take from another person or persons something of gain for themselves. Such incidents are all too frequent in our society today and can leave the individuals traumatised.

Just before Christmas 2004, the biggest ever theft from a bank took place in the Northern Bank in the centre of Belfast when £28 million was taken during a normal morning's trading. This was achieved through the assistance of two bank officials whose family members were being held hostage during the process to insure their compliance. A bank raid on a smaller branch may result in staff and customers being threatened and terrorised. In the majority of cases, physical injury is avoided by compliance. While such raids take on average eight minutes, the personal impact on those present can take months to diminish. Early crisis intervention from trained responders can assist those affected to overcome their cognitive confusion and to gain control over their painful but understandable traumatic reactions.

Staff involved report feelings of shock, disbelief and terror in the aftermath of such incidents. Delayed reactions can occur when staff realise what might have happened. Police may comment that 'They were only replica guns; you were in no real danger'. Such comments designed to reduce fear can sound irrelevant to those who have had to deal with a perceived death threat. Staff have to cope with feelings of insecurity and the fear of reoccurrence. Some may feel unable to continue to work in the same location.

Case study 6: Piper Alpha oil rig (major disaster/person-made/ large/local, national and international)

The fire on the Piper Alpha oil rig (1988) caused the deaths of 166 men. Local companies were subcontracted to Occidental, an international oil company, to drill under the North Sea. In the immediate post-crisis stage, families were advised to contact Occidental for information, but the company did not hold relevant records of those employed by local firms. This resulted in major international implications for the local community that suffered the greatest number of fatalities. The loss of so many men meant that there were many young widows left to bring up children on their own and few of them had the benefit of life assurance awards. The subcontracting system also caused many legal problems when cases of liability were being settled.

Technical disasters – transport

Disasters associated with transport create some problems that are unique in terms of providing a support network for those affected. Special features of transport disasters are now described.

Location

Such disasters usually occur away from the home location of those affected. Whether such a disaster involves one person or many people, the issue of location means that the usual community support networks are absent. The community where the disaster occurred may well react at the time of the incident, but they will not be involved in the long-term support which will be required.

The agencies responding to the incident may differ in culture and ethnic origin from those involved. Language difficulties can increase the difficulties with local legal systems (see Chapter Eight).

The distance between the disaster site and the home location of those involved may add to the stress on relatives. Relatives may have additional problems in obtaining information. They may experience additional psychological and financial stress when arranging to go to the site of the disaster. Difficulties may occur when dealing with different legal processes, methods of body identification and systems concerned with the repatriation of the injured or deceased. The injured may be in hospitals where the language and treatment methods are alien to their own culture. The lack of appropriate insurance may create problems due to costs for medical treatment and legal fees. Additional expenses will be incurred when returning to the disaster location for the inquests, the enquiry or acts of remembrance.

Lack of group identity

Those involved in a transport disaster are not a homogeneous group. They become a group because of the disaster in which they have been involved. Following the fire in the King's Cross Railway Station in London (1987), those involved were representative of the thousands of people who normally pass through a busy underground station in a major city every day. It is to be noted that one body remained unidentified for several years until new DNA techniques identified a 'missing person' who had abandoned all family contact several years prior to the accident.

Those affected by a transport disaster may have a subgroup identity within the whole such as a group of businessmen returning from a conference. The group may be homogeneous if it has been a flight following a special event such as when the members of the Manchester United football club died together in the Munich air crash (1958). When a group of day shoppers perished in 1973 on a charter flight, 50 of those killed were mothers of young families; others who perished were linked as aunts and grandmothers to these families. This disaster removed from the local society many of the children's main caregivers. In the Estonia ferry disaster (1994), when it is believed that some 999 'souls' died when the ferry capsized in heavy seas en route for Stockholm, many such subgroups were identified, including a group of civic councillors from one region.

Problem of dispersal

Those affected may be dispersed to hospitals in different areas surrounding the location of the disaster. This can mean that family members are split up, which can delay the processing of information. It can also cause additional distress for the injured as they seek information on the location and condition of other family members.

Dispersal factors can also mean that any support network established at the site of the incident may be inaccessible to those from other areas. The home community of these people may remain detached from the pain of those affected and this may be to the detriment of the support offered on a long-term basis.

Responders

Transport disasters may mean that there is a lack of continuity in the responders who provide support for those affected. The immediate responders may have difficulty in knowing the outcome of their work if the people affected are removed to another area quickly. There may be the need to establish a robust system to facilitate the transfer of those affected between different response agencies. At the time of crisis, intense bonds may be established which are crucial to the beginning of the rehabilitation process. The return to the home location may mean that these bonds are broken and other responders are seen to lack credibility, as 'they were not there – how could they understand?' People who require long-term support may not want to reinvest their trust in a new responder, and may also have a sense of grief at the loss of their first significant responder.

This phenomenon was very evident following the Kegworth air disaster (1989), where a large majority of those affected came from Northern Ireland. The support networks established in the East Midlands area were broken when the injured or bereaved returned to their homes. It was noted that patients who had been treated as 'special' in the English hospitals, following the crash, resented being treated as 'ordinary' patients on their return to hospitals in Northern Ireland.

Their perception was that hospitals in Northern Ireland could not understand their complex reactions as they were not involved at the time of the crash.

Disasters at sea

Those rescued from a disaster at sea may be taken to different ports on different rescue ships and this can make the collation of information even more difficult. It can also mean that an element of denial may remain for a prolonged period for relatives who have no news of their loved ones and refuse to accept their death. Even when they are told 'missing, presumed dead', they may still hope that their relative has been taken to some obscure port or hospital and be suffering from amnesia.

Seafarers spend long periods away from home and fellow seafarers can become a surrogate family. This means that when a fatal accident occurs on board a ship it is like the loss of a family member. Grieving for a member of the seafarer's 'seafaring family' can never be shared or fully appreciated by the natural family. Death at sea may mean that a body has to be preserved in a refrigeration unit until it can be disembarked at the next port of call. Seafarers who spend their working lives dependent on the unpredictability of the weather have a natural tendency to adhere to superstitious practices, especially in relation to death. This can create major problems on board when a death occurs. Significant problems can occur where such a death is the result of suicide. These are factors that must be understood and respected by any responder to these circumstances. When I was teaching in the Philippines on the need for psychosocial support to be available for seafarers in mission and welfare agencies on a global basis, I had to address the problem of piracy that was prevalent in the area. Smaller trading vessels may be attacked by armed boarding parties who scale the sides of the vessel. They then take over the ship, its cargo and the seafarers on board. Resistance often warrants being thrown overboard, physical attacks or sexual abuse. Legal papers are changed and flags altered as the journey to port continues. Compliance is assured by threat of death or further painful or degrading treatment. Responding agencies, such as the Seafarers' Missions, often give practical help but are limited in the psychological support they can give due to the nomadic existence of the seafaring lifestyle.

Disasters in the air

Disasters involving aircraft are usually instant and unpredictable, and involve large numbers of people. They certainly will present major problems of dispersal and location. The rescues may be difficult because of their isolation from support services. There may be multinational involvement in terms of passengers that can result in ethnic and cultural problems becoming a major feature for those responding (see Chapter Ten). News of air disasters can cause stress for other prospective travellers. Those who survive an air disaster often need psychiatric or psychological help to enable them to travel by air again.

Case study 7: the Kegworth air crash (1989)

On Sunday evening, 8 January 1989, flight BD 092 took off from Heathrow Airport, London, en route for Belfast, in Northern Ireland. At 8.26pm this British Midland 737-400 Boeing jet crash-landed on the M1 motorway, near Kegworth, while attempting an emergency landing at East Midlands Airport. The airport emergency services had been alerted and, as the crash occurred less than a mile from the end of the runway, they were quickly on the scene and prevented a major fire. The flight was carrying 127 passengers and crew, including one baby, of whom 39 died at the scene; the death toll later rose to 47. The survivors were extracted from the wreckage and taken to the three nearest trauma hospitals, in Nottingham (12 miles), Derby (10 miles) and Leicester (20 miles). No injuries occurred to travellers on the motorway.

By 11.30pm, 76 survivors had arrived at hospitals and a mortuary was set up at the East Midlands Airport. The incident was to be significant in Northern Ireland as 70% of those on board came from the area or had relatives living there.

At the time of the impact, there were relatives waiting for the flight to arrive at Aldergrove Airport in Belfast and relatives were leaving Heathrow Airport having seen passengers off on the flight. Responders were mobilised at the airports and in the hospitals where the injured had been taken. A team of social workers was established at the Thistle Hotel, on the East Midlands Airport complex, where the bereaved were taken to be close to where the mortuary had been set up. Voluntary organisations were also involved in the response.

Figure 2.1 showing the geographical area involved demonstrates how the effects of the incident radiated out from the epicentre.

Figure 2.1: Kegworth: an example of the ripple effect following a disaster

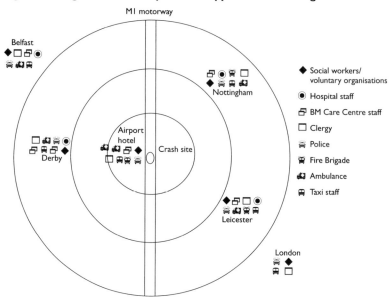

The event was like a pebble dropped into a pool with the rings radiating out wider and wider, representing more people affected and more responders needed to provide psychological and practical support. The newsflash on television that Sunday night was my first introduction to the disaster. Three days later, at the request of the social workers in the East Midlands and the Department of Health and Social Service in Northern Ireland, David Bolton, from Enniskillen Social Services, and I were sent to the East Midlands area. Our task was to assist the social workers there who were involved in the aftermath, and to enable our colleagues in Northern Ireland to set up a network of support in anticipation of the return home of the deceased, the bereaved and the injured.

As we flew into East Midlands Airport over the wreckage of the plane, I remember feeling fear, incompetence, physical nausea and a sense of being overwhelmed by the task. We were not aware of the multiplicity or magnitude of the demands that would be made of us in the next 15 days. We were based in the Thistle Hotel with the bereaved and where the police and staff from the British Midland Airline had established a control centre.

We visited the hospitals and worked alongside our colleagues and other responders. There were over 400 relatives from Northern Ireland throughout the area. We made links with resources in Northern Ireland to facilitate the repatriation of the bodies and support for the bereaved and injured when they returned home. The injured were returned to Northern Ireland when their medical conditions were stabilised sufficiently for them to undertake a flight home. Some discharges were delayed due to the reluctance of some to fly. They could not travel until they had recovered sufficiently to endure a long road journey followed by a ferry crossing.

As responders, we experienced frustration at the lack of information and the chaos resulting from the variety of needs presented by those affected. We shared in the reality of pain and sorrow. We were affected by the joy of a recovery begun and the sense of relief experienced by the relatives. We shared the weariness and stress of our fellow responders. We needed to establish a system to inform colleagues in the East Midlands area of the progress of those affected when they returned home, because the responders reported feelings of 'unfinished business'.

The Northern Ireland support network was still in contact with 54 of the families six months after the incident, and contact increased at the time of the anniversary, the inquest and the publication of the Air Accident Report.

As responders, we 'mirrored' the feelings of those directly affected. Our chaos was caused by the unique demands that the disaster had suddenly placed on us. Order came when we realised that our previous training and experience in trauma work were relevant and that we needed to adapt our skills by adding the lessons that we were learning from the dynamics of the disaster.

Rail disaster

People travelling to work on a commuter train may know each other by sight but have few links. When the Ladbroke Grove train disaster (1999) occurred on the busy line that led to Paddington Station, London, 31 people died and there were dozens of people injured. The psychosocial distress caused by the incident affected people on the train, people in the area of departure, in the workplaces to which they were travelling and people near to the accident who went to help from a local supermarket. Stress was reported by a large number of travellers who regularly used the same route, by passengers who should have been on that particular train but were not and by those on the crashed train who were uninjured. Support networks were therefore necessary in areas widely dispersed from the scene of the incident. While there was a disparate number of individuals affected, many most closely involved became a group at the time of the enquiry. Responders must also remember that their continued support may be needed at such times when issues of signal visibility and rail repairs are discussed. Seeking reasons can be therapeutic for some of the bereaved and injured, but there can also be a deepening of their distress if they hear of human acts of omission or commission that could have been preventable.

An express train travelling to Plymouth crashed into a car at a level crossing outside Reading on 7 November 2004, killing seven passengers and injuring 85 people. Immediate media attention focused on the need for more safety measures at unmanned level crossings. Another human tragedy element soon emerged when it appeared that the person in the car had deliberately stopped his car as he planned to take his own life. Psychosocial reactions for this family will also be associated with the crash but from a very different perspective.

Disaster on the roads

Each year we hear the statistics of lives lost or shattered by the injuries sustained in road traffic accidents. These figures are particularly brought to the attention of the public at Christmas time to highlight the need to separate the drinking of alcohol from driving. Drink drivers are an ever-present menace to all road users and the figures quoted in the statistics represent many personal disasters. The total toll far exceeds the death toll for many major disasters yet, because they are single events, the media coverage may be considerably less. Young and elderly pedestrians are at extreme risk as are young motorcyclists. The psychosocial toll on families of those killed or maimed is not fully appreciated by society at large. Support for such families may come from neighbours and friends. Hospital and community staff may also be involved with the rehabilitation process and care in the community. The example of road accidents reinforces the concept that people dealing with personal disasters do not normally get the level of support that is offered to those involved in major disasters. This is an issue that should challenge the providers of psychosocial support, as the needs of this group are just as painful and potentially long term.

Coach crashes and multiple crashes on motorways can move road traffic accidents into the realm of major disasters. The aspects of dispersal associated with other transport disasters can be applied.

Disasters associated with human beings' violence to one another

War

All through recorded history, humankind has been involved in the disaster of warfare that may take place on native or alien battlefields. The nature of the weapons used dictates the number and nature of the injuries sustained. While 'organised' confrontation by warring armed forces results in 'legitimate' casualties, there are always other civilians involved. The extensive media coverage of the numerous conflicts has meant that scenes of horror can be viewed almost instantaneously. Conflict is no longer an event romanticised by poets or artists in their accounts of brave deeds. We can all experience the reality of conflict in the faces of the dead, dying, hostages or homeless refugees.

Terrorism

Any consideration of a personal or major disaster must include the category of civil disturbance or terrorism. Such disasters are a worldwide phenomenon. These disasters may fit into the categories previously described, yet they tend to have additional factors that need to be considered in terms of the possible reaction by those people or communities directly affected. Global terrorism is an ever-present threat to the world in the 21st century.

Case study 8: 9/11

On 11 September 2001, passengers boarded American Airlines Flight 11 and took off from Boston Airport on a journey that was to end in tragedy. Al Qaeda terrorists were on board, who took over command of the aircraft and altered its flight path so that it flew into the North Tower of the World Trade Centre in New York. The aircraft with its passengers and full tanks of fuel became a missile that caused a fire on impact, which quickly engulfed the upper floors and spread rapidly. Onlookers at the scene and the millions around the world watched in horror as the reality of the situation became clearer. Eighteen minutes later, United Airlines Flight 175 (also from Boston) hit the South Tower and a massive explosion followed. The Twin Towers imploded shortly afterwards and fell to the ground as people rushed to escape from the burning buildings. People were seen jumping from the upper floors in a vain hope of escaping the burning inferno. Emergency

Figure 2.2: 9/11 disaster

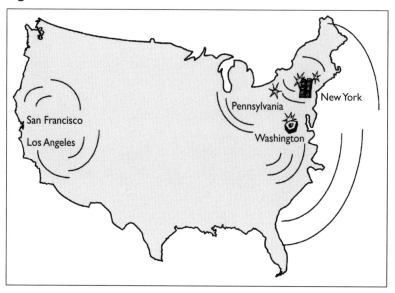

service responders who rushed to the North Tower were killed or injured as the towers crumbled to the ground.

The Pentagon, central headquarters for the US armed forces in Washington DC, was attacked within minutes of the attacks in New York when American Airlines Flight 77 crashed into the building. Due to its hexagonal design, only one side of the structure was destroyed but 184 people died as a result. A further ill-fated aircraft crashed as the passengers struggled with, and it is thought overcame, the hijackers who had put the aircraft on a flight path that could have taken it to the White House.

While the total number killed in this multi-location attack can never be completely accurate, it is estimated that 3,600 people lost their lives, thousands were injured and countless thousands traumatised as a result. This terrorist attack demonstrates clearly the concept of the pebble in the pool with the number of people affected growing as the ripples of impact spread out (see Figure 2.2). The consequence of these attacks was to alter the worldview of terrorism. The spread of global terrorism is reflected in the suicide bombers' attack on London on 7 July 2005. This incident was spread over seven locations involving the underground train network and a bus. The death of 56 people, four of whom were the suicide bombers, and the 700 injured has added the term 7/7 to the ever-growing list of terrorist acts.

Case study 9: Enniskillen bomb (1987) and Omagh bomb (1998) (major disasters/person-made/small/local and international)

The terrorist bomb which exploded in Enniskillen in Northern Ireland (1987) resulted in a small local disaster. The numbers killed were small compared with other disasters, yet it had a major effect locally and internationally. The community was bereaved; the religious divisions were put under increased tension as the perpetrators were seen to belong to one particular section of the community. As church leaders were quick to point out, a religious label was inappropriate as no person deserved the credibility of a religious title when they carried out such barbarous acts. The community was affected as its name became famous worldwide for this disaster. The words of Gordon Wilson, whose daughter Marie died as a result of her injuries, inspired many and were seen to have discouraged a retaliation attack. He told of her words of courage as they lay buried together in the rubble, and he described his reaction to the terrorists: 'I'll pray for those killers tonight and every night.' International attention focussed on the town and the many positive reactions of courage were classed as the 'spirit of Enniskillen'. Some negative feelings are still present in this community and it must be recognised that they too form part of the reaction of Enniskillen.

On 15 August 1998, a car bomb was detonated in the busy market town of Omagh only some 40 miles from Enniskillen. Crowds of shoppers were moved to the lower end of the street when a warning was given to the police. The information given by the Real IRA concerning the location of the bomb was erroneous and people were directed into the path of the bomb not away from it; 29 people died and hundreds were injured as a result. A party of Spanish schoolchildren were also involved with their young hosts who came from Donegal, in the Republic of Ireland. This fact meant that local responders had to link with other responders from Spain and other areas in Ireland as the impact of this disaster crossed geographical and political boundaries. The loss of life was the highest of any single incident of the 'Troubles'. The incident occurred at a particularly sensitive time in the fledgling Peace Process. Public horror resulted in many demonstrations for peace and of unity within the community itself and beyond. Staffcare provided assistance to nine organisations involved, including the ambulance service, hospitals, community health and social services trusts, the local council, voluntary organisations and commercial organisations. We utilised all the various crisis intervention techniques that comprise the Critical Incident Stress Management Programme (CISM) (see

Chapter Nine) to meet the multiple needs of the 647 staff seen in the first two weeks following the incident. Longer-term counselling was instigated for 72 of this total. When a terrorist bomb affects a community, the following reactions may occur:

- The response of the community may be divided as one 'side' may be seen as perpetrator and one 'side' as victim; this can result in fear of retaliation and a legacy of fear and suspicion.
- Local people have to remain within the same community and they may experience feelings of vulnerability. Their personal psychosocial reactions may be ignored as the media focuses attention on community responses.
- The event, the anniversary or any act of memorial may become politicised and personal tragedies may be used for propaganda purposes.

Case study 10: hostage-taking to achieve funding for terrorist organisations

It was a few nights before Christmas and a young family returned to their home after some late night shopping. Mum took the eight-month-old baby to feed him and settle him down for the night. Dad, who was the manager of a large supermarket, gave his young daughter aged three some supper in the kitchen before taking her upstairs to put her to bed. Exhaustion meant that she went to sleep very quickly. Dad returned downstairs having kissed his sleeping children goodnight. There was a knock at the door and Dad went to open it, thinking that it was his brother who often called in the evenings. His wife was still upstairs when she heard a peculiar stifled scream and a shout from her husband, 'Stay where you are, don't come down!' This was followed by the sound of someone being hit. She ran to the door of the bedroom to be confronted by a masked gunman who forced her and her baby son downstairs to where her husband was slumped in an armchair. There were two other armed and hooded men in the room. She was told to sit on the sofa beside one of the men. Her husband sat up and asked what they wanted them to do. The only reply he received was 'We will tell you when the time comes.' Little conversation took place; after about an hour the baby woke and Mum was allowed to go upstairs accompanied by one of the captors. Later her husband was allowed to lie down on the bed with her while their captor sat across the doorway. All phones were disconnected and they had no means of escape.

At 5am, the husband was taken downstairs to the kitchen where he saw a gun on the table. He was forced to have his photograph taken with the gun held to his head. The four bullets were then photographed in close-up to show that each one of the bullets bore the name of himself or one of his family members. He was then told to dress in his business suit and drive to the store in time for the opening at 7.30am. The photographs taken in the kitchen were to be used to persuade his office staff to cooperate with his instruction to open the safe and load all the money into a bin bag. He was then to drive to a certain location and drop the bag over the fence before returning home. He was warned that he was being watched and that, if he did not fulfil the task, in the unrealistic timescale set, his family would be shot with the named bullets. He carried out the task as instructed and rushed back to the house well behind his allocated schedule. The house was in silence and he feared the worst as he rushed upstairs to find his terrified wife sitting on the bed clutching her two children. She feared that the captors were still in the house and that her husband could not accomplish the task he had been set. After an hour, the police were called and the family removed to a safe house. The gang have never been apprehended and the long-lasting impact of this incident still haunts the family although they moved house twice in the subsequent two years.

The psychosocial implications of this incident have been long term as, from a psychological stability perspective, the captors had rendered all safe zones for this family unsafe. Their home was violated; the husband's workplace was suspect as the police felt that there had been insider information gained from that source. All members of the family were traumatised; even the baby picked up his mother's stress which affected her ability to breastfeed him.

This type of incident, while small and personal, contained many of the psychosocial factors associated with larger incidents. The family suffered a severe death threat, they became displaced from their home, and they experienced loss of control during their hostage ordeal and also over future choices of home and occupational location. Both adults suffered from Post-Traumatic Stress Disorder (PTSD) and needed skilled psychiatric and psychosocial intervention for over three years. The husband has never been able to assume a role of similar responsibility in the organisation as a result of his feelings of guilt that his job put his family at risk, and fear that he could be subject to a similar attack in the future.

The size of disaster

The University of Bradford Disaster Prevention and Limitation Unit has produced some research into the classification of disasters that takes into account the numbers of deaths:

- small = up to 20 deaths;
- medium = up to 100 deaths; and
- large = over 100 deaths.

The use of numbers, which must include the numbers injured, may be necessary to facilitate funding for relief work. In America, it is the president who defines a national or federal emergency. The government makes such decisions in the UK. The scale of environmental destruction is also an essential component when considering the scale of response that will be required.

Local

The division of disasters into local, national and international is of great significance when considering the possible support systems that will need to be utilised. This division also gives an indication of the level of media attention which can be expected. It is important to note that incidents may change their category as time passes. What begins as a local incident can escalate into the national or international category when the full facts become known. These case studies identify some examples of where this has happened.

Case study 11: Hungerford and Dunblane

The term 'local' can be used to describe incidents such as the Hungerford shooting (1987) when a small community was traumatised. The leafy lanes and roads of a small area became places of terror as the gunman stalked the area shooting at random. The town was paralysed by fear, as no one knew where he would strike next. His location could only be identified by the sound of sporadic shooting. The sunny afternoon turned into a nightmare for those affected.

While the term 'local' could also be applied to the shooting of 16 young children and their teacher in Dunblane Primary School in Scotland on 13 March 1996, the horror of the event quickly raised the category to 'international'. The horror and loss of the incident was localised in a small geographical area of the community of Dunblane, yet within this community there was also the local sub-community of the school.

In both these disasters, the gunman involved was a local man who committed suicide at the scene. Those killed and injured were local, the emergency services were from the immediate locality and the healing process was of the community itself. The community was bereaved. Outside support was necessary but the local schools, health and social services resources, voluntary organisations and churches all became involved in the recovery and rehabilitation process.

Hungerford and Dunblane developed national and international dimensions in the debates on gun laws that followed. The subject of gun laws also linked these incidents with the shootings in Tasmania, Australia, in 1996.

National

Case study 4: Hillsborough football stadium tragedy

The national dimension could be said to apply in the case of the disaster at Hillsborough Stadium (1989). The nation mourned the loss of the Liverpool football fans. Whether people were sports followers or not, they related to this national tragedy, which turned a normal Saturday afternoon activity into a nightmare. The effects of this tragedy have affected the safety arrangements for football supporters throughout the nation.

International

Case study 12: Lockerbie

The small town of Lockerbie was preparing for Christmas (1989) when an international disaster descended on it from the sky. The wreckage of the jet and the bodies of the 270 passengers fell on the area. Local houses were demolished and there were 11 fatalities among the local people. We were soon to learn that this disaster was truly international because of the 30 nationalities among the deceased. Enquiries into the cause of the crash and the search for the bombers have also been international. Many nations have been united in their shared grief. The community of Lockerbie has been linked with many people from all around the world who return to the site of the crash in sorrow seeking some peace.

Conclusion

The use of the typology and the examples cited in the case studies serve to reinforce the concept that each disaster is unique.

The classification grid may be useful in making the responder consider those factors that need to be addressed at the time of a major or personal disaster. It may also assist those with the responsibility of planning responses. The concept of classification by key elements can be used to assess the physical and psychological chaos that may exist – the 'chaos' to which 'order' needs to be brought.

THREE

Psychosocial reactions in traumatic incidents

Introduction

Figure 3.1: The continuum of psychological rehabilitation

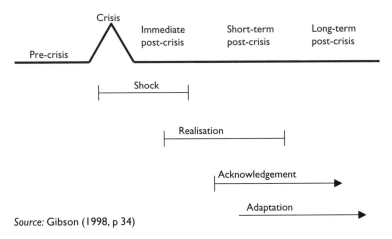

Source: Gibson (1998, p 34)

To aid an understanding of the psychological reactions that may be experienced in the aftermath of individual or major traumatic incidents, the four broad stages of shock, realisation, acknowledgement and adaptation have been identified (Figure 3.1). By adding these stages to the previous description of the concept of time as a continuum, it is hoped that this framework will be a practical aid to the assessment and application of appropriate interventions discussed in subsequent chapters. It is important to consider these stages as a continuous process rather than milestones to be achieved in a timed sequential way. Such a process may involve periods of regression as well as progression. The time periods may be short or prolonged, lasting for a few hours or days, or taking a lifetime due to the uniqueness of each individual's reaction. This conceptual framework is utilised throughout the book to aid clarity for all who seek to support individuals or communities to regain order in the chaos created by traumatic incidents.

The shock phase is associated with the immediate post-crisis stage when people report feelings of being overwhelmed by the incident in both practical and psychosocial aspects. They feel helpless; they have difficulty in cognitively processing their chaotic thoughts. Many describe a sense of detachment and numbness as feeling like an actor in a play that is unreal (see case study 13, p 75). Responders should offer practical support and use crisis intervention techniques at this stage. Responders often report that fears of finding the right words to say in very distressing situations often disable their ability to communicate. Silence, a holding of a hand and simple acts of kindness and support can be the most appropriate form of communication in such situations. The T diagram (Figure 3.2) was created by Bria Mongan, Senior Social Worker in the Belfast City Hospital, following her experiences of responding to a large group of distressed relatives in the aftermath of a terrorist shooting. This diagram is a useful aide-memoire in such situations.

Figure 3.2: T diagram

ALK	– responders must keep talking with the distressed person even where there is little information
EARS	– need to be accepted and comforted
OUCH	– may be more appropriate than words
ISSUES	– need to be readily available
ELEPHONES	– coins must be available and assistance with directories may be necessary
OILETS	– practical details are important
EA	– food and drink provide comfort
RANSPORT	– may be needed to homes, hospitals or the mortuary
ABLETS	– provision needs to be made for people on regular medication
IME	– responders need to make time to listen and to reassure people of ongoing support in the future

As the initial shock reactions dissipate, a sense of reality is experienced. This may be a painful and distressing stage often associated with anger born out of a sense of helplessness. Some 'fight' the chaos while some will 'flight' the realities of the situation with reactions that include psychological withdrawal associated with denial. Acknowledgement follows realisation. This is the period between realisation and the person being able to adapt to the changed situation caused by the traumatic incident. There can be psychological conflict as the individual seeks unsuccessfully to live life as it was, cope with the chaos of changed circumstances and create a new order in their life. Many people remain locked in this acknowledgement stage for long periods of time. Through the provision of specialist interventions (Chapter Eight) some may be helped to move through this stage to become survivors of the incident and not remain victims. Adaptation will overlap with the acknowledgement stage. Periods of progression may be interspersed with regression at times of anniversaries, legal procedures and the normal life changes that occur. Traumatised people often refer to events or encounters that appear to pull them back from adaptation to the more painful memories of earlier stages. Psychological rehabilitation should be viewed as a continuum of learning to adapt previous coping methods to deal with changed circumstances as they learn to live with the past integrated into the present in such a way that it does not disable their ability to cope with the future.

The subject of Post-Trauma Syndromes (PTS) is central to any discussion on the psychological and social outcomes for individuals affected in the aftermath of emergencies/disasters. PTS can also have an impact on those responders who have been involved in disaster work. The variety of perspectives from which such research originates demonstrates the variety of ways in which post-trauma reactions impinge on the lives of those affected. There has been a considerable increase in such research since the 1980s when the American Psychiatric Association (APA) first published its diagnostic criteria for Post-Traumatic Stress Disorder (PTSD) (APA, 1980). For the purposes of this book, the literature is discussed under two headings:

- historical perspectives, as described below; and
- theoretical models, as described in Chapter Four.

Historical perspectives

The increasing volume of research into the subject of PTS in the latter half of the 20th century would suggest that it is a new phenomenon. This is not so, although the constellations of symptoms have been variously described over the years. Humans have always had to endure, react to and cope with natural and other disasters. A study of the evolution of terms used and the underlying philosophies which led to such descriptions has great relevance for some of the contemporary attitudes on the subject. The word 'trauma' comes from Greek and is defined as 'to pierce or puncture armour'. In the context of all who are involved in emergencies or disasters of any size, this definition has significance. The nature of such incidents is that they have the potential for 'piercing' usual coping defence methods.

In 1598 Shakespeare, in his play *Henry VI* (Part 1, Act 2, Scene II) (Shakespeare, 1972), has Lady Percy describe the 'malaise' of her husband, since his return from the War of the Roses, in terms of fearful dreams, terror reactions, lack of sexual interest and times of intense feelings of helplessness. These descriptions would find resonance in more contemporary descriptions of the partners of emergency services personnel in the aftermath of 9/11, of forces returning from the war in Iraq or responders from the Asian earthquake. In my counselling work for Staffcare, I have also heard similar comments from staff who have endured a personal attack in their workplace. In the diaries of Samuel Pepys in 1666 (Daly, 1983, p 41) his description of the reactions experienced by people in the aftermath of the Great Fire of London would match the terms flashbacks, intrusive thoughts and avoidance which we use today.

The term 'Post-Traumatic Stress Disorder' (PTSD) was introduced in DSM-III in 1980. Terms used in previous editions were 'gross stress reaction' and 'transient situational disturbance'. Previous terms used appeared to be descriptive of the symptoms with which patients presented. 'Over a hundred years ago Freud had suggested that some forms of paralysis were hysterical reactions to psychological conflicts' (Shapiro, 1989, p 35).

We recognise that trauma causes psychological conflicts as the mind seeks to process the traumatic experience. It is interesting to note that the term 'hysteria' was widely used in the late 1880s and early 1900s to describe symptoms that would now be included in a diagnosis of PTSD.

Tunnel disease and railway spine disorder were terms that owed their origin to the perceived cause of the traumatic incident. The railways, closely associated with the changing face of an industrial society, created a potential source for major accidents. Those injured presented with a collection of psychological and physical injuries. As with many of the Victorian psychiatrists, Erichsen (1882) felt that concussion of the spinal cord had an effect on the brain due to neurological connections. He believed that such physical damage must account for the manifestation of the psychological distress that was also present. His description was developed for presentation in support of early compensation claims which were the result of a growing awareness of an employer's 'duty to care' by providing a safe environment for their employees.

Beveridge (1996) reminds us that late 19th-century British psychiatric theories were based on a search for the physical cause for psychological symptoms. It was felt that 'moral' causes had also a strong influence on such symptoms. Coulston (1896) was dismissive of the potential of the influence of outside incident stressors. He maintained that, if a man's brain was sound, he could withstand any degree of psychosocial stress. It was only those individuals whose brains were weakened by hereditary taint or the ravages of a debauched lifestyle, who were tipped into insanity by external events.

Combat experience was the strongest influence in the field of traumatic stress syndromes. The term 'nostalgia' was used in the American Civil War to describe soldiers who appeared to be affected by their combat experiences and not to be able to 'forget' such experiences. Terms such as 'soldier's heart', 'psychic trauma neurosis', 'nervous exhaustion', 'irritable heart', 'effort syndrome', 'traumatophia' and 'shellshock' in World War I appear throughout the literature. Recent retrospective analysis of case histories has suggested that many of the soldiers shot for cowardice, because of their refusal to engage in further traumatic combat situations, were in fact suffering from acute PTSD.

In World War II, terms such as 'combat neurosis', 'combat fatigue', 'battle exhaustion' and 'war neurosis' were used. More value-based terms, such as 'compensation neurosis', appeared in the 1950s and 1960s as the authenticity of claimants was questioned by legal systems. Legal systems were more comfortable in assessing claims for physical injuries that could be evaluated more easily.

From analysis of these combat-related terms, it seems that there is a judgemental tone emerging. There is some suggestion of personal 'weakness' if people develop such symptoms. The macho culture of many military structures appears to have had an influence throughout the history of combat-related terms. It would appear that thinking on PTS still reflected some of the Victorian attitudes of moral fortitude. Many of these attitudes appear to still prevail today.

Work by Horowitz (1986a) on adjustment disorders with Holocaust survivors offered one of the first research findings that related combat-based diagnostic descriptions to civilian populations, albeit a population created by combat. His work did much to advance the research of traumatic stress syndromes with a wider patient and client group. This growing body of research with, for example, survivors of childhood abuse and those who presented in the aftermath of disasters, identified both the similarities and the differences with combat and civilian populations in terms of their psychological reactions. His model of normal and pathological reactions to traumatic stress did much to advance the thinking of his time (see Figure 4.1, p 62).

It was the problems encountered by the returning Vietnam veterans that focused the research on PTS which was carried out in the 1970s and 1980s. This work also prompted a more vigorous search for criteria that could be used following a variety of traumatic experiences. Such criteria needed to be robust enough to withstand a largely sceptical legal analysis in an era of growing litigation against perpetrators, employers and governments.

Any study of Vietnam veterans must be set in the prevailing societal environment that existed in America at this time. It was the war that America wanted to 'forget'. Aspects of race problems were highlighted as the disproportionate numbers of those killed or injured came from the non-white population. The outcomes of brutal war methods, such as the use of napalm bombs, were visible to the world through the improved media coverage. Combat ceased to be an activity that took place far away on some foreign field. America did not 'win' the war; as a result, no glorious scenes of triumph awaited the returning forces. A society, subjected to conscription, had to witness pictures of many of their young people returning in body bags. Society also had to absorb a generation of young persons whose lives had been radically influenced by their Vietnam experience. In his book, *Stress disorders among the Vietnam veterans*, Figley (1978) reminds his readers that:

> Although American involvement ended over five years ago, for thousands of Vietnam veterans the war is not over. The individuals have had to cope not only with the tremendous stresses of combat, but also with the psychosocial stresses involved in coming home from an unpopular war to a divided, bitter country. (Figley, 1978, back cover)

Figley's seminal work was very influential in focusing on the psychosocial problems of adjustment following a trauma. This work is particularly pertinent to the aims of this book. In 1979, when working on a social work student placement in a psychiatric hospital in Indianapolis, US, I was working with a boy of 16 who said:

> I wish my Dad had been killed in Vietnam. My friend's
> Dad was killed and he came home in a body bag, but he
> came home a hero. My Dad came back but he is so different
> – he is a bastard; we can't live with him.

This boy's tragic experience of living with a father who was suffering
from PTSD gives us a vivid reminder of the infectious nature of the
psychosocial implications for the direct and indirect individuals
involved. What are the positive and negative effects resulting from the
attitudes found within the natural support networks of those affected
when they too return home from their traumatic experience?

David Healy (1993) has observed that the establishing of the criteria
for PTSD in DSM-III and its subsequent revisions represents the first
recognition by psychiatry that a psychological illness can be precipitated
entirely by external stress. In DSM-III the International Classification
of Diseases (ICD-9) (WHO, 1978) identified 'acute reaction to stress'
as:

> A very transient disorder of any severity and nature which
> occurs in an individual without any apparent mental
> disorder in response to exceptional physical or mental stress,
> such as natural catastrophe or battle, and which usually
> subsides within hours or days. (Turnbull, 1997, p 19)

When reactions lasted longer than this very limited timescale, they
were moved into the category of adjustment reactions. Again they
were described as transitory although the duration timescale was a
few months. The absence of any pre-existing mental disorder was
again emphasised. The presence of a specific external stressful incident,
the normality of the subjects and the emphasis on the short timescale
makes this a significant classification when we are considering reactions
to disaster situations.

Reactions to traumatic stress make us consider the most basic of
human reactions: survival. Colin Murray Parkes et al (1997, p 10)
describes this basic desire for survival as 'Three overlapping behavioural
systems, which explain much of the overall response to stress – the
response to threat, the response to separation and the response to
change.'

The response to threat involves the psycho-physiological enhanced
sensation response as mechanisms required for survival are activated.
Normal thought processings are put on hold and all the attention is
focused on the perceived threat. Physiological control centres in the

brain stimulate an increase in the blood flow to the organs involved in the survival response. Heartbeat and the respiratory rate are increased to enable an 'extraordinary' response to be made if necessary. An increased release of hormones is also activated. Fields and Bisson (1988) suggest that the sudden release of endorphins in the brain diminish pain responses. Adrenaline is also involved as there may be a need to react more quickly as we assess the danger and establish if the 'fight or flight' response is most appropriate in the circumstances. Parkes reminds us that, when the stress has been coped with, there may be acute fatigue as the stimuli are depleted.

The psychological responses associated with separation are often present in traumatic incidents and can be a powerful impact on the person involved. Parkes (1972, 1996) postulates that separation is particularly painful to human beings who are essentially social entities. Traumatic incidents often involve separation. It may be temporary in the initial chaos that usually exists. Many incidents contain situations of the permanent separation of death. Fear of separation, similar to that which has been experienced, can leave a legacy of insecurity many months after the traumatic incident has been resolved.

Traumatic incidents represent incidents of major change. Parkes (1972, 1996) describes that we carry within our minds our own unique and complex model of the world. This assumptive world contains images from our experience, our values and the elements by which we assess our environment and people whom we meet. Our assumptive world also provides us with the basis on which we attribute emotions such as fear, security and significant factors for us within our unique life plans. Traumatic events alter our assumptive world. This impact of change on our assumptive world is vividly described by Janoff-Bulman (1992).

Janoff-Bulman postulates, as a result of her work with individuals of rape, muggings and road traffic accidents, that we all live our lives with the assurance of three basic assumptions that are shattered by traumatic events:

- a belief in personal invulnerability;
- the perception of the world as meaningful and comprehensible; and
- the view of ourselves in a positive light.

I have found Janoff-Bulman's work to be significant and helpful to the task of responding in many post-trauma situations. Fear results from the reality born of the experience that 'it doesn't always happen to someone else'. The ordered world can become chaotic and unpredictable. Individuals often discover that they may not have reacted as positively as they had envisaged they would when confronted with a traumatic incident. For responders, some safety protocols may have inhibited their actions at the scene and may have been in conflict with their preferred reaction. This conflict may have nurtured a sense of guilt that they did not do enough to help someone. Janoff-Bulman's work and that of Parkes are helpful in classifying the elements of adjustment that are present in acute stress reactions to traumatic incidents. These aspects, which are defined in the typology of disasters, are most important when working in the aftermath of such incidents. All those affected need time to confront their 'shattered assumptions' and rebuild new ones that incorporate their traumatic experience.

Working with people who have been bereaved in such incidents, I have noted that they will often express the desire for life to 'return to normal'. What they really desire is that life should return to a second before the emergency or disaster occurred. What responders who seek to assist from a psychological perspective have to focus on is supporting them to rebuild their new assumptive world. This new world, with its new normality, has to have their traumatic experience integrated into it in a way that it no longer represents a threat to their psychosocial well-being.

This progressive refining of diagnostic classification over the years not only reflects increased attention paid to the subject by researchers but has also been influenced by global history.

The revision of DSM-III (APA, 1980), DSM-III-R (APA, 1987), was made in the light of new research findings. The revised version (see Figure 3.3) laid greater emphasis on the avoidance factors listed in Category C. This emphasis was based on the growing evidence of the impact of such elements and the need for clinicians to reflect a similar emphasis when considering a treatment regime. The revision also provided new descriptions for identifying the symptoms in children. Guilt, which can be associated with many psychiatric conditions, was relegated from a primary factor, in DSM-III, to an associated feature in the revision. Symbolic cognitive representation was given increased recognition in this revision also.

Newer classifications of post-trauma pathology need to be considered when assessing current accepted forms of intervention. The 10th edition of the International Classification of Diseases (ICD-10) (WHO, 1978), subscribes to a wider description of characteristic symptoms than the DSM (see Figure 3.4). Classification F43 of ICD-10 includes acute stress reaction, PTSD and adjustment disorder. This classification has

Figure 3.3: PTSD IV: Post-Traumatic Stress Disorder and associated syndromes

---

PTSD IV
Post-Traumatic Stress Disorder and associated syndromes

A. The person has been exposed to a traumatic event in which both of the following were present:
   (1) The person experienced, witnessed or was confronted with an event or events that involved actual or threatened death or serious injury, or a threat to the physical integrity of others.
   (2) The person's response involved intense fear, helplessness or horror. Note: in children, this may be expressed instead by disorganised or agitated behaviour.

B. The traumatic event is persistently re-experienced in one (or more) of the following ways:
   (1) Recurrent and intrusive distressing recollections of the event, including images, or perceptions. Note: in young children, repetitive play may occur in which themes or aspects of the trauma are expressed.
   (2) Recurrent distressing dreams of the event. Note: in children there may be frightening dreams without recognisable content.
   (3) Acting or feeling as if the traumatic event were reoccurring (includes a sense of reliving the experience, illusions, hallucinations and dissociative flashback episodes, including those that occur on awakening or when intoxicated).
   (4) Intense psychological distress at exposure to internal or external cues that symbolise or resemble an aspect of the traumatic event.
   (5) Physiological reactivity on exposure to internal or external cues that symbolise or resemble an aspect of the traumatic event.

C. Persistent avoidance of stimuli associated with the trauma and numbing of general responsiveness (not present before the trauma), as indicated by three (or more) of the following:
   (1) Efforts to avoid thoughts, feelings or conversations associated with the trauma.
   (2) Efforts to avoid activities, places or people that arouse recollections of the trauma.
   (3) Inability to recall an important aspect of the trauma.
   (4) Markedly diminished interest or participation in significant activities.
   (5) Feeling of detachment or estrangement from others.
   (6) Restricted range of affect (eg: unable to have loving feelings).
   (7) Sense of foreshortened future (eg: does not expect to have a career, marriage, children or a normal lifespan).

D. Persistent symptoms of increased arousal (not present before the trauma), as indicated by two (or more) of the following:
   (1) Difficulty in falling asleep.
   (2) Irritability or outbursts of anger.
   (3) Difficulty concentrating.
   (4) Hyper vigilance.
   (5) Exaggerated startle response.

E. Duration of the disturbance (Symptoms in Criteria B, C and D) is more than one month.

F. The disturbance causes clinically significant distress or impairment in social, occupational or other important areas of functioning:
   Specify if:
   Acute   If duration of symptoms is less than 3 months.
   Chronic   If duration of symptoms is 3 months or more.
   Specific if:
   With Delayed Onset   If onset of symptoms is at least 6 months after the stressor.

Source: Black et al (1997, p 25)

Figure 3.4: The ICD-10 Classification of PTSD

The ICD-10 Classification of Post-Traumatic Stress Disorder

Post-Traumatic Stress Disorder arises as a delayed and/or protracted response to a stressful event or situation (either short- or long-lasting) of an exceptionally threatening or catastrophic nature, which is likely to cause pervasive distress in almost anyone (eg: natural or man-made disaster, combat, serious accident, witnessing the violent death of others, or being the individual of torture, terrorism, rape, or other crime). Predisposing factors such as personality traits (eg: compulsive, asthenic) or previous history of neurotic illness may lower the threshold for the development of the syndrome or aggravate its course, but they are neither necessary nor sufficient to explain its occurrence.

Typical symptoms include episodes of repeated reliving of the trauma in intrusive memories ('flashbacks') or dreams, occurring against the persisting background of a sense of 'numbness' and psychosocial blunting, detachment from other people, unresponsiveness to surroundings, anhedonia and avoidance of cues that remind the sufferer of the original trauma. Rarely, there may be dramatic, acute bursts of fear, panic or aggression, triggered by stimuli arousing a sudden recollection and/or re-enactment of the trauma or of the original reaction to it.

There is usually a state of autonomic hyper arousal with hyper vigilance, an enhanced startle reaction and insomnia. Anxiety and depression are commonly associated with the above symptoms and signs, and suicidal ideation is not infrequent. Excessive use of alcohol or drugs may be a complicating factor.

The onset follows the trauma with a latency period which may range from a few weeks to months (but rarely exceeds six months). The course is fluctuating but recovery can be expected in the majority of cases. In a small proportion of patients the condition may show a chronic course over many years and a transition to an enduring personality change.

Diagnostic guidelines: This disorder should not generally be diagnosed unless there is evidence that it arose within six months of a traumatic event of exceptional severity. A 'probable' diagnosis might be possible if the delay between the event and the onset was longer than six months, provided that the clinical manifestations are typical and no alternative identification of the disorder (eg: as an anxiety or obsessive-compulsive disorder or depressive episode) is plausible. In addition to evidence of trauma, there must be a repetitive, intrusive recollection or re-enactment of the event in memories, daytime imagery or dreams. Conspicuous psychosocial detachment, numbing of feeling and avoidance of stimuli that might arouse recollection of the trauma are often present but are not essential for the diagnosis. The autonomic disturbances, mood disorder and behavioural abnormalities all contribute to the diagnosis but are not of prime importance.

The late chronic sequelae of devastating stress, ie: those manifest decades after the stressful experience, should be classified (elsewhere).

Reproduced with permission of the World Health Organisation, Geneva
Source: Black et al (1997, p 24)

great significance for this book as it distinguishes acute stress reaction as a reaction in which the symptoms typically resolve within hours or days of the incident. PTSD is a chronic disorder where the reaction type symptoms are more severe and intransigent. This timescale is pertinent to the aims of this book.

The DSM-IV (1994) again reflects the growing body of hundreds of research findings and theoretical frameworks which have been evolving with the increased interest in the subject. The APA stated that one of the aims of their field studies for PTSD, undertaken prior to publishing DSM-IV, was 'to establish the prevalence of the most commonly reported trauma-related psychological problems not currently captured by the PTSD diagnostic construction, their relation to each other and to PTSD itself (as defined in DSM-III-R)' (APA, 1994, p 179). They expanded their thinking to address the effects of chronic physical and sexual abuse of children, and other populations exposed to prolonged and/or severe interpersonal trauma such as concentration camp survivors, battered women and hostages.

Turnbull (1997) explains the complex process that led to the revisions which appear in DSM-IV. He notes that the term 'disorders of extreme distress' (DES) appeared in the literature as a result of this further debate as an attempt to encompass the extended knowledge and evidence of symptom clusters which included suicidal behaviour, sexual dysfunction, impulsive and risk-taking behaviours, as well as alterations in perception which led to guilt, shame, difficulties in maintaining relationships, the inability to trust and feelings of helplessness. As these symptom clusters co-existed with symptoms of PTSD in all but 3.4% of diagnosed cases, it was decided that it was inappropriate to develop the use of a separate category of DES but to expand the PTSD criteria in DSM-IV to include these factors. The criteria for the diagnosis of PTSD in DSM-IV differ from DSM-III-R in two important ways:

1. Criteria A (see Figure 3.3), which define the stressor, now included the term 'an event which involved serious injury to others and responding with horror', which allows for the criteria to be applied in cases of vicarious traumatisation. This is an important concept in the context of this book, which considers the impact of such activities on the people affected and the responders involved.
2. Symptoms of physiological reactivity have been moved from the hyper arousal cluster (Criterion D in DSM-III-R) to the re-experiencing cluster contained in Criteria B (see Figure 3.3).

Acute Stress Disorder (ASD) was included as a new diagnostic classification in DSM-IV. ASD remains an important diagnosis for this research as DSM-IV defines it as occurring within four weeks of the incident and usually being resolved within a four-week period. Any diagnosis associated with a response to trauma is likely to have associated co-morbidity of depressive disorders, anxiety states and incident-specific somatisation. In my experience there may also be co-morbidity with existing social dysfunction prior to the incident, which has an influence on how a person will react generally.

These DSM-IV categories will subsequently be used as a template for discussing the relevant literature pertinent to this book.

The event: the diagnosis criteria for PTSD, as declared in DSM-IV, include two elements of the event that must be present for the patient to be diagnosed as having PTSD. PTSD is the only current psychiatric disorder that identifies the external stressor or causal agent in this unique way. The two criteria identified in Category A of Figure 3.3 remind us that the event or events must be different from the normal that could be expected and contain an actual or perceived death threat or serious injury to self or others. Such actual or threatened death or serious injury must also produce intense fear, helplessness or horror in the person affected.

For the purpose of this book, this is an important consideration. Ambulance work may expose responders to many horrendous incidents, yet we need to realise that the incidents being considered may or may not be within the 'normal' expected range of their average day's work. Accident and emergency nurses also see and deal with horrendous injuries and deaths as an integral part of their work, yet they also could consider the impact of disasters as unique.

These considerations must lead us to ask the question: 'Have those responders – for example, paramedics and accident and emergency nurses – a higher threshold of tolerance than could be expected from other responders?' How far does experience influence the psychological impact of the incident? The impact of the specific type of incident is fully discussed in Chapter Two.

The type of incident has inherent factors that will define the areas that will cause significant psychological distress for those involved. One incident may be more stressful for one individual than another because of their past experiences of trauma and the specific personal attribution each makes to the events.

Category B: identifies the symptoms of intrusion that are commonly described by those affected. Intrusive thoughts, images or perceptions that enter one's thinking without apparent stimulation can be extremely distressing and evoke a sense of helplessness and lack of control. These can be particularly distressing when they occur at night-time. Sleep allows brain processing to take place and the images can be so powerful that they burst through the mind as flashbacks or nightmares. People may even dread going to sleep as a result. Poor sleep patterns are often reported in the immediate post-trauma period. This can lead to physical and psychosocial exhaustion that may require medication.

Category C: deals with the elements of avoidance which are common in the presentation of PTSD. Having undergone a 'life-threatening' experience, the person tries to avoid physical or psychological stimuli which may remind them of the incident. Many people will avoid visiting the actual scene. This reaction does not create problems if the scene was previously visited on an irregular basis. If, however, the scene is that of the individual's usual workplace or home, avoidance can create major problems for both the individual and their organisation. Sensory reminders of the incident may also evoke the avoidance symptom. Smells and sounds associated with the traumatic incident can cause a person to re-experience earlier painful reactions. Avoidance can mean that such sensory stimuli are avoided in every situation, not only those associated with the incident. The more subtle psychological avoidance symptoms may disrupt a person's social functioning, which can create problems for peers and family.

Category D: can be described as hyper arousal symptoms. These are significant in the context of both the work and home environment. Responders who have difficulty in concentrating often talk of how their self-esteem can be devastated by their apparent lack of professional competence. This lack of competence can meet with a lack of understanding from management structures.

Category E: deals with the duration factor and separates the more transient ASD from the diagnosis of PTSD.

Category F: outlines the all-encompassing effect of the symptoms on the person's functioning in all areas of their life. It also reminds us that, while the symptoms experienced in cases of the more transient ASD can be similar, it is the degree of severity and duration that segregates ASD and PTSD.

These developments in definitions of post-traumatic syndromes will no doubt continue throughout the 21st century. Parallel to this work of definition has been the development of various models by which researchers try to explore and explain the various manifestations of the syndrome.

An understanding of some of the relevant models is essential in the design of any response to emergencies or disasters. This understanding can be utilised in the pre-crisis period to help society at large increase its resilience to the impact of any such event through awareness-raising. The knowledge gained through better understanding of the models could also aid the development of a training programme, for use in the pre-crisis period, to increase awareness for would-be responders.

FOUR

Responding to psychosocial reactions

Theoretical models

The concept of Post-Traumatic Stress Disorder (PTSD) has produced a variety of theoretical models that may be used to explain its impact on traumatised individuals. These models are derived from biological, physiological, cognitive behavioural and psychodynamic frameworks. This variety is conducive to examination of the many facets of PTSD. Insights from one theoretical model appear to complement rather than contradict insights derived from another theoretical source.

PTSD is a complex condition, and no one theory appears to address all the aspects which have been identified. Over the last decade, a collaborative approach between theorists appears to suggest the best way forward in promising a greater understanding of post-trauma reactions in general and in PTSD in particular. Greater understanding should lead to more appropriate treatment interventions. Much of the research into the efficacy of interventions seems to have been concerned with treatment of symptoms, from the orientation of the clinician, rather than dealing with the total psychosocial impact of the trauma.

An understanding of some of the key theoretical perspectives is important to this book. Such understanding will be used to inform the debate on the components that would be most appropriate to include in any plan to assist in the amelioration of any negative after-effects of a traumatic experience that may occur.

Psychobiological model

From the first comprehensive descriptions of the constellation of symptoms which make up the presentation of PTSD as defined in DSM-III (APA, 1980), there has been an increase in the interest in the biological aspects of the disorder (Pitman et al, 1993). While much of the research centred on the psychological and social aspects of the disorder, biological aspects can offer insights into such symptom clusters as intrusive phenomena, arousal and avoidance. These theories can have a major influence on treatment options and can also serve to inform any debate on preventative interventions. McIvor states that:

> Blanchard's (Blanchard et al, 1986) early work showed conditioned automatic responses, such as tachycardia and increased blood pressure, muscle tension and skin resistance, in veterans exposed to combat sounds. Such work has been repeated and extended using electromyographic measurements (Pitman et al, 1989, 1990a) and event-related brain potentials (McFarlane et al, 1993). It has been suggested that [physiologically discriminated] functions derived from Vietnam veterans can significantly distinguish PTSD from non-PTSD subjects, (Orr et al, 1930) including those with non-traumatogenic anxiety disorder. (McIvor, 1997, in Black et al, 1997)

This area of research has been welcomed by the legal profession as 'hard evidence' of symptoms such as flashbacks, which could previously only have been evidenced by verbal descriptions by the patient.

The initial fear response to a traumatic event activates the amygdala in the brain to 'sound the alarm' and send urgent messages to every major part of the brain; the amygdala triggers secretion of the body's 'fight or flight' hormones. The hypothalmus is signalled to order the pituitary gland to produce CRF (corticotrophin-releasing factor) to protect the joints from injury. The amygdala and the medulla are activated to help movement and activate the cardiovascular system, the muscles and other systems which may be needed for survival. The locus coeruleus (LC) is signalled to produce noradrenaline (NA) to increase the alertness of the brain, increase the blood supply to the brainstem, limbic system and neocortex (higher centres). The hippocampus is signalled for the release of dopamine to allow for the riveting of attention. While this is a complex reaction, an understanding of the basic concepts is necessary to understand the biological impact on those who have to react and experience traumatic events.

In most cases, the impact of the traumatic event is temporary and the hyper-alerted systems return to baseline functioning levels. However, when the impact persists, feelings of loss of control and helplessness can be experienced. The brain readjusts its baseline functions and enters a state that we recognise as PTSD:

- The LC becomes hyperactive, stimulating secretion of large doses of NA even in neutral, non-threatening situations.
- The hypothalmus becomes hyperactive, continuing to promote pituitary gland secretions, erroneously alerting the body to an emergency situation which does not exist.
- The amygdala continues to signal opioid centres in the neocortex to release endorphins; this triggers a sense of numbing and anhedonia.

These responses overwhelm the ability of the brain's higher centres to shut the false alarm down. It can be seen from the description of these responses that this state of inappropriate alertness, after the initial threat has passed, is the explanation for many of the distressing symptoms reported by those affected. These symptoms are often noticed by others as they manifest themselves in social functioning.

Sleep disturbances are widely reported by those experiencing a post-trauma reaction or PTSD. It is known that the LC plays an important role in regulating sleep. Ross et al (1989) regarded sleep disturbance, and its attendant dream phenomena, as a central hallmark of PTSD. They also postulated that 'Dysfunctional REM circuitry may participate in the control of the exaggerated startle response' (Ross et al, 1989, p 59).

Those who experience sleep deprivation appear to present in two categories. Each of these forms causes distress for the sufferer and can affect the sleep pattern of a spouse or partner. Those who anticipate a disturbed night with intrusive and distressing dreams try to delay going to sleep by indulgence in alcohol or sleep medication. Many explain these acts as a means of attempting to block out the distressing dreams. Those with associated depressive aspects of the syndrome often become very anxious and distressed if a pattern of early wakening is established. These aspects can result in exhaustion and be very serious to a person's general well-being when they are trying to maintain a normal work life and relationships.

These psychobiological aspects of a post-trauma reaction are of paramount importance. The sustained inappropriate hyperstimulation of the hormonal system may have major implications for those who are called on to respond to be involved in multiple traumatic events. Opioid release produces analgesia and can contribute to psychosocial withdrawal. This may well be the explanation needed for families and friends, who report that the person remains aloof from their attempts to love, support and encourage. This can create friction within the support network when they find their efforts being rejected.

While these reactions contribute to initial survival in a threatening environment, in the longer term they may give rise to more persistent neurobiological responses which become maladaptive. Such maladaptive neurobiological responses may affect future reactions to similar stimuli. They may also affect a person's ability to process and learn from the experience. These phenomena could have serious implications for those involved in work situations that require them to be re-exposed to similar situations.

An understanding of the psychobiological reactions can help the person understand their own reaction and render them amenable to the normalisation processes. It can also assist to minimise the fear that their reaction is unique to them and the result of 'mental breakdown'.

Research into the biological aspects of trauma reactions has brought about major changes in the way initial treatment of shock should be managed. The practice of encouraging people to withdraw into the almost foetal existence of warm comforting blankets, warm sweet drinks and rest has been rejected in favour of caffeine-free drinks and encouragement to exercise normal patterns of walking to stimulate the dispersal of the excess hormonal secretions.

It is my belief that an understanding of the psychobiological model does much to guide our attempts to ameliorate any harmful and distressing after-effects. This model has many aspects that should be included in any discussion of preventative intervention especially designed for responders.

Psychoanalytical models

Freud's work (1912) on neuroses identified the need for an external stressor. His initial research had focused on a person's reaction to the stress of seduction, but he maintained an interest in war neurosis. Velsen (1997, p 117) describes trauma in a similar way to Freud as an incident '...which involved the breaching of a protective shield or stimulus barrier, which normally functions to prevent the overwhelming of the mind (ego) from internal and external stimuli, by means of managing, or binding, the excitation'.

Freud argued that 'a flood of unmanageable impulses' would cause 'disturbances on a large scale' and set 'in motion every defensive measure'. Freud drew attention to the fact that 'repetition compulsion' formed the basis for re-experiencing disturbing and catastrophic events and could be an attempt to master such memories. The person's fixation with the trauma is alternated with attempts to avoid any remembrance of the event. This analysis by Freud fits with more modern descriptions of post-trauma experience as contained in DSM–IV.

In 1926, Freud elaborated this theory by linking these reactions to the helplessness of the ego, which he felt was the core of the traumatic experience. He further suggested that anxiety could be used as a signal of the possibility of the reoccurrence of the trauma experience. This formed a link with the phenomenon of increased arousal in PTSD.

The publication of work by Kardiner in 1941 which challenged and developed all the theories which originated in Freudian analytic roots. He placed much more emphasis on the actual event or stressor. He felt that symptoms of numbing, disintegration and intrusion were caused by ego contradiction and disorganisation. In the 1950s, 1960s and 1970s, there was an increase in interest in the aftermath of experiences such as the Holocaust and the Vietnam war. It was Horowitz (1976), some 60 years after Freud, who returned to the language of information processing when he described his model in terms of the conflict created in the mind by the alternating between recalling the traumatic experience and the desire to avoid such reminders.

Most of the subjects researched in the UK were from World War II, with the emphasis being placed on treatment of war neurosis. This research led to a growing knowledge of the merits of treating veterans by group analytic and therapeutic community theories. While Freud's analytical theories underpin many of the models which we now consider 'new', evolutionary or indeed revolutionary, as in the case of Eye Movement Desensitisation and Reprocessing (EMDR) (see Chapter Nine), there appears to be more emphasis on the effects of trauma on adult psychic structure rather than theories which trace effects back to early ego regressive states. Winnicott (1974) recognised that, in the post-trauma reaction period, there may be a 'release of primitive horrors' with associative primitive ways of coping, but not a developmental regression. We need to consider these comments against Velsen (1997, p 76), who suggests that in trauma reactions: 'These established defences may be fully, or partially, superseded by other defence mechanisms.'

All descriptions of post-trauma reactions offered by dynamic models include comment on the attribution which the person gives to the traumatic event or its aftermath. Work in this area reminds us that attribution can be a very individual issue. As such, it is an area which the skilled clinician must assess and focus on in any therapeutic relationship. It is also an area which must be recognised in any design of early intervention, as attribution may be influenced by both professional training and culture.

The complexity of PTSD is reflected in the way that psychoanalytic psychotherapists appear to be adapting their theoretical approaches to aspects of trauma rather than suggesting one overall approach to the total disorder. Fear of annihilation is described as a key feature of trauma in terms of a psychoanalytic model by Hopper (1991). She believes that there is a higher risk of the development of adult PTSD following situations where people feared for their own annihilation. This approach is significant, as many disaster situations afford responders a situation in which they too may be injured or die.

Lifton (1968, 1973, 1993) based his belief in a 'psychoformative approach' on his research. He concentrates on the structure of the self and its transformation in unique ways following trauma. He describes 10 fundamental principles affecting survivor reactions based on an understanding of death and continuity or the so-called life–death paradigm.

- **Life–death paradigm**: Lifton (1993, p 12) states that: 'Although people acknowledge death as an issue, conceptual resistance to death is coupled with a general resistance to the idea of death.' He believes that the more we confront our own feelings on death personally and conceptually, the more effective we will be as responders.
- **The concept of being a survivor**: Lifton describes this as a direct corollary of the life–death paradigm. Survival is an achievement, and the survivor can either stay locked in the numbing or use such survival as a source of insight or growth.
- **The human connectedness of survivors**: Lifton views the need of survivors to re-establish a sense of being connected with wider humanity as part of their recovery process. There is a danger of an increased vulnerability to stress and dissociation during this process.
- **Post-Traumatic Stress Disorder as a normal reaction to extreme stress**: Lifton believes that we must recognise that such reactions can be viewed as a normal adaptive process given the abnormality of the trauma situation.
- **Survival, guilt and self-condemnation**: Lifton (1993, p 12) stresses the reality of psychological guilt in post-trauma experience: '…this is a paradoxical form of guilt, sometimes one can condemn the self more as a survivor or victim because the victimizer may numb him or herself'. Failure to act in a way which the person would have wished to act, due to the circumstances of the trauma,

can contribute to a sense of guilt for their inaction or, as described by Lifton, 'failed enactment'.

- **Psychosocial vitality and fragmentation of the self**: this describes the conflict between feeling and not feeling. This phenomenon is described by Lifton in terms of the standard psychoanalytic defence mechanisms. He feels that the whole issue of dissociation is central to post-traumatic reaction and survivor experience.
- **Psychic numbing – discontinuity of self**: such psychic numbing hinders the symbolisation and formative processes that are central to the recovery process.
- **The search for meaning – paradigmatic forms of self-experience**: trauma causes those involved to address their experience against their own unique and fundamental belief schema. This may lead to a period of confusion followed by a period of searching when such fundamental issues as 'good and evil' need to be addressed.
- **The moral dimensions of trauma**: much of Lifton's research involved war/torture situations which had moral issues inherent in them. This work must also alert us to the moral dilemmas for people responding to trauma victims from terrorist attacks which can be legitimised by one section of the community as justified in the pursuance of 'a cause'. This must be a consideration during analysis of the stress on responders in the aftermath of suicide bombers' attacks in Israel, Iraq or London.
- **Transformation of the self**: Lifton views 'transformation of the self' and all the aspects of traumatic reaction, which he outlined, as central not only to an understanding of PTSD but also to various strands of psychiatry and psychology. Recovery is how the experience 'transforms' the self; this may be viewed as a positive or negative transformation which underpins future behaviour and life patterns.

Psychoanalytical models have much to contribute to our understanding of how individuals react to situations of chaos and re-establish their own unique sense of order. It is interesting to trace their evolution from Freud through to present-day theorists.

Cognitive behavioural models

Consideration of the models previously outlined refers to cognitive processing and the subsequent effect on the behaviour of people who have been subjected to a traumatic experience. Models presented previously have had a different emphasis, but it is important to recognise the linking features of cognition and associated changes in observable behaviour which underlie all our understanding of models relating to post-trauma reactions.

Bowlby (1979) has written of the need for an individual who has been subjected to an extraordinary experience to deal with it by mastering the extraordinary information received from the event. Such mastery is essential if the person is to gain congruence between the new information and the person's existing mind models. This would mean that the traumatic experience becomes integrated into normal cognitive schemata in such a way that it no longer represents a threat to the person's view of their total world. PTSD would therefore be classed as a flawed integration of traumatic information into the individual's cognitive schemata.

Flawed integration of experience formed the basis of Rachman's (1980) work on 'psychosocial processing'. He drew on psychodynamic and behavioural literature when he postulated that successful psychosocial processing would result in the event causing less distress or disruption. He suggested that, where such psychosocial processing was flawed, there was a continuation of 'intrusive activity'. He also identified factors which led to unsuccessful processing which related to traumatic experiences. These factors included such features as 'intensity, uncontrollability, predictability and dangerousness', all of which relate to the diagnostic criteria of PTSD. Other factors relating to an individual include the state of the individual at the time of the event – for example, high arousal, illness or fatigue.

Horowitz (1986b, 1990) developed a model which is considered to be one of the most comprehensive to date and which addresses the most detailed explanations of how the degree to which traumatic information is processed is of paramount importance in post-trauma reactions (see also the information processing model, discussed earlier). He postulates that PTSD results from incomplete cognitive processing. The negative and overwhelming nature of such information creates problems for the individual as they seek to integrate this traumatic information into their existing schemata to regain a harmony in their lives. Such recall may be resisted by the individual in the form of denial.

Horowitz's model of PTSD is a two-phase model, with alternating intrusion-repetition and denial-numbing. He suggests that the avoidant intrusion cluster symptoms of PTSD – denial of the event, avoidance and numbness – result when the inner inhibitory control mechanisms predominate over the repetition of information into the conscious mind as characterised in the intrusion symptom cluster. At other times, the intrusion symptoms can dominate over the avoidance state.

Horowitz's model is useful when we seek to understand the intrusion/avoidance symptoms of PTSD. Foa and Rothbaum (1989) valued these features of the model but noted that it offers no explanations as to why negative psychosocial states such as fear, survivor's guilt, anxiety and depression are typically associated with PTSD. Horowitz's model offers insights which should surely serve to inform responders of the need to consider pre-crisis training as a preventative model of intervention.

Behavioural models of PTSD

Main behavioural theories of PTSD appear to use the principles associated with conditioning theories. Mowrer's theory (1947) proposes that two types of learning – classical and instrumental – are present in acquired fear and avoidance which present after trauma. Neutral stimuli, such as smells, sounds, shapes or words, when associated with painful traumatic events, can evoke painful responses. Such responses can then be described as conditioned responses to the trauma when they produce or recreate painful responses such as fear and anxiety. This model reminds us that ordinary everyday stimuli can be turned into traumatic stressors by the association with the traumatic event.

Mowrer's theory also included instrumental conditioning as an explanation of the development of such behaviours as escape and avoidance. These behaviours can be utilised as a means of reducing exposure to an aversive conditioned stimulus. Mowrer's theory can be seen in the work of Keane et al (1985) with Vietnam veterans. These authors believed that during a traumatic experience we may become conditioned to multiple sensory stimuli associated with the event. Subsequent exposure to the same or similar stimuli can elicit the same sense of fear or anxiety which was associated with the original traumatic event. Keane gives the example of veterans who fall to the ground and assume the attack position when they hear the backfire of a car because the sound may be associated with a sniper attack in the jungles of Vietnam. In my experience, there are clients who cannot tolerate the sound of thunder because they associate it with the sound of a bomb attack in which they were involved.

Mowrer's work gives us insights into how responders, who are repeatedly exposed to stimuli associated with trauma, can use escape/ avoidance behaviours in an effort to minimise the impact of the painful response which the stimuli may elicit even in non-traumatic environments. Animal experiments indicate that the longer the duration and the greater the intensity of the original trauma, the more these conditioned responses may be evidenced. A lack of understanding on how painful reactions can be triggered must surely add to the negative reactions experienced. This work would suggest that in any form of pre-crisis training there would be a need to address this possible reaction with responders in an effort to minimise the impact of such reactions in the post-trauma stage.

Cognitive models of PTSD

The theory of learned helplessness has been proposed as an explanation of the numbing effect and passivity sometimes seen in PTSD. This learned helplessness is similar to feelings associated with victimisation. Meichenbaum (1994) notes that both these situations lead to generalised beliefs about future uncontrollability and the futility of future responses.

The process by which individuals attach meaning to a traumatic event – cognitive appraisal – has been explored by several researchers such as Scheppe and Bart (1983) and Frank and Stewart (1984). Both these teams explored the concept that, if the traumatic event happened in situations which were deemed to be safe, the reactions experienced were different in severity and intensity. A rape victim who felt she was in a safe environment suffered more reaction to the rape than a victim who appraised that she was in an at-risk situation prior to the rape. Their findings, tested in a variety of circumstances, reinforce the concept that pre-existing cognitive schemata influence the individual's response to the trauma and their ability to process it successfully.

If pre-crisis training can inform an individual of the reactions they, and indeed others, might experience, can this influence their cognitive schemata? This would surely then have an effect on how they subsequently process the new traumatic information and experience, and ultimately incorporate it into their future schemata. This research also highlights the impact of internal personal variables and identifying mechanisms involved in the emergence of such factors as shame, guilt, poor self-esteem and depression – factors which are widely reported in the manifestations of PTSD.

This debate must influence our thinking on the factors which could contribute to the pertinent issue of the variability in the individual responses found in individuals who have experienced the same traumatic incident. This is an issue which often provokes much debate in employing organisations when considering how best to support responders who have been involved. It can also form the basis for viewing those who appear to be most vulnerable, because of their response, as being 'weak' and less able to 'cope'. By emphasising the influence of individual pre-existing schemata, the research offers some possible explanations as to why some individuals develop PTSD while others do not.

Cognitive models afford us explanations of some of the symptoms that contribute to behavioural changes. They also alert us to some of the factors that it may be possible to influence by pre-crisis training. However, they do not appear to address some of the more complex issues associated with the core elements of PTSD. Jones and Barlow (1990) attempted to integrate a variety of theoretical perspectives and developed an aetiological model of PTSD that was based on the process and origins of anxiety and panic. They related the connections between panic disorder and PTSD.

Solomon et al's (1985) research suggested that emotion-focused coping and distancing techniques are associated with more severe PTSD. They also emphasised social support as an important variable in the development and maintenance of PTSD.

Information processing model

One of the most significant models for understanding PTSD is the information processing model proposed by Horowitz (1973, 1974, 1976, 1986). This model was viewed as the cornerstone for the criteria established for DSM-III in 1980. While this model builds on classical and contemporary theories for trauma, the main emphasis is placed on information and cognitive theories of emotion. Peterson et al (1991), who identify the basic element of the model as 'information overload', which can occur when too much information is received at the time of crisis, use the term 'completion tendency' to describe the situation where important information is processed until reality and cognitive models match. Incomplete information processing is experienced when new information has only been partially processed and the information remains an 'active form of memory'.

Horowitz postulates that traumatic incidents involve the intake of massive amounts of new information that is outside our usual realm of experience. As a direct result, most of this information cannot be matched to a person's existing cognitive schemata. The result is information overload in which new experiences, ideas, effects and images cannot be integrated with self. As a result of extreme

Figure 4.1: Normal and pathological phases of post-stress response

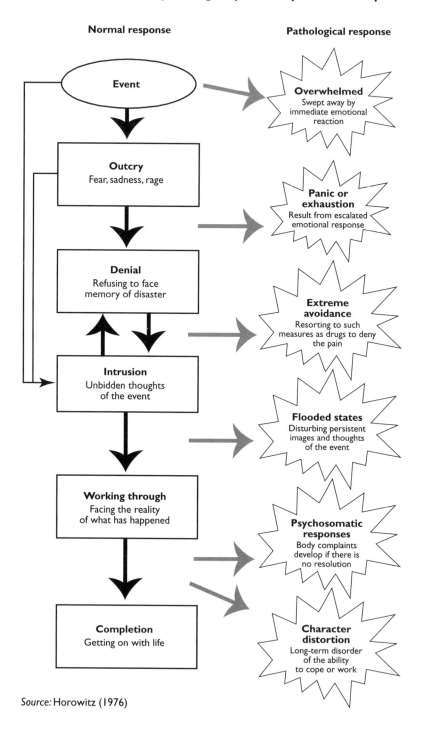

Source: Horowitz (1976)

traumatisation, a person cannot process the information and it may be shunted out of awareness. Numbing and denial may be employed as defensive mechanisms to avoid this processing. As a result, the information will remain in an unprocessed, active or raw form. This painful information will re-enter the mind at times as intrusive images or sensations due to 'completion tendency'. Horowitz (1976) views such intrusions as part of the information processing which must take place (see Figure 4.1).

Completion of information processing continues until the new information becomes part of 'long-term models and inner schemata'. Green et al (1985, p 6) believe that: 'At completion, the experience is integrated so it is the individual's view of the world and of him or herself, and no longer needs to be walled off from the rest of his or her personality'. At this point, the trauma is no longer stored in an active state. Horowitz's model of information processing is an extension of psychoanalytic concepts of trauma. Traumatic incidents continue to destabilise our psychic equilibrium until the information is fully processed.

Psychosocial model

One of the widely accepted models of PTSD is the psychosocial model proposed by Green et al (1985). It identifies factors which may aid our search for a greater understanding of why some people exposed to traumatic incidents develop PTSD and others do not. This is a very important issue which needs to be addressed in any analysis which will lead to a preventative model of intervention. As previously suggested in the discussion of the cognitive behavioural models, there is a need to adapt the person's existing internal schemata to process and integrate the new experience in such a way that it does not disable their functioning in the future. Wilson and Krauss (1985, p 114) describe this as 'psychic overload': '... a state in which the nature, intensity and meaning of the experience(s) are not readily understandable in terms of existing conceptual schemata of reality'.

They suggest that, if the person is in a favourable environment, the possibilities of working through the trauma are enhanced. Similarly, should the environment be unsupportive, the possibilities of a positive outcome of the individual's processing are diminished. Wilson (1983) and Green et al (1985) identified specific characteristics, which they deemed as important in relation to the longer-term response, as the severity of the stressor, the duration of the trauma, the speed of onset and the degrees of bereavement and displacement. The number of those involved who were affected by an actual death threat was also significant, as was the level of participation by the individual.

Green's diagram (Figure 4.2) indicates how pre-existing individual characteristics and the recovery environment interact in a dynamic way with the post-traumatic cognitive processing. Green et al (1985) argue that the influence of the recovery environment is often neglected in the theoretical formulation of PTSD. They believe that the qualities of the environment have a direct correlation with the outcome achieved.

Velsen (1997) reminds us that:

> The impact of major trauma on an individual is not in a vacuum but in a social context, often a family. Difficulties can be experienced by the families of trauma survivors, and traumatic stress symptoms exacerbated in an individual because of family dynamics. (p 244)

Figley (1988) identifies the positive and negative ways in which the family can influence the outcome for the survivor. The positive or healing influences can be:

• **Detecting symptoms of stress**: it can be the family which provides the most authentic means of monitoring post-trauma

Figure 4.2: Psychosocial framework for understanding PTSD

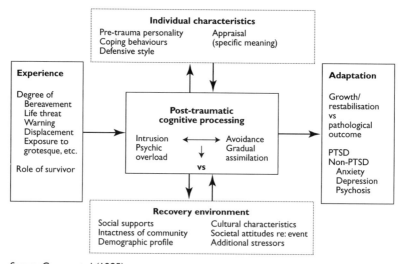

Source: Green et al (1985)

behaviours which are being exhibited and which may not be noticed by the survivor themselves.

- **Confronting trauma**: if the survivor is avoiding reminders of the incident by socially or psychologically withdrawing from the family, this can be 'confronted' by the family.
- **Encouraging revisiting the trauma**: if the family is supportive and there is honest communication and trust, then it may well be that the family context is the best environment for the physical or psychological 'revisiting' to take place. An example of this is where a father has difficulty driving a car again after a severe road traffic accident.
- **Facilitating resolution of conflict**: such conflict can be interpersonal or between organisations involved. Appropriate family support can help such conflicts to be dealt with suitably – for example, with the help of solicitors, etc.

The negative aspects of family influence are described by Figley (1988) as pathological:

- **Denying existence of significant symptoms**: this is often the result of a feeling of inadequacy to deal with such symptoms.
- **Denying need to deal with trauma**: in this situation the family is avoiding the impact of the trauma on the survivor, perhaps in the hope that 'time will heal'.
- **Reinforcing avoidance**: this can build up a situation of negative collusion in the total family unit. It reinforces negative coping skills and unhealthy communication networks. 'Family secrets' create a minefield for future relationships as all truths are questioned in a climate of general distrust.
- **Active avoidance of conflict resolution**: this non–activity can lay the foundations for future family dysfunction.

Yule (1990), writing of his work with children and adolescents after the Herald of Free Enterprise ferry disaster, noted that the children often did not want to burden a traumatised adult with their own distressing reactions as they sensed that parents could not cope with this additional burden. A conspiracy of silence prevailed and the children were denied their normal sources of nurturing and support as a result.

While the techniques of family therapy may be viewed as appropriate in such circumstances, it must be remembered that, while the whole family unit has been traumatised, allowance must be made for the individual and unique reactions of each family member, which will be varied and sometimes at variance with others being experienced. Dyregrov (1998, p 9) clearly identifies the complexities of working with families who have been traumatised, and the importance of the dual approach of total unit needs and also individual needs within the total entity. He describes the need to educate on the interpretation of post-trauma behaviours to alert families to the changes that can occur in their collective and individual communication. All these dynamics can present challenges to each member of the unit at a personal and unit level. The very fabric of parenting will be disturbed by trauma. The basic parental functions of psychosocial nurturing, education and protection can be affected. The family may have to deal with a shattering of their collective life assumptions (Janoff-Bulman, 1992, p 66). Their own collective and individual attributions will have a significant influence on how they view the incident and how it is dealt with. Family relationships can be altered by role changes which are necessary to survive. The hospitalisation of the father can alter the mother's role completely in the short term, or in the longer term if there is a residual disability of a physical or psychological nature.

In my clinical experience, responders and those bereaved or injured often note a reduction in physical contact with family members. This can result from their desire to protect the others from the painful facts of the trauma. It can be clearly seen from this that there is potential for additional stress to be caused by this phenomenon. McFarlane (1987) expressed the clear need to identify and adequately treat PTSD in parents of young children, because post-trauma anxiety was found to account for the greatest percentage of disturbed family functioning after the Ash Wednesday forest fire. Research by Fields and Bisson (1988) proved the detrimental effects on small children of the presence of depression in parents, especially mothers.

These observations bring us to ask what factors contribute to the 'resilient family' that provides the most potential for healing to the traumatised member. What factors could be developed in the pre-crisis period to nurture a resilient environment for responders who may have to face repeated trauma in their work lives? Hawley and Dehann (1996) state that, in families exhibiting warmth, cohesion and stability, children are resilient, and that a strong parent-child relationship marked by positive interaction, nurturance, affection and consistent discipline are also related to resilience in children.

The Canadian and Irish armies have embraced some of these principles in the work that they currently undertake with the families of returning peacekeeping forces. They educate the families in the possible reactions to trauma that they may observe in their family member, and offer instant support to the family as a whole and the individual in particular. They remind partners that the person who went to fulfil peacekeeping duties will not be the same person who returns home to them. It appears from this work that, when such family dynamics are explained and understood, it promotes a better intra-family environment and can prevent the development of blocks to recovery.

The support which a traumatised person receives, or does not receive, from a family unit has been demonstrated to be a crucial consideration in the psychosocial model. This must also alert us to be more aware of the added impact which could result for the responder who does not share their work or traumatic stress with other family members. There is also the impact on a responder who lives alone and returns to an empty house after a traumatic shift.

Such literature about the family may help us understand other social problems such as the effects of activity in teams within organisations, and organisations themselves, on the trauma recovery processes. The team of paramedics, or of accident and emergency nurses, who work together can be viewed as another form of family which can have the potential for a healing or pathological environment. Other responders may not normally work together, yet they become a unit, a 'family', as they share the same experiences and stressors. Members of faith communities who work together at such incidents appear to have little difficulty in transcending denominational boundaries as they work as fellow responders in the face of massive distress.

Secondary traumatic stress model

'There is a cost to caring. Professionals who listen to clients' stories of fear, pain and suffering may feel similar fear, pain and suffering because they care' (Figley, 1995, p 1). The links between the reactions of primary victims and those of responders are discussed by Raphael (1986, p 235) where she describes responders as 'hidden victims' (see Figure 4.3): 'The stressful effects on responders stem from the encounter with death, from sharing the anguish of the victims and their families, and from role stresses.'

Following a decade of research into the impact of helping on the responders themselves, Figley suggests that parallel to the criteria for PTSD, as outlined in DSM-III (now DSM-IV), there should be a set of criteria to address the needs of responders. He originally called this model 'secondary victimisation' (Figley, 1993a). Following further consultation with colleagues, he changed the title to 'compassion fatigue'. He also suggests a reconfiguration of PTSD which he names

Figure 4.3: Responders as hidden victims

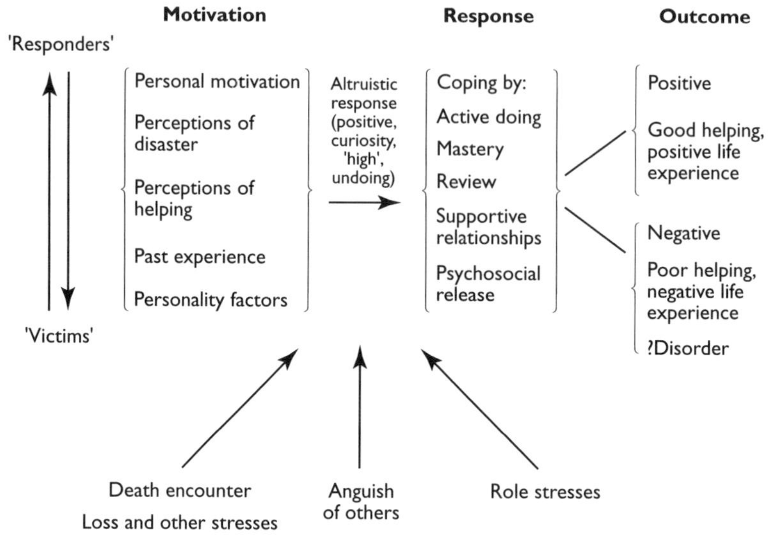

Source: Raphael (1986)

Secondary Traumatic Stress (STS) and Secondary Traumatic Stress Disorder (STSD). Figley quotes from the PTSD description in DSM-IV (APA, 1994), which deals with what constitutes a sufficiently traumatic experience:

> *The essential feature of Post-Traumatic Stress Disorder is the development of characteristic symptoms following exposure to an extreme traumatic stressor involving direct personal experience of an event that involves death, actual or threatened serious injury,* or other threat to one's physical integrity: *or witness an event which involves death, injury, or threat to the physical integrity of another person:* or learning about unexpected or violent death, serious harm, or threat of death, injury experienced by a family member or other close associate. (Figley, 1995, p 424 [non-italics added by Figley])

He feels that the italicised phrases emphasise that people can be traumatised without actually being physically harmed or threatened with harm – that is, that they can be traumatised simply by learning about the event. He notes that after the incident 'direct victims' are counted but no count is taken of those who are affected as secondary victims, family members, colleagues or responders. Figley defines STS as 'The natural consequent behaviours and emotions resulting from knowing about a traumatising event experienced by a significant other – the stress resulting from helping or wanting to help a traumatised or suffering person' (Figley, 1993a).

He also suggests that PTSD should stand for Primary Traumatic Stress Disorder rather than Post-Traumatic Stress Disorder, since every stress reaction is 'post' by definition. (Symptoms under one month's duration are considered normal, acute, crisis-related reactions. Those not manifesting symptoms until six months or more following the event are experiencing delayed PTSD or STSD [Figley, 1993b, p 8].) Figley (1993b) also notes the similarities between the criteria for PTSD and STSD in relation to responders. This set of criteria is based on the personal impact of the work.

The terms 'transference' and 'counter-transference' are derived from psychodynamic theory and are important issues when we are considering the responder–traumatised person relationship. Transference refers to the transfer of information from the traumatised person to the responder. Counter-transference is used to describe the double transfer which occurs between the traumatised person and the responder, and between the responder and the traumatised person. Counter-transference can have both a positive and negative impact on the therapeutic relationship.

On the positive side, it makes the responder more aware that, if the traumatised person's story is raising issues in the responder's 'inner world', then these issues must be having a similar impact on them. On the negative side, if the traumatised person's story raises unresolved issues for the responder that result from the responder's own life experience and values, it may consciously or unconsciously influence the responder's professional ability to support the traumatised person. Transference or counter-transference, within the helping relationship, can be viewed as the basis for STS or STSD.

While Corey (1991) defined counter-transference as 'The process of seeing oneself in the client, of over identifying with the client, or of meeting needs through the client' (Corey, in Figley, 1995, p 9), Figley notes four additional reasons why trauma workers are especially vulnerable to compassion fatigue, STS and STSD:

1. **Empathy is a major resource for trauma workers to help the traumatised**. Empathy is essential for assessing and formulating a strategy to help traumatised people. It aids the responder's understanding of the person's experience of being traumatised.

Figure 4.4: The personal impact of secondary traumatic stress

Cognitive	Psychosocial	Behavioural	Spiritual	Interpersonal	Physical
Diminished concentration	Powerlessness	Clingy	Questioning the meaning of life	Withdrawn	Shock
Confusion	Anxiety	Impatient	Loss of purpose	Decreased interest in intimacy or sex	Sweating
Spaciness	Guilt	Irritable	Lack of self-satisfaction	Mistrust	Rapid heartbeat
Loss of meaning	Anger/rage	Withdrawn	Pervasive hopelessness	Isolation from friends	Breathing difficulties
Decreased self-esteem	Survivor guilt	Moody	Ennui	Impact on parenting (protectiveness, concern about aggression)	Somatic reactions
Preoccupation with trauma	Shutdown	Regression	Anger at God		Aches and pains
Trauma imagery	Numbness	Sleep disturbances	Questioning of prior religious beliefs	Projection of anger or blame	Dizziness
Apathy	Fear	Appetite changes		Intolerance	Impaired immune system
Rigidity	Helplessness	Nightmares		Loneliness	
Disorientation	Sadness	Hypervigilance			
Whirling thoughts	Depression	Elevated startle response			
Thoughts of self-harm or harm towards others	Hypersensitivity	Use of negative coping (alcohol, smoking or other substance misuse)			
Self-doubt	Psychosocial roller coaster	Accident proneness			
Perfectionism	Overwhelmed	Losing things			
Minimisation	Depleted	Self-harm behaviours			

Source: Yassen, 1995, in Figley (1995, p 185)

Empathy is also the core of transference from those to be helped and the responder.

2. **Most trauma workers have experienced some traumatic event in their lives**. They may perceive that their personal experience means that they are better able to help a client or patient in a similar situation. Here again, there can be a danger for the responder if boundaries are not clear with the person seeking help.

3. **Unresolved trauma of the worker will be activated by reports of similar trauma in clients**. This reactivation of unresolved reactions may be injurious to the helping relationship and damage the responder through secondary traumatisation.

4. **Children's trauma is also provocative for therapists**. Inevitably, all trauma workers will have to deal with the trauma of children on a regular basis; trauma workers may have to experience the additional stress of dealing with children more than other workers in their professional peer group.

The personal impact of STS is shown in Figure 4.4.

These models of post-traumatic stress in responders are very valid to this book. They help us to distinguish the 'special' features of secondary traumatisation. They also recognise that the environment in which the responder is working can contribute to the resolution of these reactions, or it can reinforce the negative aspects of STS. In this lies the challenge – to identify organisational issues and work within such structures to raise awareness of the needs of responders and to promote preventative interventions in the pre-crisis period.

Conclusion

A greater understanding of the types of reactions which individuals exposed to trauma may experience is necessary for all who experience trauma themselves as well as for responders. PTSD is complex and multi-factoral both in origin and manifestation. The material considered has been subjective and a limited selection from the vast amount available. An understanding of such models is essential if services are to be developed to assist responders to help individuals affected in traumatic situations.

FIVE

The injured and their relatives

Rehabilitation is the bridge between uselessness and usefulness, between hopelessness and hopefulness, between despair and happiness. (Mary Switzer, Director of Vocational Rehabilitation, Department of Health, Indiana, US, 1979)

The process of rehabilitation for the survivor of a disaster, or a person injured as the result of trauma, begins at the moment of impact. In a physical sense, their injuries can be greatly affected by the way in which they are rescued. Skilled rescue workers can minimise injury. The way in which they talk to those they are rescuing can also lay the foundation for their psychological rehabilitation.

When discussing 'the injured', it is usual to deal with those who have physical injuries that may result in scars or disability. We must never forget those who have psychological injuries which leave no visible scars but who can be equally 'disabled' in life. The stages identified in the discussion of psychological rehabilitation must also be linked to physical rehabilitation.

Pre-crisis

The general health of people injured can have a significant effect on their recovery. Their previous experience of crisis can also affect how they can adapt psychologically. Their earlier experience may have equipped them with coping mechanisms which they can use as they face the new demands of the current situation. The circumstances surrounding the crisis can affect the rehabilitation stages. The questions of 'if only', which will have to be addressed in the acknowledgement stage, have their basis in this pre-crisis stage. If only the driver had not taken that one drink, he may have got home safely. If only the young mother had checked that the garden gate was locked, the toddler would not have wandered on to the road. For the injured and the family, this pre-crisis period is very significant.

Crisis

The general physical and psychological fitness of a person may affect their ability to escape from the situation, and the aid that can be provided to others. Circumstances may have been such that self-preservation was the only possible course of action. There are many reports of people appearing to have extra strengths or speed in their immediate reaction to crisis. One survivor of the tsunami of 2004, who had been swimming in a large rock pool on an isolated island in Thailand, described her experience to me as 'being a rag doll in a washing machine'. As part of her recovery process, she wrote the story of her experiences when, although injured, she organised the rescue of others. Fear of another wave at the next high tide meant that they had lifted the injured and some bodies from the beach to higher ground, using surf boards as stretchers. She spoke of the phenomenal strength she and others had needed to achieve this objective. On reflection, she wondered how they had achieved some of these tasks. The hormone adrenalin, produced by the stressful stimuli of fear, has been recognised to produce such reactions. Such situations often produce heroes. She was later described by some of the survivors as the 'Angel of the Island'. She found it difficult to accept this title as she struggled to cope with memories of those she could not save.

Immediate post-crisis

Shock may numb physical and psychological reactions at this stage. The feeling of detachment from what is happening all around is common. This period often coincides with the period of high medical activity. This is a period when other people appear to be making all the decisions. This adds to the feelings of depersonalisation recounted by many patients. Some of the drugs used following severe trauma also contribute to this sense of disassociation and low anxiety levels. While this numbness is a necessary protection for the injured, it is a time of high distress for the relatives. They may have endured a prolonged period of uncertainty following the disaster when they may have had to search the hospitals for information. Such searching may have been accompanied by the fear that the names will appear on lists of the deceased. Now, they may be searching for answers from the professionals involved as they anticipate problems of survival or disability in the future. The high level of medical activity may isolate them from what is happening to their relative. The high level of their stress may mean that they are unable to cope with or may misinterpret information that they are given. The responder may be required as an interpreter for such information and a 'sounding board' for their fears. It may be necessary to explain to the relatives the effects of shock on the injured person. The responder should try to build a relationship with the relatives at this stage that will mean that they can work together to help the injured person when their numbness diminishes. Shocked relatives may also experience psychological numbness and this can make them more accident prone. Extra care must be taken when driving a car or even when using household equipment around the home.

Case study 13: bomb victim – reactions recalled

A young woman, who had been seriously injured in a terrorist bomb attack, described her feelings of utter depersonalisation after the incident. One moment she was shopping for a new dress and the next she was caught in the bomb and was being dug out of the rubble. She recalled acute sensory impact associated with the voices of her rescuers. She remembered features of her admission to the Intensive Care Unit. She said it felt as if they were happening to someone other than herself as shock had given the events a sense of unreality. When the doctors told her that they would have to amputate her mutilated leg, she said this was just another decision that others were taking on her behalf. She felt that the leg did not really belong to her at all, and she showed little reaction. She recalled seeing herself on the bed 'from outside her body'. It was some days later that she had to cope with the psychological pain of realisation when the decision was made to amputate her remaining leg.

Case study 14: Kegworth air disaster – care of relatives in hospital

Whitham and Newburn (1991) recall in their book, *Coping with tragedy: Managing the response to two disasters*, how a decision made to structure the response to relatives proved to be best practice for the future.

A team of social workers and chaplains who were then allocated to each family group met relatives from Northern Ireland, arriving at The Queen's Medical Centre in Nottingham following the Kegworth air crash. The relatives were given a brief account of the injuries and the appearance of the injured. This description of the injuries plus some insight into the purpose of any medical equipment being used was found to be valuable. Relatives were also advised that their initial visit should be very brief. They were accompanied by their responder to the ward for the visit and then escorted to the British Midland care centre, which had been established in the hospital.

In later interviews, both injured and relatives considered this structured approach to have been helpful. They appreciated the advice on when to leave the bedside following the first emotive meeting. Their 'time out' in the supportive environment of the care centre meant that they could react without fear of adding stress to the patients. They also appreciated that someone else was making decisions for them at a time when such decision making was too difficult for them. This system was made possible by multidisciplinary cooperation in the hours between the crash and the arrival of relatives on flights from Northern Ireland. Not all situations allow time for this planning but these elements of good practice could be incorporated in pre-planning for the support to relatives irrespective of the numbers involved.

Short-term post-crisis

This stage can involve much physical and emotional pain for the injured. Physically damaged bodies are being repaired. The reality of the implications of such injuries is becoming clearer. The sense of numbness, which has buffered the person against reality, may have diminished. This state of realisation brings many concerns, real or imagined, about the future. The injured person may be preoccupied with the current state of their injuries and display limited insight into the possible long-term implications. The relatives may, at the same time, be totally obsessed by the longer-term implications. The dynamics of this situation can lead to a lot of misunderstandings and conflict. The psychological rehabilitation of the relatives and the injured are at different stages on the continuum of reaction. The responder should try to minimise this potential for conflict by discussing with each the fact that different perspectives do exist.

Case study 15: rehabilitation following an industrial accident

On a home visit to a patient whose hands had been severely injured in an industrial accident, I observed that his wife was undertaking tasks for him which he had mastered during therapy sessions in the burns unit. His newly acquired independence was being undermined. After a sensitive discussion with his wife, she agreed that this level of care was meeting her needs as much as his. During his long stay in hospital, she had felt useless and inadequate when she saw the professional care of the staff. On her husband's return home, she had been determined to show him that she was capable of carrying out similar duties. While he was in hospital, she had assumed roles in household management and in the family which her husband had never delegated to her. She was reluctant to see her husband rehabilitate too quickly and resume his original role in the family. Dialogue between the two partners was necessary if conflict was to be avoided.

The survivor syndrome

When the initial threat of death is past, there can be a sense of euphoria at survival, at cheating death; this can result in risk-taking behaviour. This 'survivor syndrome' phenomenon was noted in the behaviour of returning Vietnam veterans.

If there were fatalities as a result of the incident, the survivor may experience death guilt. This can manifest itself in such questions as 'Why did I survive when they died?' The survivors may have difficulty dealing with relatives of the deceased with whom they come into contact. There is in-depth questioning by survivors of their own actions at the crisis impact time. Could they have done more to save others? Survivors talk of their actions in an attempt to rationalise any actions they took or to justify any inaction. Did the survivor's own rescue mean that others were sacrificed?

Charles Figley deals with this phenomenon in his book, *Stress disorders among Vietnam veterans* (1978). He feels that these questions have to do with a sense of organic social balance: 'That image of exchange of one life for another is perhaps the survivor's greatest psychological burden.' Figley also noted a deep distrust by the survivor of anyone offering help. The survivors felt set apart from others by a sort of 'death taint'. Even where survivors recognised their need for help, they rejected the offer in case it would be viewed as a sign of weakness, confirming in their own minds that others felt that they were not worthy of survival. These thoughts may result in the survivors seeking help and reassurance from others who were involved. Self-help contacts with individuals or groups have the advantage that survivors do not have to explain their emotions when recalling the event. The listeners were there; they experienced similar feelings. This was the background to the Vietnam veterans setting up Rap groups (Lifton, 1973). They needed help from themselves, not from the official army system. These groups had the dual objectives of healing for themselves and of focusing their efforts to make their feelings known to the army and society in general.

Langer (1967) believes that fundamental to all survivor psychology, and encompassing all the emotions involved, is the struggle of survivors to find a sense of order and significance for the rest of their lives. This re-evaluation of life goals has been responsible for most religious experiences and for zeal for political causes following such experiences. These thoughts on the part of the survivor can be explored and extolled to others with great 'evangelical' fervour. They can cause great restlessness in the mind and actions of the survivor. This can be distressing for the family members who are most probably physically and emotionally exhausted at this stage. The survivors have a great sense of urgency to put things right in their own lives and in society. They have been given time that the others who did not survive had plucked away from them – there is a need not to waste any of these precious moments which have been rescued from death. Any responder involved in this type of situation should try to listen to all the things that the survivor feels must be achieved quickly, and try to moderate either the zeal or the timetables suggested into a more socially acceptable presentation. The survivor may become aggressive if others do not share such zeal and sense of urgency. Responders should try to advise the survivor not to make radical life decisions with too much haste. It may be necessary to inform key people such as the bank manager or solicitor of these problems. Family members appreciate the help from a professional helper at such a stage in the rehabilitation process. The intervention of the media at this time can be difficult as the survivor is very vulnerable and later may regret statements made at this stage.

The family of the survivor may share the euphoria that the survivor feels at survival, but the emotions surrounding the survivor syndrome are incomprehensible to them. The responder can also fulfil the role of interpreter of the emotions which underlie each set of actions. All those involved must assist survivors to move from the 'victim' role and return slowly to their former roles. By talking through the strong feelings which exist, survivors can begin to put events into a more acceptable timescale. Their trust that there will be a 'tomorrow' will increase as time passes and some of the urgency will ease. The concept of moving from the 'victim' role can also be influenced by the attitude of the family.

Case study 16: survivor syndrome following an air crash

A survivor of an air crash did not return to his home for many weeks due to the nature of his injuries. His departure from hospital was the cause for great celebrations and his arrival home was eagerly awaited by family and friends. However, within 48 hours of the return home, the survivor had experienced a dramatic reaction. He had become agitated, anxious and had displayed many of the symptoms of survival syndrome previously described. His wife was distraught as all her hopes of a return to normality at home were shattered. This reaction came when she was extremely weary after the prolonged visits to hospital, and she had few physical or psychological reserves to enable her to cope with these new and frightening demands. Psychiatric hospitalisation for the survivor was considered but counselling intervention was organised. The first two sessions were occupied by listening to his rapidly spoken recollections of the event. The underlying conflicts of joy of survival and guilt that others close by on the plane had perished were reiterated. Bizarre and unrealistic plans for the future were formed as the urgency 'not to waste one moment' of his future life was discussed. As days passed, the urgency and hyper alertness diminished, giving way to the possibility of discussing the sadness, guilt and pain of loss associated with the death of fellow passengers. In formed, some weeks later, the trigger for the reactions appeared to have been the silence of his own home when he had felt alone for the first time since the crash. He described the noise of the hospital, the constant feeling of never being really alone in a busy ward where activity never ceased day or night. The silence and aloneness of his own home reminded him of the similar feelings he had experienced just prior to the impact of the plane into the ground. He later said that the surgeons had saved his life and put his body together again, but the responder had given him back his life, for living.

Long-term post-crisis

An orthopaedic surgeon doing his ward round looked at the young motorcyclist, who had sustained such severe injuries to his arm that it had to be amputated, and said, 'Tomorrow is the first day of the rest of your life.' Now he had to design his tomorrows to fit in with his altered body image of today. The quality of his life in the future was dependent on how well he could adapt physically and psychologically.

For the survivor of a major disaster, there are special milestones to be coped with in the individual rehabilitation continuum. There may be the publicity of the visits from VIPs, the memorial service, the inquests, the inquiry, the litigation and the compensation claims that may follow. Such milestones can retard or arrest the rehabilitation process for a period of time.

Guidelines for responders in specific types of rehabilitation

- rehabilitation after burns injuries;
- rehabilitation after head injury;
- sexual problems in rehabilitation; and
- the use of family therapy in rehabilitation.

Rehabilitation after burns injuries

Burns injuries are associated with suffering and long-term disfigurement. When they are acquired in situations of trauma, there is the further dimension to the psychological reaction experienced by the victims. The rehabilitation of such patients demonstrates the marriage between physical and psychological rehabilitation. Badly burned patients experience severe physiological and psychological shock. If the responder can prepare the family for the initial sight of the injured patient, it is beneficial both for the relatives and the patient. If the relatives can control their reaction to the initial disfigurement in the presence of the patient, it can aid the patient's reaction. Realisation of the full implications of the long-term nature of the injuries will have to be dealt with by both parties later.

The majority of burns occur to the exposed parts of the body such as the face and hands - the areas which are particularly significant in how people assess us in everyday life. The facial expression and the type of hand extended in greeting play a major part in our instant perceptions of people when we first meet them. It is therefore necessary to consider how facial disfigurement can have damaging long-term effects for all involved. The natural reaction of the public is just to stare and then to indicate a level of rejection.

The responder involved in these situations will need to prepare the injured person for such reactions from society at large. The majority of severe burns cases are treated in specialist units where there will be some segregation of patients due to infection control. Staff and relatives may have to wear special protective gowns and masks. The line between the burns unit and the 'outside world' is usually clearly marked and labelled. This physical barrier represents a psychological barrier for the patients as well. In the unit, they experience isolation, painful treatment and rehabilitation processes, but there is an acceptance of their scars. The transition from the unit should be gradual as they face a world where they may experience less sympathetic reactions. All associated with the person bearing the scars should try to reinforce their ego and seek to remind them that they are the same person 'inside' irrespective of their scarred 'outside'. Counselling such patients may be made easier if the responder concentrates on the injured person's eyes. Focusing attention on their eyes centres one's thoughts on the personality within and helps to diminish one's reaction to surface scarring.

Many years of intermittent hospitalisation may be needed for restorative plastic surgery. The need for support can continue as such treatment continues. The point at which such surgery ceases can also be a crisis period. This is when the person realises that no further treatment will improve the scars. The person has to have time to mourn for the person they were and come to terms with the person they have become.

Victims of the Bradford fire (1985) reported greater acceptance of their scars in the Bradford area where there was community sympathy. People experiencing the rehabilitation from severe burns injuries will go through the stages of psychological rehabilitation many times, as each surgical intervention may represent a further crisis. They may alternate between the realisation and acknowledgement stages many times before adaptation is reached.

Case study 17: mother with severe burns injuries following terrorist attack

A young mother sustained severe burns following a terrorist bomb attack on the restaurant where she and her friends were attending a function. She escaped by climbing over the bodies of some of these friends who died instantly. Several years of painful reconstructive plastic surgery followed. On the day the consultant told her that her surgery was completed, the staff in the ward were pleased that her multiple surgical interventions were over. She would not have to sustain any more painful dressings or stressful physiotherapy sessions. Their joy was not matched by the reactions of the patient. She became depressed and tearful. Sensitive counselling allowed the patient to express her psychological realisation that her scars would not be improved – they now had to be accepted and 'lived with'.

Following her final discharge from the hospital, she had to begin her psychological rehabilitation. She suffered panic attacks and became more sensitive about her appearance. Counselling support coupled with behavioural modification techniques were needed to bring her through this delayed post-traumatic stress reaction. This case study is used to remind responders that physical rehabilitation is underpinned by the psychological rehabilitation process, and the two may progress in tandem or at a different pace.

Rehabilitation after head injury

The 'lamebrain' survivors of severe brain injury present as a unique group in terms of their rehabilitation process. Their needs are twofold, as there may be physical disability coupled with disturbed patterns of behaviour. Many of these people have the residual handicap of uncoordinated or 'spastic' movements. The psychological damage may be difficult to assess accurately for some time after the initial injury. Mood swings, emotional outbursts, an absence of social inhibitions, a tendency to depression, difficulties with memory or decision making are some of the common features which may be described in the all-embracing term 'personality change'. A broken limb can be seen to mend, but the presenting features of an injured brain can be frightening and perplexing to an observer or family member. The infantile behaviour, aggression and change of personality may be temporary, but in some cases time acts only to modify these features, not to cure them. Time is one of the problems associated with these cases, as compensation claims have to be delayed for some considerable time. The courts usually expect at least two years to elapse before assessments of the permanency of the collective disabilities should be carried out.

Families need a lot of support from responders involved with these situations. One young wife I counselled, whose husband had been shot in the head, put her feelings to me in these words:

> I find myself married to a stranger and I find it hard to love this person who can act like a child one moment and be very aggressive the next, if he is not given his role as head of the household. Some days I have to get away and cry before I can face him again.

Head-injured people may get large amounts of compensation because of the magnitude of their injuries, but society soon forgets those who find themselves caring for and living with 'strangers' for the remainder of their lives. Responders may have a role in supporting head-injured people to find productive outlets for their feelings and frustration if they are to gain their full potential. The support provided should extend to their families.

Sexual problems in rehabilitation

There may be specific sexual problems after an injury. In the case of such problems, responders should be prepared to discuss these subjects. They should refer the couple for sexual counselling if required. Left without discussion, sexual problems can add to the level of anxiety and misunderstanding in a relationship. This is yet another sphere where adaptation is required following a traumatic event.

The fear of being impotent or frigid, or the fear of the partner's reaction to the disabled body only increases the person's anxieties about the imperfections of their new self. The discussion of the sexuality of physically injured or disabled people is no longer a taboo subject, as there appears to be increased understanding that a disabled person will have sexual desires and feelings of frustration when these desires remain unsatisfied. Acknowledging these difficulties and reaching out to help should be an essential part of the rehabilitation process. To deny the disabled person the right to normal feelings is to treat them as less than human. D.H. Lawrence shows great insight into these problems in his book, *Lady Chatterley's lover*; he asserts that Sir Clifford ceased to be a man because of his injuries: 'he was not whole'. His wife's infidelity is excused and rationalised because 'he was defrauding her of her birthright as a result of his injuries'. This so-called 'Chatterley syndrome' is sensitively dealt with by Louis Battye in his essay of that title (1974).

The wife of a recently disabled husband may value the responder's support to discuss her reactions to the physical approaches of this changed man. The wife of a man who had suffered changes in personality as a result of brain damage said: 'I can't love this person who is not the man I loved and married.' This is a subject on which there is limited literature, and an area in which responders need specialised training.

The use of family therapy in rehabilitation

The concept of family therapy can be most useful in considering the person in the whole constellation of their family. So often, adults protect their children from a crisis and the children are left bewildered and misinformed. This may be a self-preservation mechanism by anxious relatives who feel their own anxiety so acutely that they are unable to answer the questions from their children that may stem from their natural curiosity. The ideal situation would be one where the responder could talk with the whole family before the person is discharged from hospital, and then again some weeks after discharge. By discussing with the family some of the problems which the person may have about mobility, intolerance to noise and other problems specific to living as a family, all the members could be involved in helping in a constructive manner. It is difficult for a young family to react to a recently disabled parent who is depressed. The preoccupation with self, which is evident in many people in such circumstances, may appear to the children as rejection. Mood swings and personality changes in an adult must be quite terrifying for a small child. The active and realistic involvement of family members in the rehabilitation process can make its progress easier for all. Families include all age groups, so the needs of all age groups must be recognised:

> Rehabilitation and treatment effects are undertoned to a large extent by the support which they receive from their families: it has been shown that family support in terms of active interest, acceptance and encouragement are significantly related to patients' rehabilitation response. (Goodall, 1975)

Conclusion

The process of rehabilitation is an active process and a process of growth. Abraham H. Maslow (1954) reminds us that two forces are continually at war within a person. One, with an eye on safety, is pulling us back into defensiveness and non-risk-taking behaviour; the other, with an eye on growth, is pushing us towards independence and freedom. This generalisation is especially true when trauma has been experienced. When newly disabled persons have dealt with their feelings of denial and anger, they can gain satisfaction in the processes of physical rehabilitation. These individuals are open to their growth potential within the limitations imposed by their disabilities.

On the other hand, if disabled persons become preoccupied with the dangers, fear of failing or being hurt, the accomplishment of simple tasks will be more difficult. They are likely to 'play safe' and perhaps refuse to cooperate in their own rehabilitation. Rehabilitation is a process which requires a true marriage of the psychological and the physical; then and only then can there be a positive growth process or, as the World Health Organisation states:

> Medical rehabilitation has the fundamental objective not only of restoring the disabled person to his previous

condition, but also developing to the maximum extent his physical and mental functions. It aims not only at a 'physical cure' but also a 'social cure'. (WHO, 1978, p 110)

The home environment and the level of family involvement in the rehabilitation process are very important. Some of the more scientific disciplines may see the person as an amputee, a head injury or a fractured femur; responders must see them as father, mother, son or daughter.

The relatives of the person affected will need time to go through a similar continuum of psychosocial reaction and adapt to the new situation. The responder can play a valuable role in helping both parties understand the dynamics of the situation. Relatives find frightening the changes which the injury or illness has brought, and feel anxious and unsure about the expectations being placed on them. It is hard to cope with the sight of their once fit, healthy 24-year-old son lying disabled after crashing his motorbike. The parents' hopes and expectations for his future are as shattered as his bike. Mrs G, mother of the little girl who had been injured in a road traffic accident, said that it was only after many months of acute anxiety and constant hospital outpatients' appointments, when on her initial visit to the local school for children with 'special needs', that she realised that she was now the mother of a disabled child. The responder can provide the opportunity for relatives to express feelings which they feel they cannot express or share with the person affected. It is difficult to forget the words of a wife talking about her husband whose stroke had left him with a severe speech disability which made communication between them virtually impossible: 'My husband died the day he had the stroke; now I must learn to live with a stranger who needs a lot of care.' To the outside world, this man had only a moderate degree of physical disability. The wife presented as a very capable woman who appeared to be in complete control of the situation. The relationship with the responder had developed over many weeks, while her husband attended the rehabilitation unit. Only then could she allow herself to speak these words and share her true feelings in this tragic situation. She described her inner grief as her ability to 'weep inside'. Responders must always be sensitive to those who are 'weeping inside':

> The end result of a person's reaction to crisis is an individual with a unique personality, based on his pre-crisis personality, altered to include the disability in a manner that no longer makes it a threat to his total security. (Braddon, 1968)

SIX

The bereaved

This chapter deals with the psychosocial needs of the bereaved. The general theories of bereavement counselling are discussed, and these are followed by the specific features which exist because of the dynamics of a major disaster.

Much literature exists on the grieving process which follows bereavement. Books such as Beverley Raphael's *Anatomy of bereavement* (1984), *Bereavement* by Colin Murray Parkes (1972, 1996) and *Grief counselling and grief therapy* by J. William Worden (1988, 1991) must be considered as classic texts in this subject. More recent work by Stroebe and Schut (1999) provides a welcome addition to this earlier work. Drawing on the relevant literature available, on personal and professional experience, the stages of psychological reaction are identified under the same terms as those used in relation to the injured – that is, shock, realisation, acknowledgment and adaptation.

As with the psychosocial reactions of the injured, stages do not follow in a logical sequence. Psychological reactions are a process lasting a considerable length of time and unique to each individual. Unlike the injured, for whom recovery remains a possibility and return to normality a goal, the bereaved can never replace the life that has gone. Normality for them is a life lived without a loved one in situations of complete change. New roles have to be adopted, new relationships made and a new agenda for life constructed. Some people appear to adapt more quickly than others; some find the process of adaptation totally impossible and disabling to their future functioning. 'Only people who avoid love can avoid grief. The point is to learn from it and remain vulnerable to love' (John Brantner).

Loss and grief are inevitable for us all as we go through life. There are only two certainties in this life – that we are born and that we will die. We have little involvement in the first, but the latter can sometimes be predicted or it can be totally unexpected. Death means loss of attachment and is an inevitable part of life. As we go through life, we make many attachments, and Bowlby's work on early bonding has significance when we consider attachment and the pain of separation. We experience family bonding, bonds of friendship and bonds born out of a shared workplace or recreational activity, and the breaking of these bonds has the potential to cause grief. Association with or discussions on death inevitably lead us to think about our own mortality and vulnerability.

The physical changes of death can be frightening but there can also be the peace of no more struggling with pain or distressing symptoms. In disaster situations, mutilation of a body can mean that the physical appearance can be horrendous which can add to the distress experienced. Smell and the inability to be able to recognise a corpse can have a major sensory impact, which will last long into the future for those who view or handle the body.

Death has become somewhat sanitised in our society when we consider that in pre-antibiotic times pneumonia was described as 'the old man's friend'. Many of the more aggressive interventions of modern medicine can promote feelings of isolation for the relatives. Where a death occurs in hospital, the family may feel less involved in the terminal care of their loved one, but there may be advantages: when the physical demands are removed, they have time to deal with their psychological needs. They are given time to think and to talk. Hospital staff and family should cooperate to allow the best regime to be established that allows dignity and peace for the dying person.

The pioneering work of Dame Cicely Saunders, who died in July 2005, was paramount in establishing St Christopher's Hospice (London) in the 1960s with its philosophy of total care of the body, mind and soul for those living with terminal illness. Her work in relation to the pre- and post-bereavement care of relatives was responsible for many of the developments in the care of the bereaved which have taken place in recent years. The hospice movement is now international and seeks to deliver quality care to the dying and their relatives in all cultural environments.

Advances in medical science have meant that people in hospital may experience some highly technical procedures. The epitome of technical medical advances is to be seen in intensive care units. The life-support systems mean that new questions are being asked about the nature of death itself. Terms such as brain-dead, transplant surgery, life-support systems and prolonged vegetative state are common in such units. New ethical issues are arising as science changes the role of the doctor and their team. To their role of care and cure is added the role of life 'managers' as decisions to terminate treatments have to be made.

The transplant of organs has forced the legal profession to become involved in the debate of when death occurs. The carrying of a donor card enables the person's wishes to be known. Where a family has to be approached on the subject, great sensitivity has to be used in the interests of the donor family and the would-be recipient. Some bereaved families, interviewed after they have allowed organs to be transplanted, appear to find comfort from the fact that some 'good' has come out of their loss. They appear to be able to make some positive sense out of their negative feelings of unfairness and loss. I feel that counselling should be offered to bereaved families and the organ recipients to assist them to adapt to their new situations, situations that have brought or given life out of death.

Pre-crisis period

To consider the needs of the bereaved in terms of the pre-crisis period is to consider the significance for them of the person who has died. What role in the family did the person have - husband, mother, son, grandparent? Common-law and homosexual relationships need to be considered in this context. When considering other relationship bonds, we may be considering their role in society. There are many instances where the bonds of friendship can be as significant as family bonds.

The anticipated death in old age can affect the bereavement reaction. The elderly person may have grown weary with the natural processes of ageing, and phrases such as 'he had a good life' are often comforting. Terminally ill people have themselves had to go through the pre-bereavement stage in anticipating the breaking of relationship bonds. Farewells, in the pre-crisis period, can set the pattern for the post-crisis period.

Death from AIDS can be one example of disenfranchised bereavement in our society today. There may be alienation from families, and partners can be excluded from the funeral and grieving rituals by the family members.

Newly bereaved people talk at length about the 'pre-crisis period'. It is common for them to recall in infinite detail the actions taken by them or by the dead person in the days and hours before the death. It also brings up discussion on many situations of 'if only'.

'If only' can have a very powerful effect in the bereavement process. The unfinished work, the unspoken farewell, the guilt of not being with the deceased or of being in some way responsible for the deceased's being there can cause deep distress. The suddenness and unpredictability of death in disasters can create many situations of unsaid farewells. A husband and wife had a marital row and he stormed out of the house saying, 'It will be a long time before I come back here'. He was one of the crew of the Herald of Free Enterprise who never returned when it capsized. His widow has to bear the 'if only' of the significance of their farewell which resulted from an insignificant family event.

A mother forgot to give her son the money for a school excursion. The child remembered the money as he boarded the school bus, ran back to collect it and was killed by a passing motorbike. The grieving mother had to cope with the 'if only'.

A woman dying of breast cancer has to deal with 'if only' an earlier diagnosis had been made. Her husband may find vengeance for his bereavement anger through litigation against the health authority that did not have the resources to provide an adequate screening service.

A responder seeking to support people in the immediate post-crisis stage must be aware of the factors which were present in the pre-crisis period and their possible effect on the psychosocial needs which will occur.

Immediate post-crisis period

The most frequently reported reaction of those who have been bereaved is one of shock and disbelief. Even when there has been a period of pre-bereavement preparation, as in a protracted terminal illness, the actual loss can still feel unreal. The bereaved may have rehearsed their reaction and made some practical arrangements such as who has to be informed, which undertaker to use or how the funeral is to be organised.

Where a sudden death occurs there is a real sense of shock. Following such a death, the relatives may have a total sense of disbelief especially if the person who dies is young. Many people interviewed in such circumstances recall deep sorrow that they were denied the opportunity to say 'goodbye', to express love and affection. They feel they would have wished to have been with the deceased at the time of death. Such feelings express their belief that they might have been able to save their loved one.

In the situation of a traumatic death, the issues of lack of information must be dealt with. Where a person working on a building site is killed when his excavator hits overhead cables, his identity will be known immediately by his workmates. In the case of large disasters such as 9/11 or the Asian tsunami, information is most difficult to establish and verify. The actual nature of the event can also mean, for example, that bodies may be vaporised by the intensity of the heat created by exploding aviation fluid, as following the impact on the World Trade Centre, or washed out to sea, as following the tsunami wave.

If relatives or friends were also present at the time of the disaster, they may express the wish that they had perished also, reflecting their belief that they cannot live on without the deceased. All responders must deal sensitively with such feelings.

The way in which the information that a death has occurred is relayed to people can have a major effect on their grieving process. Hospitals may have procedures where only a doctor can tell relatives of a death. Police have to carry out this task in many cases or it may fall to a general practitioner, clergyman, family member or friend to share such information. In situations of large loss of life, lists are collated of the missing and these are reduced, or added to, as facts become known. Following the Omagh bombing in 1998, the community was advised to go to the local leisure centre for information. Lists of names were created from the information gained from anxious enquirers. As police collated names of individuals admitted to hospital or who had returned to their own homes, the information was announced to the waiting crowds. Those left waiting after each announcement grew more pessimistic as they anticipated that they were more likely to be the bereaved. One young member of staff in the leisure centre, who was involved in reading out the names, said that he felt like 'the angel of death' as he announced the names of the living and realised that the names that remained on the list were likely to be of those who had been killed. He knew many of the people on the list.

Following the terrorist bombing in London (July 2005), authorities were criticised for the apparent delay in the identification of the dead. Such anger was understandable from the perspective of distraught relatives who sought confirmation of the facts. However, the sites of destruction were scenes of crime and every care had to be taken to gather forensic evidence from the sites and from the bodies. Indeed, the identifications were proceeding while bodies were still being removed from the rubble in the underground tunnel at King's Cross Station. This situation serves to remind all responders that there are many diverse human perspectives from which a disaster is viewed.

In earthquake situations, the names may never be known, as whole family units may be lost leaving no one to record them missing or to instigate a search. Mass burials may be necessary to avoid perceived health hazards. Following the Asian tsunami, the presence of thousands of foreign tourists in the area made the identification of those missing or who had died extremely difficult. Forensic experts from other countries arrived to assist in the process, as distressed relatives rushed to the area in an effort to find loved ones.

The breaking of bad news can create a difficulty for many people. Truth with sensitivity should be the key to this process. Avoiding painful words such as killed, died or missing does not give clarity of communication. We must remember that shock and disbelief will lead people to have difficulty in fully grasping what is being said to them. Sensitivity must be shown when deciding where people are told. Every effort should be made to provide a private space. The bereaved people should be separated from a crowd. They may have one or two close relatives or friends with them. The bearer of the news should speak slowly and clearly, and be prepared to repeat the facts surrounding the death. Psychological chaos may occur for the bereaved. They hear, they realise, and then disbelief and numbness may follow almost immediately. Facts are believed and disbelieved almost instantaneously. If phrases like 'called to higher things', 'passed on', 'is at rest' are used, these only add to confusion. Words of sympathy and comfort are frequently used but often they sound like, and indeed are, much used clichés, such as 'he didn't suffer', 'you wouldn't have wanted her to survive if she had been a cripple'. Words are necessary but may be difficult at such a time. Responders dealing with distressed people often say, 'I didn't know what to say'. I believe that an honest statement such as 'It's hard to find words to say to you at the moment' express empathy in an eloquent way. The communication of touch can say more. A hand held in comfort, an arm around the shoulder may convey more of our concern and care than any words.

If the person breaks down and tears flow, the hand should still be held. The responder can demonstrate that such a reaction is acceptable by making time to stay with a distressed person. The bereaved person may apologise and be embarrassed by their reaction. Such feelings are compounded if the bearer of the news remains 'professionally aloof' and leaves quickly. One suspects that their professionalism, in such cases, is more about the protection of their own feelings than their ability to care enough to share the distress of another human being.

Newly bereaved people will need a protected personal space to begin to process the reality of their loss. They may wish to 'say' their farewells and take their leave of the deceased. They may indicate this by asking people to leave them alone. This request should be respected, unless there is a danger of self-harm.

Death by suicide causes extreme distress to the bereaved. The bereaved may experience intense feelings of guilt that they ignored warnings or failed to give enough support to the deceased. There may also be a sense of anger that they are being punished by the deceased by this wilful act. Such grief is particularly poignant in the situation of a young person.

The type of death is the key consideration in defining the type of response that will be needed. Where there is an anticipated death, family or friendship support may have been mobilised. Procedures such as who has to be contacted may have been rehearsed. Where there is an unexpected death, the responder may be crucial in providing a method of mobilising practical support networks. Their role must be based on their understanding of the psychosocial reactions of the bereaved. People in shock have difficulty in:

- **Comprehending** what is being said to them. Information must be given slowly and clearly. There may be a need to repeat instructions.
- **Remembering instructions**: the responder should try to write down simple notes to give to the bereaved on what needs to be done or what they have done.
- **Concentrating**: too much information causes confusion at a time when cognitive dysfunction can exist. Assistance may be needed to perform simple tasks such as searching for telephone numbers.
- **Decision making**: the psychological confusion and cognitive dysfunction inhibits the usual decision-making processes. The responder must be aware of this difficulty and assist where appropriate.

These difficulties can make the bereaved more liable to accidents. Many bereaved tell of household accidents or near traffic accidents because of the factors outlined above.

Short-term post-crisis period

The sense of numbness will begin to give way to the pain of reality. The rituals associated with the death and the funeral are often instrumental in this process. At such times, families and friends gather around and offer support. In considering such support, there is a need to be aware of demographic changes in society that may erode this traditional support network.

The way in which people grieve must be considered in a cultural context. In the book, *Death and bereavement across cultures* (Parkes et al, 2003), various experts define the rituals associated with a wide variety of cultures. They emphasise the need for responders not only to respect such rituals but to accommodate the processes required, if at all possible:

> Rituals define the death, the cause of death, the dead person,
> the bereaved, the relationship between the dead and others,
> the meaning of life and societal values. Failure to undertake
> them in full may leave people confused about all of these.
> (Rosenblatt, 2003, p 49)

These rituals of death represent the final act, and denial is less possible. The belief or non-belief in an afterlife greatly affects the way in which these rituals are viewed. Death may be seen as final or merely as a transition to another existence. Many people use their religious traditions as a means of making 'order' from the chaos of grief.

A young Asian woman, married to a British diplomat based in Thailand lost her husband and her total family of three children, aged 9, 8 and 6 years in the tsunami. She found the bodies of her two older children on the beach when the wave receded. Her husband's body and that of her youngest son could not be found. She took the children's bodies to a Buddhist temple near her home in Bangkok. The Western traditions would have suggested that she should cremate these bodies together due to the great uncertainty that the other bodies might ever be found. With the support of her husband's family in Britain, she decided to delay the cremation. In her Buddhist tradition, she wanted the bodies of her total family to be reunited at the time of the cremation. Her husband's body was identified some seven weeks later, but she again delayed the plans for the cremation and a memorial service that the embassy wanted to arrange. It was six months after the tsunami that her youngest son's body was identified through DNA matching. Five hundred family members, friends and colleagues attended the ritual in the temple when she cremated her complete family. She had prepared and produced small pictorial memory books of her family which she distributed to all who attended the ceremony as her 'way of thanking those who had supported her and who were honouring her family by their presence'. I have no doubt that her ability to fulfil the traditional rituals has helped her on her long and difficult road of rebuilding her life.

The gathering of the relatives allows the social structure to begin to establish new roles and 'reallocate' the role of the deceased. The death of the elderly mother may cause the role of matriarchal head of the family to move to the eldest daughter. The widow may suddenly realise that she has the responsibility for decision making in areas which were previously the prerogative of her husband. The son may realise that he is now the male head of the family. It is not uncommon to hear relatives say, even to a young boy, 'You are the man of the house now – you will have to be strong and look after your mother.' Such phrases should be discouraged as they lay an inappropriate load of responsibility on the shoulders of a young person who is already shattered by the loss of his father. If, in future weeks, the mother appears to be placing too many demands on such a son, he may be angry and reject her increased psychosocial investment.

'Anyone counselling the bereaved needs to be familiar with the broad range of behaviours that fall under the description of normal grief' (Worden, 1988, 1991). The key word in this quotation is 'normal'. The fact that the bereaved have both psychological and physiological reactions can be a great source of comfort to those who are frightened by these alien feelings at a crisis period in their lives. Many describe symptoms of feelings of hollowness in the stomach and tightness in the chest that can be associated with breathlessness. There can be general physical debility, lack of energy and headaches. One bereaved person described feelings of depersonalisation as 'walking down the street and nothing seems real, including me…'. The bereaved have been reminded of their mortality and they may begin to fear for their survival on both a physical and psychosocial basis.

Strong emotional reactions arise when past relationships with the deceased are remembered. Past actions and experience are used to justify any overwhelming feelings of anger and guilt. The anger is sometimes focused on the deceased themselves. This can be a most difficult aspect for the bereaved to cope with. Throughout the funeral rituals, the person becomes almost deified and yet the loved one may now experience anger against the person, anger that they have left them to cope. Such feelings indicate that the pain of grieving now becomes a reality. There is a sense of yearning, pining and restlessness. This is associated with the bereaved person's searching for the deceased person in psychological terms. There does not seem to be any purpose in going on to an uncertain future. This feeling is particularly prevalent where there has been a long-term relationship such as in marriage. The years of marriage have made the two people as one. The loss of a spouse is like the loss of half of oneself. With the older widow or widower, life without 'one's other half' seems pointless. Readjustment may take longer or it may never take place. For the younger widow, demands of the family and the need to support the family financially may force her to continue life quickly but she must also make time to grieve.

It is not uncommon for the bereaved person to hold on to physical reminders, such as clothes and personal possessions, as a means of retaining the past and the closeness of their loved one. The bereaved may seek to carry out their original patterns of daily living totally and express anger if anyone would try to change them. Medical problems experienced by the deceased may be replicated in the bereaved.

Bereaved people facing such challenges try their previous coping mechanisms. Some may prove adequate and will be retained. Others which fail will be rejected and new ones sought for the future. Stephen Murgatroyd and Kay Woolfe describe this process as a learning process in their book, *Coping with crisis* (1982). Order out of this chaos comes when some sense of control returns for the person affected. Mastery over a small area of life can give some confidence to seek control in more major areas. Gradually, the bereaved can cope with separation from the deceased and risk going forward to a future that does not include that person.

During the short-term post-crisis, much of the support from friends begins to diminish. It is as if society is saying that there is a 'grieve by date' when the period of grieving should be over. The bereaved person may feel totally alone with their grief. Tears are less acceptable in public, so crying is done in private. Friends may seek to return the bereaved to their previous social networks. Such attempts may be resisted or the bereaved person may decide to try to accomplish this. The effort may be tremendous, in psychosocial terms, and not fully appreciated by others. A young widower persuaded by friends to join in company some weeks after the death of his wife suffered for days before he finally went to the function. An observer remarked, 'He wasn't long getting over her'. The bereaved can be said to be in a no win situation no matter what action they choose to take. Their recovery or rehabilitation is a long and painful journey with many milestones where progress may seem limited and regression may occur. Reality has moved from acknowledgement of the loss and adaptation is beginning.

Chaos in practical terms may also exist. If the main provider in the home has died, there are many practical issues to be dealt with. Professional help from solicitors, mortgage companies and financial advisors such as bank managers should be sought. Often people speak of making other major life changes such as moving house or changing jobs; these decisions may be made on present evidence only, without the knowledge of what the changed future is really going to be like. Where possible, other family members such as the children should be involved in the process of change. They are part of the change and must be included if their feelings of worthlessness and isolation are not to be compounded. A bereaved parent may become overprotective of members of the family as they experience the real fear of losing them as well. This process is easily observed in reverse as children experience acute anxiety that they may lose the remaining parent (see Chapter Seven).

'No-one ever told me that grief felt so like fear. I am not afraid but the sensation is like being afraid. The same fluttering in the stomach, the same restlessness, the yawning. I keep on swallowing' (C.S. Lewis, 1966). Depression is a common feature of this stage. 'It does seem true, however, that as time passes anger and pining grow less, while episodes of apathy and depression remain' (Parkes, 1986, p 106). This depression is difficult for friends and relatives to cope with. They may have given as much support as they can and still the bereaved person needs more help. It is at this stage that support from a responder may be particularly significant.

Anyone speaking with a bereaved person who is depressed must be prepared to listen and support them as they perceive their needs. Platitudes such as 'I know how you feel' must be avoided. A more appropriate comment could be 'Tell me how you feel. I can only imagine how painful it must be for you.' Attempts to 'cheer the person up' must be avoided. The use of inappropriate comments will result in the bereaved person's withdrawing into their private feelings and not risking sharing their feelings again. We may be able to help the bereaved recall another period in their lives where they experienced similar feelings and were later able to cope.

Long-term post-crisis period

It is unwise to attempt to use time as a measure in the case of the grieving process. Adaptation means that the loss of the deceased has been integrated into the life of the bereaved in such a way that it no longer causes acute pain. The psychological chaos which existed has been reshaped into some semblance of order. There are times when people who have been bereaved many years ago can experience an acute sense of loss again. Bowlby (1979, p 101) quotes one widow as saying, 'Mourning never ends. Only as time goes on it erupts less frequently.' The term 'erupt' is a very valid one. Feelings of loss and sadness are never erased, only put into a new perspective.

The bereaved person, who is experiencing a normal grief reaction, will find that the sad days become fewer, and that painful memories become mixed with happy memories of past life events with the deceased. Interests in current life become more important. The bereaved person may feel more confident to risk planning for a life without the deceased person. At this stage, the bereaved has completed the 'tasks of mourning' as identified by Worden (1991):

- to accept the reality of loss;
- to work through the pain of grief;
- to adjust to an environment in which the deceased is missing; and
- to psychosocially relocate the deceased and move on with life.

I have always found Worden's work particularly apposite to most bereaved people. Grieving is hard work and, if viewed in terms of tasks to be worked through, this can be a help to the bereaved in giving them a sense of progressive stages. Bereaved people often reflect feelings of lack of recovery in such statements as 'I was beginning to make some progress but now I feel that I am back to pain of the beginning again'. This fluctuation is well described in the research carried out by Stroebe and Schut (1999) when they describe the feelings and activities which result from bereavement under the two headings of loss and restoration. People experience distress as they experience the transition from living a life in a relationship to living a life without the relationship. Stroebe and Schut's dual process model describes in a realistic way how the bereaved person searches, consciously or unconsciously, hoping that the person who has died may return. This activity is based on loss and entails looking backwards, and it may render them incapable of looking forwards. Restoration in the dual process model is used to describe the things which people do to get back to some form of normality and to rebuild their social lives. They try to get back to work or to resume some of their social links without their relationship which previously existed. The dual process model sees both activities associated with loss and restoration as vitally important to the recovery process. In the transition process, loss may predominate early activities with restoration following later, or there may be an oscillation between the two. Abnormal grieving may result in a fixation with loss and an absence of restoration activities. This model allows for a greater understanding of how people grieve in their own unique way in the context of diversity in cultures, gender and age differences. It can also be used to explain why some people can laugh or talk of future plans at a funeral, or why someone who has coped well with the changed circumstances in the first post-bereavement year can still break down when they revisit feelings of loss and loneliness. The model also suggests that men tend to use a restoration-oriented approach to grieving and internalise their emotions. Women tend to deal with their loss through more open displays of emotion, which is then followed by restorative activities.

Anniversaries of the death, birthdays and the first Christmas may be difficult to cope with. Many bereaved people fear such dates. They fear that any progress they have made may be shattered by these 'special days'. Often the anticipation of the day increases anxiety, and feelings of psychological panic and chaos re-emerge. Some people may choose to spend 'special days' alone, to visit the cemetery or a place of happy memories. Of most importance is that the wishes of the bereaved should be acknowledged and respected by responders and friends.

If there is a reawakening of some of the deeper pain of loss, the bereaved may need the reassurance that this is normal. They may fear that all the work they have done to readjust has been lost. The responder should listen to what is being said and try to tell the bereaved person that they have learned a lot about coping in the time since the loss, and that these lessons remain. Some bereaved people find that the first anniversary of the death is a milestone of progress. They have experienced a year of 'firsts', now things must get easier. They have coped with the first wedding anniversary without a partner, the first birthday without the child, or the first Christmas without a grandparent. The second year can bring disappointment that things are not suddenly better. The bereaved person may become depressed that, in spite of all the efforts they have made, there is still the loneliness, still the sense of loss.

In a healthy bereavement process, in time, the grief becomes less disabling; feelings of hopelessness give way to hope; there is renewed vigour to look forward not back; new roles feel more comfortable and less threatening.

Abnormal grieving

There are those who appear to be locked in their grieving, those whose grief is 'abnormal'. There are those who fail to grieve. Anyone seeking to help bereaved people should recognise these complications of grieving and realise that psychological or psychiatric help may be necessary.

Failure to grieve may be a result of the relationship which existed prior to death. The bereaved person may have ambivalent feelings about the relationship and such feelings complicate the ability to grieve. Where there was an intense dependent relationship, as a result of this dependency the bereaved has to overcome a change in the established self-image. 'For the person who loses an excessively dependent relationship, feelings of helplessness and the self-concept of being a helpless person tend to overwhelm any other feelings or any ability to modulate this negative self-concept with a more positive one' (Worden, 1988, p 54). Where a degree of uncertainty exists over the death, this may block the ability to grieve. If no body is found, the bereaved may refuse to grieve by holding on to hope. In war, or peacetime disaster where someone is reported 'missing, presumed dead', the family may hold on to hope even though all the evidence indicates that the person is dead. Lazare (1979) suggests that, where there are mass deaths in an earthquake, aeroplane crash, fires or where many members of one family are lost, the grief is so overwhelming that the bereaved person may close down the mourning process. Television pictures of shocked bereaved people wandering aimlessly among the ruins of their homes in Iran (1990) were indicative of this reaction.

Where a person has had a history of depression, there is an increased risk of a complicated grief reaction. Past experience of loss can affect how a person will react to the current loss. Where there has been unresolved grief, the current loss may reactivate all these feelings. It is important to try to find out if there is any such history that will need to be addressed.

People who tend to protect themselves from strong psychosocial reactions in their normal living and develop coping mechanisms to avoid feelings of helplessness may have difficulty in grieving. They deal with such feelings by shutting them out; this may not be a positive way to cope with grief.

A bereaved person may feel the need to be strong for other family members. The bereaved father may feel he must be strong to help his children. Such 'strength' may block the expression of grief not only for the father but also for the children. It would be healthier if they could share the feelings with each other and then help each other.

People living alone or those with a restricted network of friends may have fewer support networks to assist them to grieve normally. This will surely become more common as the traditional patterns of nuclear and extended family continue to change. Restricted family networks and living alone are not the only forms of isolation. It is possible for a bereaved person within a large extended family to be 'alone'. Widows, who were particularly angry following the deaths of their husbands, were found in Parkes' study in London (1972, 1996) to have become 'isolated' by their attitude. Their rejection of help offered meant that they were approached less often with such offers. This then became a self-perpetuating phenomenon of feeling rejected and becoming more angry.

Types of abnormal reactions

Chronic: the reaction is prolonged and people appear to be stuck in the past, or in the 'loss processing', as described in the dual process model. They are so fixated by the past that they have little time to think about the future or the restoration process. Their loss never seems to have a satisfactory conclusion.

Delayed: this is where the person is inhibited in grieving at the time of loss by circumstances or personality. This can happen where there are multiple practical issues to be resolved or attended to. A person may not have the time to grieve because of the demands of others.

Exaggerated: it is normal to have periods of feeling depressed or devoid of hope after a bereavement. Exaggerated grief is where this remains at a level which totally disables any growth towards the future without the deceased.

Masked: a masked grief reaction may present in a physical symptom. The person may not recognise this in themselves because a physical problem may be more acceptable to them in seeking help. Such symptoms may be similar to those experienced by the deceased. Shoor and Speed (1963) suggest that some forms of delinquent or maladaptive behaviour may also result from a masked grief reaction. This is noticed particularly in children and adolescents.

Death in a major disaster

Responders must consider the additional factors surrounding a death in a major disaster (see Chapter Ten). The dynamics of disaster are evident in this account of how one mother learned that her son had been crushed to death at the Hillsborough football disaster in 1989.

A mother out shopping in Liverpool hears two shop girls talking of a newsflash they have heard that there has been some serious crowd trouble at a match at Sheffield Wednesday's ground. She realises that Liverpool are playing Nottingham Forest – isn't that the match her son and his friends were going to? A frantic dash home confirms her worst fears as neighbours begin contacting each other. They watch with horror as the scenes develop on the television. They decide to go to Lime Street Station to meet the supporters who were returning by train. They search anxiously among the sad and dejected fans who file off the train in subdued mood. Everyone is beginning to realise the magnitude of the disaster. Happy friends and relatives rush forward to meet some fans. Others stand and wait. For them, the nightmare is becoming a reality.

They get the car and drive to Sheffield. There is chaos at the hospitals and at the ground, and no one seems to have information although they know that the death toll is rising. There are media people everywhere as people are directed to the makeshift mortuary. After hours of waiting, they file in to search among the photographs for their son - they all look similar. Their eyes fall on the face of their son – so normal yet so unusual – he is dead. Their emotions are in chaos. He was so young, he loved football and he never missed a match. What will his sisters say? Who do we need to tell? How can we contact them? What do we do now? His father says he will identify the body but his mother wants to go too. Until she sees her son dead, she will not believe it. The formal identification follows after another long wait. There are so many around in the same situation. There are many people there to help, yet the parents are strangely alone in their personal hell of loss among other grieving families.

Other issues

Information: the person affected may have to endure a prolonged period of time until the death is confirmed. These are hours of intense stress and uncertainty. The linking of a responder to each family at this stage is desirable to help the police in the identification process. The responder may help facilitate passing on information of identification from the bereaved to the central casualty record office or bureau. The Cullen Inquiry (1997) into the Dunblane tragedy criticised the delay in telling the bereaved parents. Lord Cullen describes it as 'unacceptable'. The fact that the small children had changed into sports clothes and some had put on another child's shirt, coupled with the fact that the teacher who knew them best had also been killed, added to the delay. The terrible news had to be accurate news.

Identification: the responder should work with the police and be available to the bereaved if they request their help. It is particularly effective if the same police officer and responder can work with the same bereaved family. Where no body is found, the bereaved experience added stress. They feel that they have no tangible focus for their grief. They have no means of 'leave taking'. They have no grave to visit. They feel that their loved one has not been laid to rest. Participation in rituals can be particularly helpful in the absence of a body.

Supportive help: the responder should be available to support the bereaved through the practical and legal requirements following a death. The quality of this relationship can form the basis for the future role of a responder. If the bereaved feel positive about the supportive help they receive at this stage, they may feel more confident in using help in the future.

Rituals: responders need to be sensitive to ritual acts such as gifts of flowers and tokens which help people to express their sympathy.

Longer-term post-crisis period

Bereavement counselling: in a disaster situation, the bereaved have not only to cope with their own reactions but they are part of others' grief also. It is important to deal with the traumatic aspects of the death before bereavement counselling can proceed. This requires a willingness on the part of the responder to listen to the difficult memories before progressing to support for the restoration processing:

> To listen to stories of psychological trauma is to come face to face both with human vulnerability in the natural world and with the capacity for evil in human nature. To study psychological trauma means bearing witness to horrible events.

With these words from her book, *Trauma and recovery*, Judith Herman (1992) reminds us that the trauma element of death can delay, postpone or block the natural grieving process.

The very event has brought together people in shared grief. Fifty deaths at a disaster are not the same as 50 individual deaths, as the incident itself has its own dynamics. The dynamics of disaster are such that the bereaved may have the increased pressure of media and public events.

There may be visits from VIPs and this may signify to those affected that society is sharing in their tragedy. The majority of people welcome such visits; some express the feeling that they are an inappropriate intrusion into their private grief and designed for the media coverage they receive.

A memorial service has become a feature of recent disasters. These occasions allow for a communal recognition of what has happened. They are important for the bereaved, the survivors, the responders and the community. The presence of eminent people can help the families feel that the wider community wants to be associated with them. The selection of those who should attend often causes friction. Anniversaries are also times of shared grief and memories. The affected have requested that a service be held to mark the first anniversary of some of the recent major disasters. The responder needs to be aware of the possible effects of such events on group grieving, and be available to assist the bereaved with their individual grieving process.

Terminating contact: the timing of the termination of contact must be sensitively handled. If we believe that the role of the responder is to assist the bereaved, at a time of psychosocial chaos, to achieve a state of order to enable them to cope, then we must recognise a time when continued contact is counterproductive to this process. The responder must not foster this dependency but keep reminding the bereaved of their inner strengths and giving positive reinforcement to any progress which is being made.

Conclusion

Bereavement is something which we will all experience in life. It is stressful for virtually everyone. Death in the circumstances of a major disaster produces additional stress for the bereaved person. Many people move through the process of grieving with the support of friends or family. Some will benefit from the support of responders beyond the family, such as those associated with Cruse Bereavement Care. Groups may provide a suitable forum for some of the bereaved. 'Interaction with members of an accepting group is enormously beneficial as long as it is not to the exclusion of all other social interaction over a prolonged period of time' (Staudachel, 1987). Groups for extended family members such as grandparents were found to be very helpful following the Dunblane shootings. Psychiatric help may be required for those who have complicated or abnormal grief reactions.

Bereavement is a natural process. It can be described in the same terms as the healing process which takes place in a wound. When a child falls and cuts a knee, the wound is open and bleeds freely. Healing commences and the wound closes. If it is knocked, it will bleed again. There may be delayed healing due to infection that needs treatment. The scar develops and, although a knock will hurt, it does not bleed. In time, the healing process results in a surface which bears a scar and can take knocks without bleeding. For the bereaved person, scars remain but a healed scar can be lived with. 'The pain of grief is just as much a part of life as the joy of love, it is perhaps the price we pay for love, the cost of commitment' (Parkes, 1986).

SEVEN

Crisis situations associated with children

Children may be directly or indirectly involved in many crisis situations associated with personal or major disasters. They themselves may be survivors of, or bereaved by, the event. This chapter deals with some of these situations. In the UK from 1995 onwards, we have seen an increase in disasters involving children such as minibus crashes, a vicious attack on children in a nursery school in London, and the fatal shooting of children and their teacher in Dunblane Primary School in Scotland. The shooting of students in the Columbine High School near Denver in the US in 1999, and the terrorist attack in Beslan School in Russia, 2004, when parents, teachers and children were first held hostage and then many killed by gunfire and bombs, shocked the world when the usually safe environment of schools was violated. Many children lost parents in the 9/11 attacks. Following the Asian tsunami wave, the number of children lost was very significant as their light body weight meant that they were easily wrenched from their parents' grip and tossed into the raging waters from the beaches.

The needs of children are sometimes overlooked by responders as they are seen as appendages to adults. Parents may resent a responder speaking with their child because they see the support and nurture of their child as exclusively part of their parental role. This is particularly difficult where parents are distressed and cannot understand that their distress may be blocking the child from receiving the usual degree of help and support from them. The age of the child is significant when assessing needs. Responders need to see the child as an individual with unique needs.

The death of a child is particularly distressing for parents and the extended family. Few can remain emotionally aloof when a child's life ends in either a personal or a major disaster.

Death of a child

A child's death represents the loss of the child itself and of its potential life, which will never be realised. There always seems to be an increased sense of injustice that such a loss should have happened in the natural order of things. Death in later life can be expected, but a child's death leaves few unmoved in societies where better healthcare has eradicated many of the former causes of child mortality. In some areas of the world, the expectation by parents that not all their children will survive to adulthood can result in larger families being produced. The cultural context associated with the death of a child must always be an important consideration for any responder. 'Serving dying and bereaved people from other races and creeds provides us with the privilege of learning from them' (Parkes et al, 2003, p 7).

Miscarriages are rarely seen by outsiders to be as significant as they may be to the would-be parents. The woman feels guilt that some action of hers has caused the loss. The husband may also feel this way. He may find that he is the object of his wife's anger. Professionals often deal with the strong feelings by reassuring the woman that she should try for another child as quickly as possible. If it is the first pregnancy, there may be fears that the woman may be unable to bear a child. Anxiety for the future becomes entangled with feelings of loss on the part of the mother. Grief work needs to be done and responders should seek to support the parents through this process. Stillbirth causes great anguish for parents and hospital staff. Circumstances can mean that the cessation of life is known before the delivery takes place. Labour and delivery may mean the same physical effort for the mother, but all such effort is accomplished with the knowledge that the child is already dead. To facilitate future births, the mother may be advised that the delivery has to be delayed for some days or weeks. Many mothers recall anguish when they talk of living through this time. One mother described it to me as 'walking around with death inside me. This "thing" that I hated was the baby I longed for'. This is a personal disaster of great magnitude. The mother may feel responsible for the death, the father may feel isolated and unable to help, and, where there are other children in the family, they may not understand the parents' reaction. Society, that has seen the mother pregnant, may not understand that she has not got a healthy baby. It is important that the parents are given the opportunity to grieve for the loss of their child. The parents may feel that they want to hold the child and say their farewells. Many hospitals now assist this process by photographing the child and offering the photograph to the parents when they are ready to request it. A hospital book of remembrance can also help.

The responder needs to be aware of the psychological chaos that surrounds such an event, and to allow the parents to talk, if they wish, of their disappointment and loss. Their bereavement reaction needs to be resolved before they embark on another pregnancy, which will inevitably be an anxious time as they fear the same result. The mother needs to have restored her psychological equilibrium and progressed her mourning for the dead child, which only she has felt alive within her womb, before she can reinvest her love in another baby.

Cot deaths due to sudden infant death syndrome (SIDS) cause great distress when apparently healthy infants die suddenly. There is shock, numbness and a sense of unreality. The parents must grieve for the baby, but all their hopes and dreams for their baby have also been lost. Research continues as to the cause of such tragedies, but no one cause has yet been agreed. The sudden nature of death means that there is a need for an investigation. Police may be involved in these enquiries. Their participation adds to the parents' feelings that they were in some way responsible. Recently in the UK, there have been several cases where a 'miscarriage of justice' has occurred, as expert evidence has been disputed and mothers convicted of killing their babies have been released. All parents seek causes of the tragedy from within their care of the baby. Did they neglect physical symptoms? These feelings may cause the parents to blame one another. Members of the extended family may become involved in this 'blame' process, as they, too, seek answers.

Emotional chaos can also exist for other siblings. The arrival of the baby may have produced a feeling of resentment that this new person had displaced their role in the family. Children may feel acute guilt if the object of such 'wrong' feelings has died. They may feel that they were responsible.

Parents often have severe difficulty in grieving for the lost child and dealing with the multiplicity of feelings of guilt, anger, fear and confusion. It is often helpful to talk to other parents, who have sustained the same loss, through the national organisation SANDS (Stillbirth and Neonatal Death Society) which exists for this purpose. The parents may benefit from bereavement counselling, and further support may be needed during subsequent pregnancies. Some mothers have said that they were afraid to allow themselves to anticipate or enjoy the next baby in case they lost it too (Bryant, 1989).

The diagnosis of a terminal illness in childhood is a time of intense stress. Participation in treatment and care can allow the parents to feel involved in the process of maintaining life. In certain types of illnesses, there can be anticipatory grieving interspersed with periods of intense hope. One mother referred to it as a 'roller coaster of hope and despair'. Treatments can be difficult for the child to bear and the parents often have feelings of despair. They may experience feelings of conflict as they encourage the doctors to continue the treatment, have to cope with a distressed child and question within themselves whether the treatments merely act to postpone the inevitable. With the increased instances of cure, the responder must seek to support the parents' hope.

If the prognosis is poor and the terminal stages are reached, the parents should be encouraged to stay involved in the physical care of their child. The dying child often gives words to the parents' fear and, by giving unconditional love, brings a sense of normality to the situation. Parents should be encouraged to talk to their children about their illness. Children ask direct but simple and profound questions. They may display their fears through play or art. Parents often find some comfort in the child's uncomplicated understanding of the issues of life and death. Many parents who have lived through the child's process of illness with an intense fear of the moment of death later recall a sense of peace and intense love.

The parents' grief is acute and painful. Other children may remind them of their loss: 'When I came back from the hospital, I couldn't bear the other children near me. It seems an insult to her to be cuddling them.' These words of a bereaved mother are quoted by Lindy Burton in her book, *Caring for a child facing death* (1974).

The birth of a child with a disability can represent a personal disaster for a family. Parents may need support to accept the 'imperfect' child as the product of their union. Some go through a period of self or family blame. Grandparents may be involved if the disability is viewed as a flaw in their family's genetics and ability to produce a perfect child. Parents need to grieve for the child they hoped to bear and the associated dreams they had for its future. They need to adapt to and acknowledge the child they have. The need to provide additional care often deepens the love that develops for this special child.

The presence of a sick or disabled child in the family can have major effects on the other family members. The other siblings may feel unloved and outside what is happening. Family plans appear to revolve around the sick or disabled child. It is not uncommon for a sibling to display psychosomatic symptoms to gain attention. The death of a child can have wide repercussions on the psychological well-being of the wide circle of people involved.

A major disaster involving children

Case study 18: Aberfan

On a cold wet October morning in 1966, the mothers of Aberfan, in Wales, said 'goodbye' as their children left for the village school.

Prolonged rain had loosened the unstable foundations of the coal slag that had been built up above the school. Suddenly, it slipped and with unrelenting speed engulfed the school. Its black mass wiped out 116 children's lives as they sat at their lessons. Twenty-eight adults also died, some of whom were teachers.

The large loss of children's lives made this particular disaster especially significant. Tony Austin (1967), in his book about the disaster, described the desperate attempts of the miners as they clawed at the rubble and sought desperately to find the children:

> They worked with a will that was a fervour for hours, sometimes days without a break. Silent men with sad faces, hardly believing that what they were doing could be, men with faces smudged and blacked hands wiping away sweat and often tears. (p 27)

The name Aberfan became the centre for worldwide sympathy. Apart from the individual families bereaved, Aberfan itself became a community of grieving. The community also had to come to terms with the fact that the National Coal Board, which had provided employment over the years, built their homes and built their school, had also become the 'murderer' of their children through their mismanagement of the slag heap. The effect of the loss of one age stratum in the community is still felt there today. Children who had survived the tragedy, because they were not at school that day due to illness, were ostracised by the bereaved parents. The community was inundated with outside help, but the real grieving and recovery came within the tight social network of the village itself. It was one of the first disasters in the UK where the psychosocial needs of the individuals involved were considered. It was also the first time that the differences in the way that the fathers and mothers grieved were recorded. Mothers were able to cry and express their loss. They appeared to be able to draw much of their support from peers and family members. Those responders who tried to reach out to the fathers found they were much more introverted in their grieving processes. They rarely talked of their pain or sought support. This appeared to change when a male voice choir was formed and the men used their common love of choral music as a means of expressing their feelings and gaining support from peers. In 1996, the media focus returned to Aberfan. The stories told reminded us all of how the aftermath of such disasters is ever present, even after 30 years.

The bereaved child

Adults who have been bereaved call on past methods of coping and adapt these methods to meet the new demands. It may be a long and painful process. An understanding of this process allows us to appreciate the difficulties of a child who has been bereaved. When things go wrong in a child's life, he turns to his parents for love and support. What a dilemma it must be for a child who cannot fully understand what is happening, when their usual sources of help cannot help because of their own grieving. The response of a child depends on their age and stage of development. Adults tend to exclude children from their conversations about death or their fear that a relative is dying. Children may feel excluded and that such exclusion means they have done something wrong. If possible, children should be given basic information and an explanation commensurate with their age:

> Allowing children to deal with death openly, as a natural resolution of life allows them to grow intellectually and to trust that you and other adults, upon whom they rely, will tell them the truth. I am convinced that the realities of death will frighten children far less than evasive answers or lies. (Kastenbaun, 1977, p 141)

There has been limited research into the specific reaction of children following major disasters. Professor William Yule (1990), who was involved with children following three disasters at sea, feels that children as young as eight can suffer Post-Traumatic Stress Disorder (PTSD) which is almost identical to that reported in adults. The symptoms can last up to two years. He feels that normal screening instruments miss some of the psychopathology. Parents, teachers and responders are reluctant to ask children about their feelings in the belief that if they are not expressed they do not exist. Perhaps we fear how we will cope with a distressed child who, in the innocence of youth, can graphically recall every detail of the incident.

Yule lists 10 common reactions which he observed in his work:

1. Sleep disturbances. These were very common in the first few weeks. There were reports of fear of the dark and of being alone. Bad dreams and nightmares persisted over many months. He found that the use of a personal stereo and music tapes helped at bedtime.
2. Separation difficulties. A bereaved child clung to the surviving parent and talked of fear of losing them also.

3. Children reported concentration problems at school.
4. They had problems of remembering new material they were given. Former skills such as reading music could also be affected.
5. Intrusive thoughts about the incident caused distress. Such reactions could be triggered by environmental stimuli which reminded them of the incident.
6. Many children did not want to talk to their parents because they feared causing them distress.
7. Talking with peers was felt necessary but the children needed to control the timing of such discussions.
8. Children reported a heightened alertness to danger and risk situations.
9. Children were anxious to live each day to the full as the disaster had shaken their faith in the future.
10. Many of the children developed fears of travelling in similar circumstances.

Yule advises that children need reassurance that others share such feelings and that they will pass. Children need permission to talk about them freely in a safe environment. Dr Dora Black, writing of her contact with children following the Bradford fire disaster, notes:

> The children who are given the opportunity to talk and cry about their dead father, recall the good (and bad) times they had together, make sense of their mother's grief, and are reassured that she continues to love them and that the whole community will care for them until their mother feels better, should cope with their loss. (Black, 1985a, p 56)

Black also suggests that children should be offered help directly in a group situation. Support can be given through an established widowed parent circle, where parents gain support from other bereaved parents. When children are told of a death, they tend to take a very practical approach. They may ask simple yet profound questions which need an answer. They tend to integrate the news into their lives on an unemotional level and are concerned about how the change will affect them personally. This can be interpreted by adults as unfeeling and cause some anger. Such a reaction from adults typifies the contradictory approaches that adults tend to take when talking to children in these circumstances. They do not allow them to share in the process as adults, yet they expect them to have adult reactions. A boy of 11, told of his father's death, shared his mother's grief. When, later in the day, the mother explained about the funeral and gave him the opportunity to choose to attend or not, she was met with the question, 'Will Daddy's old body that hurt with cancer be in the coffin at the Church?' 'Yes', came the reply. 'Then the sooner we get rid of it the better, as he is not in it. I'll go to help you to see that they do it right.' Simple, practical, profound, and yet inspirational to the mother.

Some children may react by angry outbursts or periods of difficult behaviour. Care must be taken to recognise that these may be related to the bereavement. Adults may take time to reinvest their affections following bereavement, but children tend to seek alternative relationships quickly. Children's ability to grieve is dependent on their level of perception of death as permanent or temporary. Be prepared to match the type of response provided to the age of the child.

A child's perception of death evolves in relation to its physical and age developments. An infant or toddler can quickly sense and react to anxiety or distress in the adults around or handling them. They may become fretful and demanding if changes in routine or in their carer occur. Young children between the ages of two and five are particularly sensitive to any form of separation. This is very obvious where there is the death of a parent. They are not able to grasp the finality of death and may talk in terms of when 'Daddy comes home from the graveyard'. Some children envisage a heaven in the skies and long for an aeroplane to take them there. Separation can also be sensed when the usual caregiver is not able to give the same physical or emotional attention to the child because of their own need created by the loss.

From the ages of eight to 10, children develop a sense of the finality of death. They can also develop a deep curiosity about the issues and rituals associated with death. They appear to have difficulty in ever considering that death can occur in a peer. From the age of 10, children ask questions about death which need to be answered as honestly as possible. As the child gets older, they grow in their understanding of the finality of death. Research by Bluebond-Langer (1978) suggests that at age 11 the child begins to conceptualise the future in terms of potential losses.

Children's experience of pets can help their perceptions. However, a dead goldfish rapidly replaced by parents can suggest that all people who die can be replaced in a similar fashion. Consideration of age can give some guidance, but there are other factors such as intellectual ability and previous experience of death which also need to be considered when assessing the child's reaction and possible bereavement pattern. Young adults who are faced with the grieving process can experience the additional problems of the normal adolescent's processes.

They feel that they should be independent in their grief, yet they long to return to the dependent child role. The loss of a parent against whom they have been 'rebelling', in the normal process of growing up, can add acute feelings of guilt to their loss.

If a child has had a normal loving home life, the loss of a parent, grandparent or sibling can destabilise their view of the world. The perceived loss of their safe and stable base can lead to an undermining of self-esteem. They question whether they did anything to bring about the loss, they fear their own demise and also that they will be left alone and unloved. They may try to replace a deceased sibling in their parents' attention.

The eventual outcome for bereaved children is dependent on the support they receive at the time of loss and also on a longer-term basis. The way in which the adults react to the grieving process has a major effect on the child's own reaction. As with adults, there may be a need for professional help if bereavement becomes pathological.

Guidelines for helping bereaved children

- Share as much information as possible with children.
- Use clear language to children – 'Granny has gone asleep and gone to heaven' can result in a fear of sleep in the child's mind. If they go to sleep, will they go to 'heaven' too?
- Involve the child in family rituals if possible. Do not send the child away to neighbours or relatives.
- Keep reassuring the child of the continuity of care, security and love. Physical cuddling is important.
- Allow the child to see adult tears and explain why crying is necessary.
- Try to maintain as many of the normal routines of mealtimes and bedtimes as possible. This will help to maintain a sense of stability for the child at a time of total confusion.
- Allow the child to help in the house but do not expect too much.
- Involve the children's friends to ensure that normal play and recreational activities continue.
- Try to minimise practical changes in the child's life.
- As adults work through their bereavement reaction, share the happier memories of the deceased with the child. Give them 'permission' to talk of the deceased. Artwork and writing can help the child to communicate. The making of a scrapbook of memories of the bereaved can be beneficial to children at the time of loss and in the future.

- Be aware that even the child who appears to be 'coping' well may have periods of sadness and need to talk about the loss. Adults need to be available and sensitive to these needs.
- A bereaved mother may over-invest emotions in her children. The child must have rights to be treated as normally as possible, to be free to develop as an individual, confident person.
- A grieving parent can let standards of behaviour and discipline slip within the home. Not all bad behaviour can be excused as a result of the bereavement. The child still needs to understand that boundaries have not changed. This can be particularly difficult when the death of a parent is involved.
- The school can be used to help the bereaved child.

The school as an aid to the traumatised child

School is where children spend a major part of their lives from the ages of 5 to 16 or 18. Attendance at playgroups and pre-school classes extend this period further. It is, therefore, important to utilise the support of teachers in the rehabilitation of children affected by the trauma of personal or major disasters.

In the case of a child who has been ill or injured, the re-entry into school should be managed sensitively. A staged re-entry period is advisable. Other children may be very curious to look at the child and should be prepared by the teachers if there is any major alteration in physical appearance. Children are naturally curious, and straightforward answers to their questions will often suffice and divert their attention elsewhere. Involving children in support of their peer may be a very positive way to channel their enthusiasm. A rota of children to carry the schoolbag of a child on crutches can produce a sense of caring in the group.

Children who have been bereaved and are returning to school may long for the normality of school routine after a home that has been disrupted. Routine may represent security in the fact that life is continuing in spite of what has happened. Staff who support the children, and assure them of their care and concern without making them feel 'too different', must display sensitivity. The teacher can allow children to talk about what has happened when they are ready to share their thoughts. Responders involved in post-trauma work often find that adults block their attempts to reach the child and dismiss the need for the children to have access to support. The teachers should be aware of the availability of counselling and access it, through the school networks, if appropriate. Parents should be made aware of these decisions and encouraged to support the child in the process. Art or writing stories may allow children to express their feelings in a non-threatening way. The teacher 'can observe the course of grieving and may witness behaviours that indicate need for discussion, explanation or reassurance' (Sterweis, 1984). The teacher is a key person in the child's life, but may not be as emotionally affected as the family members and therefore able to meet some of the needs of the bereaved child. The grieving parent may be cross and irritable at a time when the child needs tolerance and understanding. Family patterns at home may have been altered and normal routines, such as discipline patterns, may have become inconsistent, adding to the confusion for the child. Bereaved parents may idolise a deceased child and this can mean that they place unrealistic expectations on the surviving child. Teachers can help moderate parental attitudes and help them make decisions that affect the surviving child.

Schools can be an important resource for a community under stress. Mooli Lahad and Alan Cohen in their book, *Community stress prevention* (1988), write of the value of using the education network in Israel. Education in stress management as part of the school curriculum appeared to aid the participants. Following a major disaster, the responder should attempt to involve the schools in the area. Teachers should be included in any meetings between the coordinator and voluntary organisations, and they should be made aware of counselling services available for those affected. This will enable them to advise the pupils or their parents. Disaster awareness training courses should be available to teachers. The school should be encouraged to maintain as normal a schedule as possible. This can help to restore and maintain a sense of 'business as usual' for individual children, their families and the whole community. The responder should help parents to see that the teacher and the school can form an important support network. Teachers themselves should be made aware of any support networks for responders. They are themselves responders and may become traumatised.

Discussions on death and loss now form a normal part of the school programme. Surely all schools should discuss these subjects as part of living. Such discussions must be sensitive to ethnic views and traditions. Teachers may need training or the support of specialist counsellors to fulfil this role.

EIGHT

Responders and the process of responding

The role of responders following major or personal disasters will be as varied as the disasters themselves. Different circumstances will demand different responses on an organisational and personal basis. To discuss the role of responders, a major disaster is considered. However, much of the discussion is also applicable to helping in the circumstances of personal disaster. When a disaster occurs, there are two types of responders:

• those by circumstance; and
• those by assignment.

Responders by circumstance

These responders may themselves be involved in the disaster. They may have survived and been able to render immediate help to others affected. Other responders by circumstance are those who happen to be present at the time and rush to give aid. They may simply be bystanders or have a professional training which they volunteer to use in the situation. If they declare their training, they usually command attention and may become natural leaders because they are perceived by others to have expertise. Such responders become part of the incident themselves, as they may share much of the shock and impact of the event.

On a short-term and longer-term basis, the family, colleagues or the community itself can become responders by circumstance because of their pre-crisis links with those affected.

Assigned responders

These are responders who, because of their role in a professional or volunteer capacity, are assigned to the disaster as their expertise is needed. Their training may have prepared them for the task. They bring to the disaster situation their previous skills and professional experience, which they will need to adapt to current challenges. They also bring their own experiences of life, which can have a positive or negative effect on their ability to carry out their tasks. A previous experience of family loss may render them more vulnerable to traumatic stress. Experiences which involve the ability to adapt their coping mechanism can give them the confidence in dealing with the new demands placed on them.

Responders are regarded as those who will be able to aid the individuals affected regain equilibrium in their lives. These people have an expectation of responders that they will know how to act, how to elicit needed resources and how to answer questions.

Those experiencing the psychosocial impact of the emergency or disaster will be seen as vulnerable, and there is an expectation that they will be grateful for the help they are given. It must be remembered that those people also bring their life experiences to the situation. Such experiences, as with the responders, may make them less or more likely to be able to adapt and cope.

The elements of the disaster

Consideration of the disaster as a unique event but one which contains the elements of cause, location and size (see Chapter Two) allows for a degree of prediction to take place.

The type of people affected

- The ethnic origins of those affected must be of paramount consideration. Minority races may be disadvantaged in terms of the resources that they can access for practical and emotional support. Cultural attitudes to gender roles and traditional attitudes to receiving help will affect the acceptability and effectiveness of the help offered. Cultural perceptions of the event will affect the emotional aftermath and can have a major consequence for those affected. Responders of the same ethnic background should be assigned to the helping tasks if at all possible. Language compatibility must be considered vital. If the unique needs of those affected are to be adequately met, then information must be made available in their own language. Teachers or lecturers in language could provide invaluable help with translations or interpreting.
- The needs of the sensory impaired are often neglected in these situations. When people with a hearing or sight impairment are involved, responders skilled in such work should be assigned as

soon as possible. They can help to ease the additional feelings of isolation which result from such impairment.

- The gender of those affected and that of responders is another element which needs to be considered when assessing need and the help that should be provided. Those who view the male as dominant may be more accepting of a male 'responder' in situations where assertiveness, power and authority are needed. This can be observed in the immediate post-crisis stages where chaos exists and information is difficult to obtain. The female responder may be viewed as more able to empathise with emotional reactions. Those traumatised are probably more likely to show distress to a female responder. In a male–male pairing, distress may be inhibited for fear of appearing weak or unmasculine. Gender issues can also influence the way in which distressed persons will share their problems or life experiences. The female responder may be expected to understand issues of female health problems, problems associated with child rearing or sexual problems because of their own life experiences. The converse is often expected of the male. A woman feeling very vulnerable following the death of her spouse may transfer some of her feelings, consciously or subconsciously, on to a male responder. A male volunteer responder, helping with the young family of a widow bereaved in traumatic circumstances, found that the children quickly put him in the 'father' role. When the situation progressed to the point when the volunteer was advised to withdraw by his supervisor, the children regressed and viewed it as a further instance of 'bereavement'. Co-working with male and female responders may have been more appropriate.

Accessibility and acceptability of the help offered

The need to seek help may be alien to the life experience of many of those affected by disaster. Issues of class, race and gender all need to be considered. If help is offered from a social services office, those seeking help may be deterred because of the traditional stereotyping of social workers. The use of the title, 'member of the Crisis Response Team', may improve the acceptability of the team in such circumstances. It may be more accurate as a description of all the disciplines which integrate their skills to meet the comprehensive and complex needs which are created in such circumstances.

Many of those affected by the disaster may wish for the security of confidentiality in accessing help through a helpline or a help unit designated for the specific disaster. Their resulting vulnerability and perceived need for help can place high expectations on the role of the responder, which can put stress on them as they seek to help. Disasters, by their very nature, affect all, irrespective of class, gender, race, age or role. This fact is nowhere more evident than in the Asian tsunami.

Pre-crisis stage

Responders bring a variety of skills to the task. Such skills may involve duties essential in disaster relief. Staff in accident and emergency departments, fire brigade, police and ambulance personnel are trained in dealing with crisis situations where there may be injuries or death. Experience of the personal disaster situation involving car crash fatalities must prepare them for reacting to major disasters. However, mass injury and death demand even more from responders involved.

Training for disaster work is considered expensive when assessed in relation to the probability that all staff will have this type of experience in their normal working life. Some countries, such as Norway, have adopted the practice of having a team of well-trained, experienced disaster workers who will be flown to the scene of a disaster as quickly as possible. They see the advantages of the 'A Team' approach as being that the personnel are highly trained and have the advantage of working together on a regular basis. This model is viewed as more cost-effective in terms of expensive training and equipment. The 'A Team' model has the advantage of recognised experts being available to aid local responders.

In terms of local need and the availability of long-term support, this 'A Team' approach has certain disadvantages. While expert advice may be necessary, there may be a resentment of 'outsiders' being in charge. Local people have a greater understanding of local resources in both physical and personal terms. Cultural and regional differences may be reflected in the attitudes associated with receiving help. Such attitudes may be counterproductive where 'outside' help is involved.

From my own experience, I feel that the best preparation that responders can have for their task in a disaster situation is to have a network of responders trained in disaster awareness within relevant organisational systems (see Chapter Twelve). This network approach has been formalised in the 2004 UK Civil Contingency Act with the need to establish local Resilience Teams. The 2004 report, 'Working together to support individuals in an emergency or disaster' (www.redcross.org.uk), which was a European initiative facilitated by the British Red Cross, also demonstrates this model on a European basis. Australia and the US have similar networks. Where a network exists in local areas, then these local networks could link together when a disaster occurs across geographical or organisational boundaries. Responders who maintain good standards of practice every day and have been given critical incident training are the best basis for any response to a crisis.

Crisis stage

The main focus at this stage is on saving life and minimising damage to property or the environment. Emergency services should have up-to-date plans for such situations, including contact with social work departments to activate the necessary practical and emotional support networks for those affected. Voluntary organisations should be part of this network. All responders involved in this 'impact' stage should have an awareness that they are at the beginning of not only the recovery but also the rehabilitation stage. The way that they act, the way in which they treat people, the words they say, can all have an infinite influence on the possible psychological outcome for those affected.

The skills of their professional training need to be adapted to meet the demands. Such skills should include training in caring for the 'whole' person. Treating people with respect and attempting to protect their dignity as human beings are an essential part of the responder's role.

The immediate post-crisis stage

Responders at this stage may be those involved through circumstances and those assigned to the task. Their role is essentially that of 'hand holding' or giving support. Supportive help may be both practical and emotional. As previously discussed, the people affected are in shock. Responders should be sensitive to their feelings of emotional and practical chaos, and seek to aid them in a way that does not add to their feelings of being overwhelmed. Good pre-planning should stop too many responders 'swooping in' on the individuals. If the size or nature of the incident warrants it, a rest centre for the 'walking wounded' or distressed should be established as soon as possible in a safe location near to the scene of the disaster. A Family Assistance Centre may also be established to allow all the helping agencies to be easily accessed at one location by those people affected. Following the London bombings (2005), such a centre was established, but the name was later changed to the 7/7 Support Centre as it was found that those requiring support were not only family members but friends, work colleagues, fellow travellers from the damaged trains, bystanders and other witnesses. Such centres need to afford privacy and confidentiality to the users.

Guidelines for responders in the immediate post-crisis stage

- Make sure you identify yourself – name badges and identifying tabards should be worn if at all possible.
- Whatever type of area has been provided for the support of the individuals affected, try to create a safe place to talk to people that is away from others who may be involved. Refreshments and toilet facilities are important. People may be reluctant to move away from the immediate area if they feel they are being distanced from any sources of information.
- Be proactive in approaching those affected. Such approaches must be supportive and non-threatening. Remember that those affected may have difficulty in making decisions because of shock.
- It is important that all details of your contacts are recorded. You may gain information concerning missing persons, and this information should be shared with the police casualty bureau as soon as possible. Confidentiality must be protected and information shared on a 'need to know' basis only. The growing practice of using one set of forms compatible to the police casualty bureau forms should be encouraged.
- Information about those killed or injured will be of paramount importance at this stage. Responders should be aware of the dangers of speculation or rumour. They should seek facts from those in authority and avoid the danger of adding to speculation through discussions between responders that may be overheard.
- Telephone links are important for relatives. Responders should establish a means for providing such links and have change for payment of the telephones or phonecards if necessary. Remember that, although mobile phones are in common use, batteries will quickly run down. In the event of a major disaster, the police in the UK have the capacity to shut down the networks for public use to facilitate communications between the emergency services.
- Local taxi firms or transport provided by voluntary organisations may be needed to transport families to hospitals or mortuaries. Records must be kept of where families go and any contact telephone numbers that are appropriate. This is essential if further details become known when they have left the scene.
- Responders should be linked to one or two family groups only, if at all possible. The fewer people with whom those affected have to

relate, the better. In the case of the bereaved, this is important and can act as a resource to the police who have to carry out the identification processes. Many police forces now have teams of trained Family Liaison Officers (FLOs) who will be linked to individual family groups. My support for this method of co-working with the FLO is based on the experience of supporting a mother while she supplied identification details at the mortuary as we feared that her 14-year-old son was one of the bodies which had arrived from the site of a multiple terrorist shooting. In her emotional state, she was having difficulty understanding the questions and in responding to the sensitive questioning by the FLO. When she stumbled over describing what her son might have been wearing, she turned to me and started talking about the difficulty she had experienced in matching the wool for his sweater. I took over the conversation and gently led her through the details needed by the FLO. She appeared to value talking about normal things to another woman who was not from the police. She ended her description with the comment that she had needed enough for two sweaters exactly the same. It was then that we realised he had a twin brother and that we had the description of the body that lay in the mortuary. The mother asked us both to accompany her to the viewing.

Guidelines for responders involved in relatives' visits to a mortuary

Relatives may have to make a formal visual identification; others may choose to go to view the deceased for their own emotional needs. The timescale, size and type of the disaster will dictate the method of identification used. In either situation, the relatives should be advised that the body 'belongs' to the coroner until released by them following full identification and the completion of forensic evidence testing. These methods cause additional stress to those who must wait. Responders may be instrumental in helping ease this stress by explaining the reason for the delay.

Mortuaries may be permanent and have established routines, as in the case of a hospital or community mortuary. In these situations, it is to be hoped that such arrangements are sensitive to the needs of relatives. In the case of major disasters, temporary mortuaries may need to be established in airport hangars, swimming pools or tented accommodation. Even in these emergency circumstances, responders should try to influence arrangements to minimise the trauma to relatives.

The size and nature of the Asian tsunami caused major problems with regard to mortuaries. Sites were usually established in or near Buddhist temples or hospitals. The overwhelming numbers and the fact that so many of the emergency service personnel themselves were involved as victims or as family members added to the chaos. Bodies subjected to the force of the waves, the effect of the sea water and the heat quickly became discoloured and contaminated. This situation caused additional distress as distraught relatives searched among the rows of bodies arranged on the ground in makeshift mortuaries.

No matter what the circumstances are, every effort should be made to show sensitivity in relation to:

- religious symbols that are visible;
- seating in a private area before and after the viewing;
- the possibility of seeing other aspects of the mortuary work (for example, body bags or pathologists at work);
- sounds that can be heard in the surrounding area;
- sights and smells that may add to the discomfort of the situation;
- the provision of flowers, which can often 'soften' the harshness of the scene;
- flowers provided to relatives, which can facilitate their need to leave a token of their grief with the body; and
- the provision of practical support, such as the provision of water, cups of tea, boxes of tissues and toilet facilities, which should be accessible to the relatives.

Responders working in collaboration with FLOs should:

- have had previous experience of viewing a dead body;
- equip themselves with as much information as possible prior to the viewing on issues such as the physical state of the body and whether relatives will be able to touch it. Will relatives be allowed to place treasured tokens with the body? Parents of dead children often place a beloved teddy with the child. Who will be present at the viewing? Relatives often resent the presence of 'officials' at what is essentially a very private and distressing moment in their lives.

If there is pre-training and pre-planning between the organisations involved, fewer problems should arise. The central need is for the dignity and privacy of the deceased and relatives to be protected in the most humane way possible. A basic consideration for responders should be: 'How would I like to be treated if my role was that of a relative?'

The responders' task will be to provide both practical and emotional help to those affected. Practical issues such as accommodation, travelling arrangements, financial aid and help with contacting relatives appear to dominate this stage. It is important to establish the commitment of various organisations in the provision of such practical help. The organisations which are involved in the disaster, such as an airline, may also become involved in this process of responding. It is interesting to note that, at a later date, such help from a company involved may be rejected as 'blood money' when the anger of the relatives may turn against that company or organisation.

Funding for the provision of practical assistance and counselling services should be part of the pre-planning process. Normal resources may be used, but problems arise where the demand on these resources is such that a local area cannot bear the expense. In many circumstances, those requiring services do not come from the area required to provide the service.

Those affected by a disaster may feel more comfortable in seeking help with practical matters, but a sensitive responder can use these presenting problems to begin to offer emotional support or involve another responder trained in these skills.

Short-term post-crisis stage

The supportive help provided at the immediate post-crisis stage forms the basis for any other interventions in the future. The coordination group established at the time of the disaster should carry out an assessment process to aid a structured approach to estimating future need for services. Such assessment must include consideration of both the elements of the disaster and the relevant research on various possible methodologies.

There are three accepted methods for providing short–term and longer-term post-crisis support. These different methods may be used at the same time or at different stages in the response.

Proactive approach

If early intervention can minimise the long-term effects on mental health, then surely it is advisable on economic and humanitarian grounds? Research to date appears to have concentrated on the needs of those who have been involved in disasters (Figley et al, 2005). There are few specific studies into the effects of one method of intervention against another.

This research is welcomed by those helping agencies who have advocated and adopted early intervention or the proactive approach in many of the recent disasters in an attempt to minimise the longer term effects. The proactive approach is a departure from the usual methods employed by helping agencies. Social services, in particular, have a number of clients referred to them by virtue of their statutory role, as in the case of child abuse or mental health. Some find a conflict in adopting a proactive approach as a result. However, two factors are important in this debate:

- Those affected are not 'clients' as they are usually perceived in normal social work practice. These are people who, because of the circumstances of a disaster, are suddenly thrown into the situation of emotional and practical chaos. They may be bereaved or injured, or homeless and without possessions.
- Shock means that people have difficulties in decision making. Part of this problem may be that they are uncertain of how to access help or decide to reject it.

The proactive approach usually entails:

- Direct contact, with all those affected, at the scene of the disaster, the hospitals or mortuary. This may also be done by letter advising them that a responder will call at a specific time. The opportunity exists for the person to reject this offer. A leaflet based on the Red Cross leaflet, 'Coping with a major personal crisis', may be included in this letter. One of the problems of this approach is that contact is made with those directly affected. Traumatised members of the extended family may not feel that the contact can include them.
- The distribution of leaflets which identify the normal reactions to a crisis situation and local access to support resources. After a recent train disaster, these leaflets were made available at railway stations for commuters who usually travelled on this route to work. Leaflets should be given to key people in the community such as general practitioners, representatives of the community nursing services and members of the faith communities.
- Publicity about support services via the media, through the overprinting of the leaflet.
- Contact with the people known to be affected at the time of the anniversary, inquests or the publication of the report.
- Having responders available at public events associated with the disaster.

Reactive approach – accessing support services

The support services offered may form part of the established network of responding agencies and constitute areas of the usual social service systems that may be perceived as stigmatising by those affected. Such people may feel that they are being categorised as having mental health problems. They may never have had any association with helping agencies before, or have a negative attitude to social services and feel the stigma of being deemed 'inadequate' if they admit to needing help. They may attempt to access help through their general medical practitioner, although some have reported that this feeling, this choice, establishes them in the 'sick' role.

The issue of class can affect the numbers who will seek help. If the individuals affected come from a disadvantaged group in society, they may have fewer resources in terms of influence. This may have a direct effect on the choices that they have to make. If their homes are damaged, they may have to wait for the authorities to repair them. They may not have insurance policies that can be utilised. Those with financial security may have the ability to mobilise instant practical help. The wait for financial compensation may not be such a problem for those who have greater financial stability.

Self-help groups

As previously discussed, a bond is built up between those who have had a shared experience. If this common bond of experience is the basis for a self-help group, the members feel that they can talk freely and that their feelings will be understood. The group enables members to make sense of the experience and deal with feelings associated with the survivor guilt syndrome.

The group can also be used to circulate information on the support networks that exist and details of legal procedures, and they may become a pressure group to facilitate change. The Lockerbie family group, united by grief, found strength from each other in their crusade for information and the improving of airport security. This joint action was a creative way of dealing with their emotions of anger and frustration for the benefit of the group. Brooke (1990) discusses three reasons for promoting this form of intervention. It is:

- **Cost-effective.** A responder may be needed at the initial stage to aid the setting up of the group, which will soon establish its own leaders.

- **Non-stigmatising**. A group may be viewed positively by those who do not want to seek help through a helping agency.
- **Empowering**. The community and the people involved can take ownership of the group. Disasters can have the effect of taking power and control away from the local community. Long-term recovery must be in the community itself.

The group of parents of Dunblane made a video of their experience at the time of the first anniversary and they felt help from each other was of paramount importance. They had found a focus for some of their grief in the Snowdrop Campaign which successfully worked for the ban on the possession of handguns.

Long-term post-crisis stage

Counselling is an overused word. It is used to cover many activities that constitute helping. Some people associate it with psychotherapy and psychiatry. They feel that they are 'out of their minds' or mentally inadequate if such help is needed. The use of the word 'counselling' may reinforce the feeling that the counsellor has all the answers and they will make things right. The responder involved in counselling following disaster should be regarded as a facilitator or enabler. The affected person is enabled to adapt their usual coping mechanisms to meet the challenge of the new stress that has unbalanced their usual psychological equilibrium.

Counselling in these circumstances is a dynamic process that involves the responder and the person seeking their help in a partnership. This partnership needs to be based on mutual respect and the assurance of confidentiality. Responders need to recognise their own strengths, weaknesses and limitations. They must be prepared to refer the person to a more appropriate professional counsellor if necessary. A psychiatrist, priest or psychologist may have specific skills needed at particular stages throughout the helping process. A referral must be done in such a way that the person affected does not feel rejected or 'dumped' at a time of additional emotional stress. It is not unusual for the person to feel angry if such a referral is made. Unless the referral is sensitively handled and a dual interview or visit arranged between the two responders and the person, there can be regression in the recovery process. A person under stress, with the possible associated low self-esteem, may well interpret a transfer as a further indication of their low self-worth and guilt. Such a perception may mean that there is reluctance to accept help from another responder. Fear of a further rejection may inhibit the development of the necessary trust relationship.

NINE

Theoretical approaches to responding

Those who are responders to the psychosocial needs created in the aftermath of a personal or major disaster may be asked to fulfil a number of tasks. They will have to utilise a variety of methods that are based on a range of theoretical approaches. The art of responding is to be skilled in taking a flexible approach. The main determinant of the method to be utilised is the person to be helped and their individual needs. Strategies of responding need to be constantly reviewed and new objectives set as appropriate. The structured supervision of responders is an essential element in the process. Supervision monitors the quality of the help being given and can also support the responder in their task. Responders may be asked to help individuals or groups of people, such as a number of affected people in an organisation, a family or the community itself.

Crisis intervention

One of the pioneers in the study of crisis intervention and the psychosocial reactions presented by those affected was Dr Gerald Caplan of Harvard University, US. He chose to research the reactions of mothers and families who had sustained a premature birth. He observed that the outcome achieved by those affected was not wholly predetermined by pre-crisis personality or 'inner strength' but by the kind of help the person received: 'During a period of crisis a relatively minor force, acting for a relatively short time, can switch the whole balance from one side or the other – to the side of mental health or the side of mental ill-health' (Caplan, 1968, p 74). Further work by Howard L. Parad and Erich Lindemann (1968) developed this theory of short, intensive intervention. Their work provided the basis to justify a proactive approach being adopted following a disaster experience. Crisis intervention techniques are based on the opportunity for the person to ventilate feelings about the crisis situation in a safe and supportive relationship. Crisis intervention, which deals with the crisis as the centre of the process, can be described as psychological first aid and preventive in outcome. The nature of disaster situations themselves can make scientific research difficult due to the multiplicity and magnitude of acute human need. Major ethical issues arise in such matters as establishing valid control groups when testing the efficacy of the provision of, or the withholding of, an intervention technique in situations of human distress.

However, the practical experience of many responders and clinicians in such situations, in addition to comments from people who have been the recipients of crisis intervention techniques, is most positive especially as a method of ameliorating symptoms of acute reactions through education on normal healing processes, methods of self-care and knowledge of how and when to seek longer-term methods of treatment.

Recent valuable research into 'Effectiveness of employer-sponsored crisis interventions after a major disaster' was presented by Charles Figley and Joseph Boscarino at the 8th World Congress of the International Critical Incident Stress Foundation in Baltimore, US (February 2005) (see Boscarino et al, 2005). Their work evaluated the outcomes of 1,681 adults following 9/11. It was the first rigorous scientific evidence that suggested that post-disaster crisis intervention in the workplace significantly reduced mental health disorders and symptoms up to two years after the initial intervention. Analysis of their findings reinforces the validity and robustness of the methods and theories of responding identified in this book.

Following disasters, friends and families may weary of hearing those affected recount their trauma experience repeatedly. Responders can allow time to listen to this repetition as people seek to make sense out of their jumbled reactions. Listening and helping people to cognitively process what has happened to them are the essential features of the helping process.

Critical Incident Stress Management programme

The International Critical Incident Stress Foundation (US) has developed a comprehensive multifaceted Critical Incident Stress Management programme (CISM) to provide a structured approach to the multiple needs of people and communities experiencing trauma. I have been trained in and have practised under this system for most of my professional practice as a responder in many emergency and disaster situations. I have found it to be robust enough to meet the multiple demands created at all stages of providing a crisis response in a wide variety of disaster situations in a number of geographical and cultural settings. The programme provides responders with a 'toolkit' of different crisis intervention techniques that can be used. These techniques have been designed to meet the needs of organisations and communities as well as individuals. As such, the programme can have a valid use in the pre-planning stage as well as in the in-training programmes for responders.

There are 10 components in the CISM programme:

1. pre-crisis education;
2. demobilisation and staff consultation;
3. crisis management briefing (CMB);
4. defusing;
5. critical incident stress debriefing (CISD);
6. individual crisis intervention one-to-one – SAFER model;
7. family CISM;
8. community and organisational consultation;
9. pastoral crisis intervention; and
10. follow up/referral on (adapted from Everly and Mitchell [1999]).

1. Pre-crisis education: this component of CISM involves work, in society generally and within organisations specifically, to increase psychosocial awareness of the impact of major disasters. This awareness promotes the need to prepare emergency plans that include those to support the people who may be involved. This awareness can also help to promote caring attitudes towards those who face situations of personal disaster. An organisation may prepare staff to form a CISM peer support team or link to a Crisis Response Team (CRT) to prepare responders to meet the needs of individuals or groups.

The pre-crisis preparation can also be considered a form of psychological 'immunisation' in relation to the training of responders. The goal is to lessen potential vulnerabilities and enhance psychological resilience in such individuals. 'Pre-incident preparation also consists of behavioural response preparation and rehearsal. This includes familiarisation with common stressors, stress management education, stress resistance training, and crisis mitigation training for both frontline personnel and management' (Everly and Mitchell, 2000, p 213).

2. Demobilisation and staff consultation: this intervention, which can last for 10-30 minutes, is primarily a stress prevention technique, which may be instigated immediately after the responders are stood down from their deployment in a crisis situation and before they return to normal duties or to their homes. Demobilisation techniques were developed for use with emergency personnel who encountered either an individual person in crisis or a large-scale traumatic event. The team leader conducting the demobilisation can show their appreciation of the efforts made by the team, encourage them to look after themselves and get some rest. Demobilisation techniques can also be adapted to support staff involved in smaller incidents, such as a difficult shift in the accident and emergency department of a hospital, or police personnel who have been involved with a difficult crowd control situation. In my experience, these techniques can help responders begin to gain control of any psychological reactions they may feel as the result of their tasks. The use of such techniques can help to promote a culture of care for staff within an organisational context.

3. Crisis management briefing (CMB): this is a method for use with large groups of people, either in communities or within organisations, following a traumatic incident. It will take 10-45 minutes, can be provided for 10-300 people and has four phases. The first phase consists of bringing people who are associated with the incident together. Depending on the circumstances, this can be done for a total organisation, a community or for individual classes – for example, where a school is involved. Phase two involves someone with credibility, who may be known to the participants, explaining the facts about the incident as they are known at the time without breaking confidentiality. Information can be supplied on facts that are not generally known, and it helps to suggest ways in which updated information will be made known to the participants when it is available. This phase will help to control rumours, reduce anticipatory anxiety and return a sense of control to the participants. In phase three, a trained responder from the CRT discusses relevant psychosocial reactions that may result from the incident, and identifies common signs and symptoms. In phase four, personal coping skills and methods of self-care will be identified. Peer support should be encouraged, and sources of additional helping services can be identified and contact information supplied. Leaflets covering the information on possible reactions, suggested ways of coping and access to any additional resources should be supplied to all participants. An example of where CMB was most appropriate was when Staffcare was asked to provide a response to the tragic death of a student nurse in an accident on her way home from lectures. She was driving the car that crashed, and her three passengers, also student nurses, were seriously injured. The CMB was conducted by the College Principal and a CRT responder from Staffcare to an assembly of 150 of her fellow nurses. Other components of the CISM programme were available when appropriate, and the availability of counselling and other treatments underpinned the process.

The CMB meeting can take from 10-45 minutes, but has been proved to be valuable in reducing rumour, encouraging peer support and demonstrating that feelings can be talked about openly. CMB can also be used to good effect pre- or post-deployment of staff to a crisis situation.

4. Defusing: this is a small group process, which is instituted after any traumatic event or critical incident powerful enough to overwhelm the coping mechanisms of the people exposed to it. The defusing, which takes approximately 45 minutes, has the three stages of introduction, exploration and explanation, and is a shortened version of critical incident stress debriefing (CISD). Defusing can be used much earlier in the post-trauma response and can be particularly appropriate on the same day as the incident itself. The defusing, which is carried out by responders trained in CISM techniques, offers an opportunity for people involved in a traumatic event to talk briefly about their experience. It also provides for the initial teaching on stress management techniques to help the participants to deal with their own reactions in the most appropriate way. A carefully delivered and well-managed defusing may eliminate the need to do a debriefing, or it can enhance any subsequent CISD if it proves necessary to organise this more in-depth group process.

5. Critical incident stress debriefing (CISD): the CISM programme includes a model for the small group practice of CISD. The CISD process can best be defined as a confidential group meeting or discussion for a homogeneous group in terms of their exposure level to the traumatic incident. The model employs both crisis intervention and educational processes, targeted towards mitigating the psychological distress associated with a critical incident. The model uses a 7-phase structure which must be followed for the maximum benefit for the participants, for safe practice and to minimise any retraumatisation. Responders undertaking this work should be fully trained and experienced in the process. They should work in pairs, and one at least should have mental health training. CISD is a multiphase, structured group discussion, usually provided within 24-72 hours of the incident or when the threat created by the crisis is over for the participants.

The seven stages are:

1. introduction phase;
2. fact phase;
3. thought phase;
4. feeling/reaction phase;
5. symptom phase;
6. teaching phase; and
7. summing up/re-entry phase.

The model also advocates the availability of refreshments in the room at the end of the CISD to allow the participants to relax, promote peer support and have individual contact with the responders. The responders will use this opportunity to provide additional support to specific individuals who would benefit from further intervention or treatment.

In addition to mitigating the psychosocial impact of the incident, CISD allows for the enhancement of peer support and the opportunity for the trained facilitators to assess the need for follow up. The CISD may be followed by intervention on an individual basis with those individuals who require it. Referral for more formal mental health intervention may then be encouraged in discussion with the individual participant involved. The usual standards of confidentiality apply, and these are discussed with the participants in the introduction phase of the model. If the facilitators fear that a participant 'may be at risk to themselves or to another person', and where the participant refuses to seek help, mandatory reporting is essential to get them the psychiatric help which is indicated.

The purpose of CISD is not to provide a treatment for Post-Traumatic Stress Disorder (PTSD) or any other psychological disorder but to enhance the natural recovery processes in the immediate post-crisis period. It also helps to remove the stigma of seeking help by those who later find they experience delayed reactions. I feel that the use of this model, and indeed all the interventions advocated within the CISM programme should be viewed as health promotion techniques.

In recent years, this model has received some adverse criticism. The critical research that suggests that CISD should not be offered as an early intervention following a traumatic incident seems to influence the latest UK National Institute for Health and Clinical Excellence (NICE) guidelines (2005) which state:

> If you have been in a major disaster, you should NOT
> normally be offered a single session of psychological therapy
> (often called 'debriefing') immediately after the event
> because research shows that this is not very helpful and in
> some cases could make you feel worse later on. Instead,
> you should be offered practical support and advice about
> how to cope over the following weeks. Healthcare
> professionals may offer treatment in the first four weeks
> after the trauma if your symptoms are very severe, but will
> usually wait and see how you are after a month has passed.

Following the publication of the NICE guidelines (2005), the British
Medical Report headline read 'Debriefing not effective as a treatment
for PTSD'. The article then commented that Eye Movement
Desensitisation and Reprocessing (EMDR) and Cognitive Behavioural
Therapy (CBT) were recommended as the most effective treatments.
This concurs with the philosophy of the CISM programme, which
uses CISD as one of the crisis interventions designed to ameliorate
early reactions. CISD is not designed as a treatment for PTSD, which
cannot be diagnosed for at least 30 days after the stressful incident.
CISD promotes self-care and peer support. It also provides an
opportunity for the trained responders to assess the need for additional
support and referrals for further treatment. We need to keep in mind
the crucial fact that CISD is not a stand-alone intervention but part of
the total CISM programme.

Many of the research findings, cited in the Cochrane Report (2000)
and used to criticise the CISD model, have been found to have resulted
from interventions with individuals, even though the model was
designed for groups. One of the most often cited research findings of
harm being caused by CISD is that by Bisson et al (1997), which
looked at the effectiveness of debriefing in acute burns trauma victims.
Thirteen months after the trauma, those who received the debriefing
intervention scored significantly higher compared with the controls
on both the anxiety and depression subscales of the Hospital Anxiety
and Depression Scale (HADS) and the Impact of Event Scale (IES).
The prevalence of PTSD was also higher among those who had
received the intervention. It appears that the research sample had more
serious injuries which had necessitated a longer stay in hospital. The
CISD was used with individuals and not with a group. The intervention
was offered to individuals or pairs for an average of 44 minutes (30–
120 minutes) and was carried out by a nurse and psychiatrist trained
by the author of the report. The question of bias must be addressed, as

must Dyregrov's (1998) caution that it is clinically unsound to use CISD interventions with patients who have severe burns and who must be preoccupied with aspects of their physical healing in the early days after their injury.

In response to the growing confusion over the debate on CISD, a report was commissioned by the British Psychological Society (BPS, 2002). The report concludes that 'debriefing' has become a very loaded word in the last decade and means many different things to different people, leading to a great deal of confusion. The report also states that there has been little empirical evidence to 'demonstrate the effectiveness of psychological debriefing in accelerating normal recovery process following trauma'. The findings of Rose (2000), Kenardy and Carr (2000) and Orner et al (1997) were critical of the CISD model. In his evaluation of psychological debriefing, Yule (1990) cites studies by Robinson and Mitchell (1993), Griffiths and Watts (1992) and MacFarlane (1998). These studies might be described as neutral in their outcomes, as they do not report psychological debriefing as harmful but neither are they clear as to which debriefing intervention was used. There appears to be no standardisation of debriefing procedures used or evaluated. A study by Hytten and Hassle (1989), comparing debriefed and non-debriefed groups of firefighters, reported that there was no significant difference in the IES scores between those who had been debriefed and those who had talked informally to colleagues. These studies, it can be argued, do not constitute evidence to abandon CISD as an early intervention, as many of the outcomes were based on evaluation methodologies that evaluate the outcomes for longer-term treatment of PTSD.

The British Psychological Society report (BPS, 2002, p 75) concludes that 'there is still work to be done before it is possible to prove that "CISD" is effective as an early intervention following trauma exposure'. It can also be reasonably argued that the case against the efficacy of CISD has not been proven. As previously argued, any research undertaken must reflect that CISD resides within the integrated and multi-component programme CISM. It is hoped that Figley et al's (2005) research will be linked to this debate in the future.

Emmerick et al (2002) and Seligman (1995) believe that the decision to provide debriefing is not necessarily based on findings from only empirical research. Reports of satisfaction or perceived helpfulness by participants might be sufficient reasons to continue to offer debriefing.

Interestingly, the British Psychological Society's (2002) report also found that debriefing has generally been regarded positively by its recipients, and that this has led to 'anecdotal' reports of its effectiveness in the use of the group model with individuals; this should not deflect us from the fundamental truth that it is very likely that it will facilitate survival messages to be assimilated into long-term memory in time. Studies of the biology of memory processing make it very likely that the making of a comprehensible narrative account of the trauma will help. Training and experience are essential for the facilitators of CISD to maximise the benefit for the participants and avoid retraumatisation.

6. Individual crisis intervention 1:1 – SAFER model: this model is designed as a first basic intervention to deal with a traumatised person who is distressed. The model allows the responder to help **s**tabilise the situation for the person, **a**cknowledge the impact of the incident, **f**acilitate them to relate their story if they wish to, **e**ncourage them to be involved in the next actions to be taken and **r**efer them for further support if necessary.

This model is useful to provide a structure for responders who may have to provide 'on site' support. Under this approach, trained CISM responders are organised in advance of the incident. 'On scene' support services may lessen the impact of a traumatic event and block further deterioration of the individual, so that there is less need for time off for prolonged physical and emotional distress (Everly and Mitchell, 1997, p 145).

Following 9/11, several reports of intervention on the site, later to be known as Ground Zero, detailed the experiences of responders. Some responders made themselves available to the construction workers by distributing leaflets at the refreshment point and putting posters up in toilet facilities and locker rooms. SAFER model techniques were also important as responders sat on the rubble and talked with workers who were taking breaks. The SAFER model can also be utilised with telephone contacts.

7. Family CISM: family support services should be part of any properly integrated CISM programme. Any person who is part of a family unit and has been affected by crisis, trauma or disaster brings the crisis home to the members of the family. 'The crisis can spread directly to family members through abuse, abandonment, violence or neglect, or it can spread indirectly through isolation and withdrawal' (Mitchell, 1997b, p 57).

Mitchell, in a personal contact context, described to me how he had provided a CISM programme for the spouses of the firefighters after 9/11. It was significant that these spouses were not the bereaved, but needed support as the firefighters were spending a high proportion of their time with their peers and sleeping in their Fire Station accommodation. It appeared that they needed to gain support for their grief for lost colleagues by staying in their 'work family'. Family problems were arising at home as a direct result.

8. Community and organisational consultation: All the components that make up the CISM programme are interdependent and it is vital that close collaboration is maintained through ongoing consultation with the communities and organisations involved. Those responders managing the response need to involve the key personnel in the assessment and strategic planning processes. Clear briefing on the components of the plan which are available, how they can be accessed and for whom they are appropriate, must be maintained from the immediate post-crisis stage to the longer-term period. Consultation is also important at times of the anniversary, inquest or public enquiries.

9. Pastoral crisis intervention: disasters, whatever the numbers involved, are life-changing events. Such changes can make people consider the deep impact on the fundamental questions of life and death. Janoff-Bulman (1992) described this process as 'shattered assumptions'. Faith professionals from all faiths who have been trained in trauma care are a valuable resource at the scenes of disasters, hospitals and at rest centres. They can also be involved in the longer-term follow-up response. It should be noted that they should not be there to evangelise on their particular faith perspective, but be willing to deal with those who have no faith or who are questioning their own existing faith.

10. Follow up/referral on: it is important that any 'on scene' support services, demobilisations, defusings or CISDs are supported by a safety net of higher forms of intervention such as trauma counselling, Cognitive Behavioural Therapy, EMDR or psychotherapy. Prescribed pharmacological interventions may also be appropriate. Any crisis intervention should receive some type of follow up. Follow-up services should include telephone calls, station visits, small group meetings, meetings with commanders, peer visits, one-on-one services and family contacts.

The total CISM programme contains most of the tools which a responder would need to have in their 'toolkit' for crisis intervention support. Such techniques require training and skills practice. The art of CISM is to know which tool to use in response to the needs of the people affected who come for support either as individuals or in groups.

'Leaky sac' model, in support of early intervention

Recent events around the world remind us that being prepared to respond is essential if the multiple needs of those involved are to be met. A study of the needs of those affected by the larger incidents can also aid our understanding of the comprehensive and complex needs of those who have experienced any individual traumatic incident in their lives.

This model was devised in collaboration with Dr Gordon Turnbull for a presentation to emergency responders at the Emergency Planning Society's annual conference in York in 1999. It was later published and has been found to be useful to a wide range of responders. We presented a model which draws on other theorists and is designed to encourage a proactive response. We believe that early management of acute stress reactions can help to ameliorate symptoms which can lead to the development of chronic PTSD. Some of the confused criticism of CISD has meant that some practitioners have misinterpreted the criticism as advising that no intervention should be offered in the initial post-crisis intervention period. We strongly dispute this conclusion and we believe that this model encourages a proactive approach. People can cope and gain mastery over their symptoms by a better understanding of what reactions can be expected. Psychosocial education and practical help can often save hours of anxiety as the natural healing processes are encouraged. The model (illustrated in Figures 9.1 to 9.4) is presented to aid a general understanding of what happens psychologically as a reaction to an abnormal or traumatic incident.

The criteria for PTSD were defined in the Diagnostic and Statistical Manual of the American Psychiatric Association (APA) (DSM-III), published in 1980, and were later revised in DSM-IV (APA, 1994). The criteria define the incident as a specific event 'which is beyond normal experience' and is represented in our model as a 'bolt of lightning'. The symptom clusters defined in the criteria for PTSD can be defined under the headings:

I. intrusion;
II. avoidance; and
III. arousal (see Chapter Three regarding symptoms of acute stress reaction (ASR) and PTSD).

These symptom clusters are also present in stages 2 and 3, but vary in intensity and severity as the stages progress.

Figure 9.1: Three-stage model

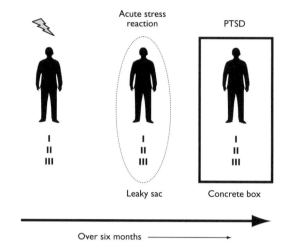

Figure 9.2: 'Leaky sac' Stage 1

I   Intrusion
II   Avoidance and numbing
III Hyper arousal

**Stage 1
The incident**

Figure 9.3: 'Leaky sac' Stage 2

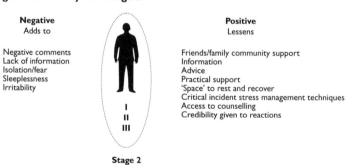

Figure 9.4: Stage 3: PTSD or the 'Concrete Box Stage'

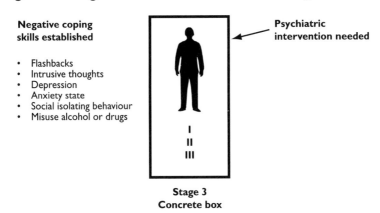

Negative coping skills established

- Flashbacks
- Intrusive thoughts
- Depression
- Anxiety state
- Social isolating behaviour
- Misuse alcohol or drugs

Psychiatric intervention needed

I
II
III

**Stage 3
Concrete box**

Normal individuals experience an ASR as a result of a traumatic incident. An ASR is a 'normal' reaction to an abnormal incident that threatens life and brings about a powerful emotional reaction such as intense fear, horror or helplessness. This is not a psychiatric disorder, although the symptoms are very similar to the chronic version known as PTSD when they persist for more than a month. The 'leaky sac' represents the ability of the core symptoms of intrusion, avoidance and hyper arousal to leak away through the 'porous membrane'. Of course, the pores would allow the influence of further (secondary) stresses to maintain the sac or even increase its size by leaking in.

Negative features listed on the left of Figure 9.3 increase the distress when they seep into the sac. Unhelpful comments such as 'you should be able to pull yourself together by now', or 'I don't know why you are upset; you should be thankful that you are alive' can add to the trauma and make people feel isolated and nervous of talking about the impact because they fear that others may treat them as 'mad' or 'weak'.

Positive features listed on the right side of the diagram help some of the tension to 'leak out'. Many of these represent crisis intervention techniques or 'psychological first aid'. Information sensitively sought and delivered is of paramount importance. Individuals affected appreciate small kindnesses such as sensitive delivery of bad news or someone staying with them during the hours of anxiety.

It is common experience that 'talking things through' with trusted relatives, friends or colleagues makes matters clearer. CISD should be recognised as only one element of a wider CISM.

If the 'leaky sac' stage results in deflation, then the ASR will have been resolved. Progress to the hard, encapsulated PTSD stage (the 'concrete box' in Figure 9.4) implies that recollections of the impact of trauma have not been processed and are accompanied by deepening intrusion, avoidance and hyper arousal. Generally, the more interpersonal the trauma, the more likely it will be to progress to PTSD. For example, natural disasters generate 5% chronic PTSD, road traffic accidents 10%, combat and terrorism 25%, assault 50%, rape 75% and torture 90%. The symptom complexes are the same as in ASR but are 'locked away' in what has become a steady state of suppression. Once the 'time-capsule' containing historical material is broken into and an attempt is made to process the contents, then this can be achieved quickly and successfully.

This model should help inform those involved in responding to the needs of traumatised people of the importance of early intervention from the moment that the traumatic incident occurs, which has an influence on the recovery process. This model is not based on philosophy, opinion, speculation or hope. It is firmly rooted in biological science. The model also challenges organisations to support their responders appropriately if they are not to become secondary victims, because they too can relate their reactions to these three stages.

Tehrani model for individual debriefing

Noreen Tehrani in her book, *Trauma in the workplace – concepts, assessment and interventions* (2004), comments that most of the negative criticism of debriefing arose from people using the group models, such as the Mitchell model in CISM, with individuals. She notes that there are few protocols for a debriefing model for use with lone workers who have been traumatised in the workplace. She presents such a model which she developed, in conjunction with Robert Westlake, in her work with the British Post Office. Her model has five stages and has been proved to be a very valid tool in this context. As with all crisis intervention, it has great potential as an assessment tool for the need for more structured interventions on a long-term basis. I commend this model and we have used it widely in our work in Staffcare as a first meeting assessment for individuals referred for counselling following a traumatic incident.

Cognitive Behavioural Therapy (CBT)

This is one of the longer-term interventions which is recommended by the NICE guidelines (2005). This well-established and much researched intervention has been proved to show good outcomes for people suffering from PTSD. Post-traumatic reactions, many of which can present with the co-morbidity of anxiety disorders, depression or phobias, are also considered amenable to trauma-focused CBT. While such conditions may not meet the strict criteria for the diagnosis of PTSD, we must never forget that the symptoms are similar and can cause great distress for the sufferer and their family members.

CBT must be delivered by a qualified practitioner who is in receipt of clinical supervision. The therapy has two aspects – *cognitive* and *behavioural* – and requires the active and motivated participation of the user. The most commonly used behaviour-changing techniques are desensitisation, relaxation and breathing exercises. When one considers the symptoms associated with a traumatic experience, these therapies, especially where a therapist has additional training in traumatic reactions, have a lot to commend their use.

Eye Movement Desensitisation and Reprocessing (EMDR)

This method has been pioneered by Francine Shapiro and appears to be most beneficial where the cognitive processes are 'blocked' by a traumatic visual memory. The method uses a rapid hand movement by the therapist across the eyes of the traumatised person as they focus their thoughts on a painful visual memory. Some therapists use sounds or light to create a similar stimulation of both lobes of the brain. By repeating the series of brain stimulations, while the person continues to focus on the sight which is disturbing for them, it appears that they rapidly reprocess their reactions and appear to be able to lower their sense of associated fear or anxiety. Uncertainty still exists as to the total reasons for the effectiveness of EMDR. However, it has been proved to be of particular use in cases where a person's cognitive processing of a traumatic event has become blocked. Treatment patterns usually involve three to six sessions, and the rapid improvement can in itself be beneficial to a person who is weary of coping with the painful ongoing memories of their traumatic experience – memories which are hindering their desired wish to rebuild their lives again. EMDR can be a useful additional tool to use in specific cases. It should only be used by fully trained therapists as part of a total treatment regime.

Perlman's theory of partialising problems

Many people involved in disasters talk of being totally overwhelmed. There are too many things happening to them at the same time. It is not unusual to hear phrases such as 'What is wrong with me? I start to do one thing and I get diverted to other things and nothing gets done. This is not like me, there's just so much to do, I don't seem able to get started.' Such a reaction is the result of shock and a sense of being overwhelmed. Consider the example of survivors from the Marchioness river boat tragedy (1989). They were shocked as they learned that so many friends had lost their lives. They were devastated by their feelings of loss, memories of the sinking boat and the sense of relief that they had survived. There may be elements of 'survivor guilt'. The lives of survivors are filled with good wishes from family and friends; there is medical treatment, and insurance and compensation claim forms to be completed; there are contacts to be made with solicitors, workplaces and other survivors; and there is a need to sympathise with the families of friends lost in the incident. They may also be subjected to media attention. There will be many practical issues to be handled such as lost credit cards, bank cards and driving licences, all of which require form filling and explanations that reactivate their acute emotional responses.

Perlman's theory of partialisation of problems can be appropriate in the helping process. The theory identifies the four 'P's of person, problem, place and process. It allows the identification of the totality of the problems that are combining to give the sense of being overwhelmed. The responder should then suggest that the total load is made up of smaller components which it might be possible to deal with individually. Some part of the problem should be identified and a strategy devised to work on it. A person who participates in this process may regain some confidence in their ability to achieve control. Any gains should be reinforced and encouragement given to work on another piece of the whole problem. The responder should assist but allow the control to stay with the person seeking help. This method of partialisation is valid in many situations that arise following disasters: 'The intent of the casework process is to engage the person himself in working on and coping with the several problems which confront him by such means which will stand him in good stead as he goes forward living' (Perlman, 1957, p 9).

Core principles of responding

This was one of the essential elements in the helping relationship which was identified by Felix Biestek (1934). He reminds us of the uniqueness of each person in terms of 'heredity, environment, innate intellectual capacity and volitional activity' (MacLean and Gould, 1988). Unless the responder recognises those features of the person that cannot be changed, such as the ethnic or cultural background which has given them their unique view of the world, the process of helping will be impotent.

Providing a safe environment for the expression of feelings

Roger (1988) outlines three basic qualities which are necessary if a helping relationship is to provide the safe environment needed for the expression of feeling:

- **Empathy**: 'the ability to experience another person's world as if it were one's own without ever losing that "as if" quality.' Empathy is different from sympathy which offers emotional comfort and support to distress. There is a need to check out what is being said so that the helper does not put their own interpretation on the problem being expressed.
- **Warmth**: people need to feel safe to share feelings and to feel that they are accepted and respected for their individuality and uniqueness.
- **Genuineness**: Roger warns responders against 'acting' as superhelper. People will soon detect the lack of authenticity. Being an active listener is important. The responder's own personality naturally forms part of the relationship. Roger warns against the dangers of self-exposure by the responder, which may inhibit people from sharing their feelings as openly as they should. Genuineness can contain an element of confrontation. If the person says, 'I'm coping better and my children are not upset by the death of their father', the responder may need to refer to the evidence observed and gently encourage discussion.

Confidentiality

Trust is the basis of any relationship. Confidentiality is part of such trust. Responders need to be realistic about this value and recognise with the person the boundaries which exist. These are where the person presents a risk to themselves or to others. Disclosure of criminal activity must also be shared. The transfer of such information to another agency should not take place without the person's permission. If trust exists, then the person can be helped to see the necessity of sharing. Trust and the sharing of sensitive information put a great onus on the responder not to abuse such trust.

Appropriate level of involvement by the responder

Appropriate level of involvement by the responder means that they always retain a sense of the worth of the person being helped. The responder must not take over the problem and solve it for the person. Allowing the person to retain power over their own life is so important. This is particularly so where shock following a disaster may render people inactive and submissive to tasks being done for them. In post-disaster work, it is easy for responders to become too involved. Such over-involvement may be meeting the responder's needs more than the needs of the person seeking help. Supervision of responders can monitor this situation and help counsel staff as to when the withdrawal or termination of a relationship may be the most appropriate action.

Client self-determination

Self-determination is one of the core values of responding. Often the person is feeling vulnerable and unable to make decisions and may pressure the responder with questions such as 'If you were me, what would you do?' Eric Berne (1964) describes this in transactional analysis terms as the ego state of the 'child seeking the parent' (responder). To be placed in the power position may seem attractive to some helpers, but their task is to aid the person to grow to the parent/adult role and so enable them to become an equal. Decisions that are self-determined will elicit commitment from the person. Decisions that are imposed by the responder will bring little participation.

Following personal or major disasters, the helping relationship required is one that will promote a state of order from the emotional chaos. The relationship should provide the support necessary to allow those involved to adapt their individual coping mechanisms to take on the additional features of the situation and restore equilibrium to their lives.

TEN

The response of systems to traumatic events

The previous chapters have dealt with the tasks and processes involved in responding to the psychosocial needs of those affected by a personal or major disaster. The dynamics of any disaster are extensive and involve many systems in society. Family units must respond, communities may be involved and many organisations have a role to play. Disasters are by definition events that overwhelm existing resources. Organisational responses are therefore difficult to plan for because disasters are unpredictable, but there may be a need to respond at any time.

The role of a health board, local authority or other statutory authority organisation in providing a response to the psychosocial needs of a community in the aftermath of a major disaster

Historical perspective

The role of local authority social service departments in many disaster plans has been seen as that of the provider of practical help, such as shelter for the homeless and care for elderly people or children who may be involved. When disasters such as flooding occur, residential homes and day care facilities are often crucial in the rescue procedure. The growing awareness of the need for psychological as well as practical support to people following disasters has involved social service departments in a new way: they are being called on to provide staff who can not only access the necessary resources but who can also utilise their counselling skills; this development has been welcomed.

Responding to psychosocial needs following trauma is not a new phenomenon for social services. Their work in relation to child abuse cases and to some mental health problems are only two examples of 'everyday' casework that includes trauma work. Social workers in hospitals are also experienced in this work through their work in accident and emergency departments and intensive care units. Bradford Social Services (1985) recorded the lessons that they had learned in their response to the tragic fire in a football stadium. Subsequently, other social service departments have drawn on their experience and adapted the lessons learned to meet the needs that 'their' disaster has presented.

Models for the delivery of a social service response have therefore developed in a piecemeal way with lessons from one incident passed on and refined. Brooke (1990) criticises the way in which social workers faced with responding to a disaster have asked 'What did you do?' rather than 'Did it work?' Response to any disaster must be based on assessment, evaluation and coordination with the voluntary and private sectors. The expectation of the general public has been raised over the years and the need for psychosocial support has been recognised. Such recognition has led to expectations that it will be available.

'Disasters – planning for a caring response', report of the Disasters Working Party (HMSO, 1991)

The British government established a national working party in February 1989 to prepare guidelines on the provision of social and psychological support in the aftermath of disasters. It was funded through the Department of Health and the Home Office, with Cruse Bereavement Care acting as the coordinating organisation.

The 15 members of the working party included representatives from social services, emergency services, voluntary organisations, local authorities and psychiatric services who had direct experience of disasters in their professional capacities as either managers or practitioners. I represented Northern Ireland social work on this working party. The deliberations of the working party were greatly enhanced by the insights from the relatives' perspective provided by one of the members.

The initial recommendations of the working party were discussed at 10 symposia held throughout the UK in the spring of 1990. Their deliberations helped to shape the report and added authenticity to it. The working party recommended that social work departments should play a lead role in terms of coordinating and organising the psychosocial support required for those affected at the time of the disaster. The report was well received by government and the organisations involved, but unfortunately such support was not backed by the necessary financial funding to enable the recommendations to be implemented. However, the recommendations formed the basis of a 'best practice' guide for many organisations and, as a result, influenced strategic planning. Many local authorities established teams of staff who, in collaboration with local voluntary organisations, undertook joint training and established protocols for response activation. Such work laid the basis for the changes that contributed to the 2004 Civil Contingency Act.

The 2004 Civil Contingency Act

Since the publication of the Disasters Working Party report (HMSO, 1991), statutory organisations in the UK have experienced a series of organisational restructuring processes. They have continued to respond to community needs that have been the result of emergencies and disasters. Political changes and the development of global terrorism have brought about changes within emergency planning. Emergency planning was no longer a matter of national responsibility but had to be achieved at international level which reflected interdependence.

The 2004 Civil Contingency Act was the UK response to these global changes and to the experience of the fuel crisis and severe flooding in the winter of 2000. The overall purpose of the Act is to establish a single framework for civil protection. The Act is separated into two substantial parts: local arrangements for civil protection (Part 1) and emergency powers (Part 2). An emergency is defined as:

- an event or situation that threatens serious damage to human welfare;
- an event or situation that threatens serious damage to the environment; or
- war or terrorism, which threatens serious damage to security.

Part 1 deals with local arrangements for civil protection and divides local responders into two categories:

Category 1 responders, to include local authorities, government agencies, emergency services and NHS bodies. These responders will have the responsibility to assess local risks and use this to inform emergency planning which includes plans for business continuity. Information to the public about civil protection matters and the arrangements to warn, inform and advise the public in the event of an emergency are seen as of paramount importance. The duty to share information with other local responders, in order to enhance efficiency, is also defined.

Category 2 responders have placed on them the lesser duties of cooperation with voluntary, statutory and private organisations, providers of public utilities, public communications (landlines and mobiles), transport organisations and the government's health and safety executives. There are local arrangements to cover devolved powers to regional assemblies.

The Act requires local planning to take place in multi-agency forums that come together at a strategic level under a regional coordinator. These regional coordinators have the responsibility, under the Prime Minister and other relevant cabinet ministers, to coordinate and collaborate with systems across regional boundaries in the event of a nationwide emergency. (The Act and all relevant documents can be found at www.ukresilience.info/ccact/index.shtm.)

As a result of this legislation, the key role for local authorities remains to assess, plan and advise through the Local Resilience Forums. The advent of the 2004 Civil Contingency Act, and the fact that emergencies and disasters are now considered beyond national boundaries, prompted some recent pioneering work to consider a European dimension in emergency planning for responding to the psychosocial care of individuals affected by emergencies and disasters. With European funding, the British Red Cross was responsible for managing the extensive process of consultation that took place. Representatives from government and non-governmental organisations (NGOs) from all the European countries pooled their experience in the production of the May 2004 report 'Working together to support individuals in an emergency or disaster' (www.redcross.org.uk). This document is an invaluable record of past experience being used to inform the predicted demands of the future. The main purpose of the project was to establish a common code of practice across political and geographical boundaries. Such a code will inform training and understanding of how the psychosocial needs of people have certain common features even if they occur in different geographical environments.

The Civil Contingencies Secretariat, established to implement the Act, has developed a report entitled 'Responding to emergencies' (2005). This relates directly to how local and regional Resilience Forums need to plan to respond. As well as a chapter on management and coordination at local level, a chapter is devoted to issues concerning the media. This publication and the Red Cross European Report (www.redcross.org.uk) should be used as handbooks for responders and responding organisations.

Pre-crisis stage

There is a need for the director of social services in each area to identify a senior social services manager who will have the responsibility for planning the provision of psychosocial help. It is this manager's responsibility to be aware of the other emergency plans of the organisations that constitute the Local Resilience Forum. Pre-planning should include regular contact with voluntary organisations; they should provide details of the type and volume of help that they could provide. Some local Crisis Response Teams (CRTs) may be recruited on a multidisciplinary and inter-agency basis.

Responders should be an integral part of pre-planning, and joint training will allow responders from different organisations to learn of each other's skills. This collaboration could avoid some of the inter-agency rivalry that can arise. Practical issues that should be addressed in the training and pre-planning stages include:

- the supply of name badges, car stickers and identifiable fluorescent tabards;
- the creation of an agreed protocol for the 'call out' and a pro forma for collecting information;
- a plan for supporting the psychosocial needs of the responders.

Crisis stage

Tasks for the manager

- Activate the 'call out' procedure as appears to be appropriate and identify an on-site team leader as soon as possible. All responders should report to the team leader who will assess needs and coordinate response.
- Establish an operational centre, with a computer information system, at an appropriate location as soon as possible. Administrative staff should be part of this call out procedure.
- Set up a helpline if appropriate.
- Act as media spokesperson or delegate this responsibility to a prearranged public relations officer.
- Sanction the use of resources necessary to the response.
- Collaborate with other disciplines and voluntary organisations to avoid duplication of resources.

Immediate post-crisis stage

Tasks for the manager

- As soon as is practical, the manager should call a coordinating meeting for other disciplines, voluntary organisations, faith communities, etc. This group should establish plans for the immediate post-impact stage, and longer-term plans should also be identified.
- The role of the coordinating committee is important in keeping everyone informed of developments and dealing with any difficulties which may arise in the service delivery. Plans to support responders should be activated immediately.

Short-term post-crisis stage

Tasks for the manager

- Decide on the need for additional responders and deal with all associated issues.
- Decide on the methodology most appropriate for the provision of longer-term support. The decision may be to establish a disaster team, which may include personnel other than social service staff. The selection and accreditation of such team members is the responsibility of the manager, but can be carried out in collaboration with the voluntary organisations if their members are to be included. The system for the supervision of the team must be established. Payment and length of contracts should be established. The manager must consider how long the team should remain in operation. This is important for the responders and the people affected. There is a need to provide help at times of additional stress such as inquests, memorial services, anniversaries and the publication of inquiry reports. The literature on this subject suggests that support should be available for up to two years after the event. This timescale is, of course, dependent on the type of disaster as well as geographical and demographic features.

Longer-term post-crisis stage

Strategic planning

It is necessary to consider the longer-term implications of the incident and to undertake inter-agency strategic planning. Such incidents create the need to plan not only for the individual needs of those most affected but also for collective needs within the community itself.

Plans need to be considered for how support will be delivered. Tim Newburn (1993), who carried out research into the social work response to the Hillsborough football disaster (1989), concluded that 'it should not be assumed that setting up dedicated teams is necessarily the most effective or efficient way to respond to a disaster'. Some of the social workers involved in dedicated teams reported to Newburn that the intensity and isolation of the work caused high levels of personal stress. They felt ostracised by their peers who regarded them as elitists who had been selected for this high-profile work. Return to normal practice was very difficult for the staff involved and many reported demotivation where normal duties were concerned. Those staff who had carried out 'normal duties' plus some disaster cases had suffered many conflicts in allocating their time, but had fewer problems of reintegration when the response was terminated.

Case study 19: strategic planning – Dunblane

The Dunblane tragedy on 13 March 1996 shocked the world with the horror of the murder of 16 small children and their teacher in the primary school in the rural setting of Dunblane, Scotland. The families bereaved and those whose children were injured were offered support by social services in the initial period. I was involved on two levels at the request of Stirling Council. At one level, I was asked to organise and deliver support to the family support workers, as a group of staff (see also Chapter Eleven). I was also asked by Stirling Council Strategic Overview Group to undertake brief focused research into the strategic and operational plans for the psychosocial response to be delivered by social services, the health board and the education services. A series of interviews was carried out with the staff involved. Each system had reacted at the time of the tragedy, and their staff had their own visions of the longer-term implications for their individual organisations. In writing the report, I drew on experience and research, and used the core concepts identified in this book.

Using the typology described in Chapter Two, Dunblane was person-made and largely experienced locally, but it quickly moved into the international category. It was 'small' in the terms of the number killed but 'large' in terms of those affected. Its unique features were in terms of the age of the children killed and the fact that their teacher, acting in loco parentis, was also killed. The incident contradicted fundamental beliefs in the sanctity of childhood and the safety of schools. The horror of the incident was localised in a small geographical area, but it was also contained within the 'subcommunity' of the school. The suicide of the perpetrator removed from the scene the direct focus of anger and blame. All these elements added to the devastation felt by the community.

The need to avoid labelling people collectively as 'the bereaved' or 'the injured' was very apparent. These groups were part of a traumatised community, each of which had their own unique way of reacting. The planning of any response had to be person-centred. Those involved in strategic plans recognised that they needed to 'ensure that children, families and community define the direction of provision and response ...'.

The comprehensive needs presented in the aftermath of Dunblane required collaborative working with statutory, private and voluntary organisations. There was a real danger of overzealous altruism causing duplication of resources. The wider community might have also grown to resent the attention being focused on 'the tragedy' for too long. The aim of strategic planning had to be to deliver services to the whole community of which the response to the disaster was only a part.

Strategic planning must take place on the micro- and macro-levels. These levels are interactive and they evolve as time passes within other cultural, social and political considerations. Strategic planning challenged us to form a vision of how Dunblane would judge the response in 5 or 10 years' time. Strategies to support the bereaved had to promote their natural grieving processes in such a way that they would begin to 'live' again and not just exist. They would never forget, but they would remember with less pain. Their attitudes would affect the next generation of Dunblane, who would have the tragedy as part of their family and social history.

The efforts of the education services to support pupils and schools that had been directly or indirectly involved could be helped to ensure that the educational standards were equal to the normal level that would have been expected if the tragedy had not occurred. The general physical and psychiatric morbidity of the community would indicate the long-term success of the medical and psychiatric intervention made in the short-term post-crisis period. The juvenile crime rate, the extent of drug abuse, the level of marital breakdowns and the value of housing in the area could all be used as measures by which the statistics of Dunblane could be judged against comparable societal norms.

While such issues may appear academic at the post-crisis stage, they are necessary if survival is to be achieved. The name of Dunblane will always be associated with the tragedy. Strategic planning and the sensitive delivery of services could also mean that the name of Dunblane was associated with a community that healed and developed creatively in the aftermath. Current indicators would suggest that these issues have had a positive outcome, but on-going monitoring will be required.

A network approach – Crisis Response Teams

To prepare for the response to crisis situations, a social service or social work department should consider setting up a Crisis Response Team (CRT). Staff should be identified by management because of their location or previous experience, such as hospital work or mental health experience. Management should recognise that not all staff may be willing to act as responders. There must therefore be an element of self-selection or volunteering. Staff who go through the disaster awareness training must be allowed to 'opt out' if they feel unable to carry out this role. Such opting out should be sensitively handled and the staff member should not be made to feel a 'failure'. Management may also need to counsel out any staff member whose abilities are not found to be appropriate to the perceived task during the training.

The use of the Critical Incident Stress Management (CISM) model (see Chapter Nine), as defined by the International Critical Incident Stress Foundation, outlines a multifaceted, multi-component programme for responders and responding organisations. The interventions outlined are appropriate for a training programme. One of the most important features of this programme is that it trains responders to assess the vulnerability of the individuals involved. This assessment allows for appropriate follow up or referral on to a more appropriate level of treatment intervention.

The CRT leader

A team leader should be identified to deal with ongoing operational issues for team members. This will include maintaining contact with team members and organising ongoing training, on a six-month basis, which allows the skills to be maintained and personnel contact records updated. With information circulated from the Local Resilience Forum, the manager and team leaders should be responsible, with administrative staff, for establishing and maintaining a number of emergency boxes at strategic locations. The emergency boxes should include local maps, essential telephone numbers and basic office equipment such as referral forms, phonecards, petty cash, vouchers to local traders, boxes of tissues and lists of local resources (for example, residential homes, day care facilities, hostels for the homeless, car hire firms and voluntary organisations). Extra name badges, car stickers and identifying tabards are also useful.

The use of the CRT

The existence of this CRT would provide any social service managers with responder staff who have the necessary training to react appropriately in a crisis situation. If the demands on CRT members in one geographical area were overwhelming, the manager could enlist other CRT members from another area. The agreement to take this action should be part of the area disaster plan.

Advantages of this model

This model is most effective given the nature of emergency and disaster work. If a network policy is adopted for joint training and practice exercises, then all the responders should know the majority of their colleagues.

I have had experience of establishing such a team in my own area and of helping other regions to adopt this network model. When trained, team members have been asked to react to cases such as family distress following a murder, a family in the aftermath of the death of a family member by suicide and a family rendered homeless after a house fire. Their role in these situations has enhanced the services offered by their organisation and provided the opportunity to develop their skills. They have also undertaken joint training with staff in the local airport as part of the disaster plans for the airport.

Non-governmental organisations (NGOs) or voluntary organisations

The role of NGOs and voluntary organisations in the support of those affected by both personal and major disasters has been significant over the years. Such organisations typify the sense of altruism experienced by most members of society when they learn of human distress. The history of organisations such as the Salvation Army, the Red Cross and St John Ambulance is closely linked with situations of disaster. Society expects to see the uniforms of these organisations in the midst of the rescue operations. The basic practical care of those affected, and responders, by the provision of food and drink by the Women's Royal Voluntary Service (WRVS) or the Salvation Army has been a key feature of many relief operations. The uniforms of such organisations mark these people out and can be a significant factor in situations of chaos. People know what such uniforms mean and they have certain expectations as a result. Uniforms clearly define roles and these help to bring order out of chaos.

The Samaritans are well known for their telephone support to those who are distressed. They have also played a more proactive role in recent years by identifying themselves as a source of trained voluntary help with helplines where their telephone skills could be valuable.

Cruse Bereavement Care, started some 50 years ago, has developed into a national organisation that provides trained voluntary bereavement workers for all who have been bereaved. They have built up an expertise in helping in situations of personal disaster. As a result of recognition of this expertise, they became involved in post-disaster work when they provided a team to assist British people in New York in the aftermath of 9/11, and teams at Heathrow and Gatwick Airports to meet families returning from the countries affected in the aftermath of the Asian tsunami. The WRVS, Relate, Victim Support, Raynet (amateur radio operators) and youth organisations may all become involved in responding at various stages of personal or major disasters.

The involvement of voluntary organisations should be coordinated and achieved under the terms of the 2004 Civil Contingency Act. A database of these resources should be established and maintained. Joint training can have the advantage of increasing understanding and determining common standards of best practice. The voluntary sector can also have a significant contribution to make to training.

The police and the coroner

The management of an immediate disaster response is the responsibility of the local emergency services – the police, fire brigade and ambulance service. While each has specific duties, these interface closely with each other. The armed forces may also be involved. The role of the police includes helping to save lives, preserving the scene of the incident as a crime scene and gathering evidence as to cause. They are also involved in managing the collection and dissemination of casualty information, and they assist in the identification process as agents of the coroner, or the procurator fiscal in Scotland. They work to ensure that all information on casualties and the dead is accurate. This process can create long delays for the relatives, which can result in conflict and additional distress. If responders have an awareness of the procedures involved and an established collaborative role with the police, they can support the relatives through the identification procedures.

The coroner's duty is to establish who the deceased was, and how, when and where the death occurred. The coroner is required to carry out such investigations where the death of a person is sudden, violent or unnatural. The coroner remains legally responsible for the bodies until they are handed over to the next of kin, or to those entitled, for burial or cremation.

The location of the bodies is important and photographic evidence is also collected. Following Lockerbie, some 800 square miles had to be searched for bodies, personal items and debris from the plane, all of which was of paramount importance in the process of identification and investigation. Major logistical and practical problems occurred in the aftermath of the Asian tsunami as many bodies were washed out to sea. After a few weeks, the bodies that washed up on the beaches were unrecognisable.

Following disasters, bodies are taken to a mortuary where a pathologist carries out post-mortems. The pathologist may need the assistance of fingerprint experts, or dentists to compare dental records. In some cases, identification is simple and straightforward because visual identification is possible. However, if the nature of the disaster has distorted the body, DNA matching may be successful. Even with the use of every sophisticated method of identification, it is not uncommon for some bodies to remain unidentified. These circumstances are more likely to occur following an incident involving large numbers of an anonymous general public.

During the process of identification, a police officer will be responsible for gaining ante-mortem details from the relatives. This is a very stressful process for the relatives, yet it is essential that they are asked very basic questions. This process requires great sensitivity. In some areas, Family Liaison Officers (FLOs) work in partnership with responders from the local CRT to aid the process and avoid additional distress for the relatives. From a psychological point of view, it is beneficial if continuity of personnel involved can be achieved. Distressed people form intense relationships with the police and responders at this stage, a relationship on which may well depend their ability to accept help in the future. If the same responder works with the same team of police personnel, a trust builds up between them. This trust may also provide a supportive network for those who are working together to help the relatives.

The police also manage the casualty bureau information and liaison with the coroner's office. Close liaison is essential between the casualty bureau, the mortuary and the point where anxious relatives are seeking information. Brief descriptions gathered from the relatives and hospitals' accident and emergency departments help the police in the identification processes. Accurate identification depends on accurate information. All responders should be aware that in conversations with those affected they can gain some vital pieces of information to pass on to the police.

Evidence is emerging to substantiate the belief that seeing the body after a death aids the grieving process. Raphael et al (1983) carried out research into the reactions of relatives who had and had not been given the opportunity to view the bodies of their relatives after a rail disaster. They interviewed 44 relatives; of the 34 who had not seen the body despite being advised to do so, 22 regretted their decision after 18 months. This was compared with a sense of regret expressed by only eight of those who had viewed the body.

The viewing of the body may provide a valuable opportunity to say farewell. The visual reality may be less horrific than the fantasy that may develop. Viewing the body may aid the person's understanding of the reality of the situation and confirm for the relative that no mistake in identification has taken place. The use of photography can help the relatives in the future if they later wish to view the deceased. Photographs should be filed carefully and only made available if specifically requested. These photographs have also been used in a case where a seriously injured relative was deprived of the opportunity to participate in any of the usual rituals because of his hospitalisation.

A particular problem arises when children are involved. 'Some children are naturally curious but hold back because they sense distress in adults' (Cathcart, 1988, p 87). Adults should be sensitive to the feelings of isolation that children feel at such times. Children often adopt a very practical approach to the whole subject of death and they need to be included by the family at whatever level is deemed appropriate.

Where a doctor did not see the deceased for a specified period of time before death or after death, the death must be reported to the coroner. The coroner is involved in situations where death occurred in custody, or in the case of a child in care, during or immediately after an operation, where there are suspicious circumstances or the reason for the death is believed to be industrial injury or disease, or where there has been an accident. The coroner may establish that the death was due to natural causes and that there is a doctor who will be able to certify the cause of death. The coroner then issues a certificate, and the death is registered. If this is not the case, then the coroner can arrange for the body to be removed for a post-mortem examination to be carried out.

The inquest can be a difficult process for relatives as they hear details of the incident. There may well be renewed press interest. This can be an additional factor of distress. Some of the bereaved may hear explicit details of how their relatives died. These details may have been withheld at the time of the death for fear of adding to the level of distress. Responders may be needed to support the relatives at this time.

The words used by the coroner in describing the incident can have a profound effect on the bereaved. There are many coroners who display great sensitivity to the bereaved by addressing them directly to express sympathy and understanding.

Points for consideration by responders

- A knowledge of the procedures involved and the role of the police and coroner is essential.
- There is a need for the police to have procedures to liaise with responders in a structured way to ensure that confidentiality is protected and adherence to the 1998 Data Protection Act maintained.
- Provision of an area for relatives at the mortuary and in the court used for the inquest is important. Such space should be protected from the press, and be a comfortable area with access to responders, telephones, refreshments and toilets (see Chapter Thirteen).

The role of the police is central in any disaster situation, be it major or personal. Their work interfaces with the injured, the bereaved and all involved with the provision of practical or psychological help. Good pre-planning and a sensitive understanding of each other's roles are essential if police, coroner and responders are to work as a team to the advantage of those affected.

Case study 20: multi-agency working following bomb blast in Belfast

In 1995, a large van bomb was detonated without warning by terrorists outside a forensic laboratory in South Belfast. It was close to private housing and the Belvoir Housing Estate. The prompt action taken by the two neighbourhood policemen when they noticed the van saved many lives. No one was killed but 1,002 homes were damaged and some 40 people sustained relatively minor injuries. Community amenities such as churches, the schools, the library and the health centre were badly damaged. Electricity supplies failed due to the damage caused; the residents used their car headlights to illuminate their homes. All emergency services were mobilised and the Crisis Support Team (CST) members were called to the scene. Neighbours helped neighbours; the home helps in the area left their own damaged homes to run to the aid of their vulnerable clients. One clergyman got the elderly members of his congregation, who had been at a meeting in the church, to hold hands as he led them out of the devastated church and took them to their homes, which had also been damaged. Even when CST members visited devastated homes, they were often told, 'We are coping, you should go to those houses over there; there is a young mother on her own with kids, and an old lady in that one.'

Alternative accommodation was organised in the local council leisure centre, which was the only building with its own generator. People did not require this accommodation as they wanted to stay in their own homes if at all possible. Collaborative working between agencies resulted in the establishing of a 'one-stop' help centre in the leisure centre, and the media were used to tell residents of its availability at 8.00am the morning after the incident. As the dawn broke, we observed a phenomenon witnessed at other such incidents. The surge of activity and courage displayed in the immediate aftermath, when the adrenalin flowed, diminished. People wandered in the area in silence and with a sense of disbelief at the magnitude of the destruction. The sight of churches and homes devastated provoked intense sadness and quiet sobbing. Realisation brought anger and a sense of being emotionally overwhelmed.

Residents came to the help centre where the agencies had gathered together. The police representatives, Castlereagh Council representatives, the Compensation Agency, the Social Security Agency, the Law Society and representatives of the local Health and Social Services of South and East Belfast Trust (SEBT) worked together to attempt to meet the multiple needs. Refreshments were provided by the trust and all their resources of nursing and social care were coordinated from the centre. The CRT helped with those experiencing emotional reactions to shock, and coordinated voluntary responders and church groups to support families in their own homes. The Red Cross provided a crèche for children who could not play in their own homes because of glass in the carpets, or their own gardens because of glass in the grass. It was noted that the children were reluctant to be separated from their mothers, even when a safe place to play was waiting for them. The Samaritans supported the helpline. Youth groups and volunteers helped to distribute food to homes left without cooking facilities.

Some residents expressed their anger and grief to those working in the centre. These staff often had to cope with misplaced anger as they struggled to satisfy the acute demands. Staff, too, needed support, and the CRT provided debriefing sessions. The usual SEBT staff visited the homes of known clients and the philosophy of 'business as usual' was supplemented with additional resources. Many valuable lessons were learned from this response, which formed the basis for future standards of practice for responders. These were as follows:

- Pre-planning aided collaborative working and inter-agency meetings were organised each day.
- The council's role was paramount in providing accommodation for the help centre and coordinating the 'clean up' operation with their own staff and voluntary groups.
- SEBT personnel present on the night were the CRT, the home helps and staff of the mental health hostels and hostels for those with learning difficulties who rushed to help their clients. Later, the SEBT coordinated the psychosocial response by supplementing normal services and providing support to voluntary and community groups, which made resources available to visit residents in their homes.
- The one-stop help centre was vital to this response as people were too shocked and tired to travel to different locations. It also provided a meeting place where they could talk in a 'safe place'.
- The SEBT supplied food, and it was found that bowls of 'Irish stew' served in disposable containers with plastic spoons were preferred as you did not need 'clean hands' to eat it. It was hot, nourishing and acceptable to most age groups.
- The Mayor's Relief Fund was coordinated from the centre. The many offers of practical help received were recorded and either used or acknowledged later by letter.
- The council produced a newsletter each day, and then weekly, to keep people informed of the help that was available. Youth organisations were utilised in their distribution.
- Damage to the inner lining of chimneys necessitated the presence of the Coal Advisory Board at the help centre to advise not to light fires due to the risk of toxic fumes.
- Looters and disreputable builders added an unwanted complication to the response, but the police acted quickly to warn vulnerable residents.

- Critical Incident Stress Debriefing (CISD) for staff and responders was essential. Home helps were given a debriefing session in groups of eight. These sessions were invaluable in expressing gratitude to them for their efforts, in allowing them support for their own emotional reactions and in notifying needs of their clients.
- The SEBT established a central database to coordinate information and avoid duplication of resources.
- Two years later, the area won the award for the 'Best Kept Estate' in Northern Ireland.

The role of the embalmer and funeral director

The role of the embalmer and funeral director is twofold: the care of the dead and the responsibility for arranging funerals. The care of the dead involves embalming and the preparation of the body for burial. This is a skilled task, which includes the injection of a preservative to avoid discoloration and deterioration of the corpse when it is seen by the relatives. Great sensitivity is required in this task, and religious and cultural requirements must be strictly adhered to. The traditional washing of the deceased by relatives in the case of Hindus is an example of such rituals.

Where there has been a traumatic death, the embalmer may advise that the body should not be viewed. The police will be part of such a decision at this stage. Where there is gross disfigurement, every effort is made to improve the appearance of the body, although it may not be possible to make a visual identification. The relatives' wishes should be considered in such cases.

Disasters involving fire, chemicals, explosion or water can mean that the remains are difficult to identify. Many of the advanced identification techniques such as DNA, dental records and finger-printing may be utilised in the identification processes. Information gained from the relatives, and from personal effects, can also assist. The embalmer's work follows that of the pathologist. The recovery, examination and embalming of the bodies can vary greatly with the circumstances of each disaster. The time factors involved at this stage can add additional stress where cultural rituals demand burial within a specified period.

The funeral director will be involved with the police in displaying the bodies to the families. Every attempt should be made to provide privacy and some sense of dignity in this process. Here, the support of a responder may be appropriate. When all forensic evidence has been gathered, the embalmers will return the personal effects found on the body, such as rings and watches, after having cleaned and restored such items. When the local coroner procedures allow, the body is released to the family for burial or cremation.

The funeral director is responsible for arranging the funeral in accordance with the wishes of the bereaved. The funeral director should deal with all the paperwork involved and negotiate times of services, etc. with the religious establishment involved. The nature of disaster is such that many nationalities may be involved. There are sometimes special emigration and immigration arrangements to be made. It is the responsibility of the funeral director at the site to arrange this paperwork. The arrival of the body at its home destination can mark the beginning of the ritual grieving or mourning period. Such rituals, no matter what form they take, are important in the grieving process. The grave site, or the place where the ashes are scattered or buried, is an important focus for future grieving.

Mass burial following a disaster is the favoured option in some areas. After the Asian tsunami that washed many people out to sea, other bodies that were washed up on the shore were placed in mass graves in some countries. This may be a preferred option on health grounds. Families who do not wish this to happen must make their wishes known to the authorities as quickly and forcibly as possible, but it is not always possible to achieve the practice requested.

Responders should seek to facilitate this process by advice and support to the bereaved that is based on their knowledge and experience. They should support the bereaved in requesting clearly whatever form of burial or ritual they prefer. The responder should be sensitive to the need for the family to have time to say farewells to the deceased. They should be available but be careful not to intrude. Even in situations of mass death, each individual body must be treated with equal respect and dignity.

Funeral directors and embalmers, too, may need mechanisms to share their feelings after such events. They usually seek support from their colleagues. However, access to confidential counselling should be available.

The role of religious belief in crisis

At times of stress, fear and loss, when people feel overwhelmed and inadequate, they may seek support from sources beyond their own resources. Primitive humans thought that the natural disasters that befell them resulted from presumed offences against their gods. Disasters can render people helpless and hopeless. It is not unnatural that they should turn to someone or something that offers them support and hope. The role of religious belief is significant in the person's perspective of what is happening. At a time of crisis, even those who have lapsed in their religious practice or have little religious belief seem to turn to God for comfort. Survivors from a disaster often speak of prayers being said as they waited for the impact or while they awaited rescue. Those rescued are often greeted by 'Thank God you're safe'. Those who have a faith in God often find that such faith is their only channel for real comfort and help. They seek answers and strength from within their established religious practices. However, some people who have a faith in God find that they begin to question its validity against the backcloth of crisis. Frequently, they find themselves asking, 'Why did God let this happen to me?', 'How can I still believe in a loving God when He allowed this to happen to my son?'. God may become the focus of their anger. The responder must be sensitive to the inner turmoil that such reactions can bring. The person may benefit from the counsel of an understanding priest or clergyman – not one with bland biblical platitudes but one who can share the pain and pray on behalf of the person if they feel they cannot pray themselves.

Unbelievers may find that in crisis situations their anger, too, turns against any form of God. The pain and devastation they see may be a confirmation to them of the non-existence of God. Grey (1989), discussing the effect of the death of a parent on an adolescent, noted that those who professed a religious belief exhibited less depression. It was a way of their finding some meaning in this major life crisis. Parkes and Weiss (1983) noted that the dimension of meaning is an important one for understanding the psychopathology of bereavement. Responders must be sensitive to the effect that the dynamics of religion can have on people, and must be very careful not to impose their own beliefs or attitudes on those who are so vulnerable at the time of a crisis. The responders' own faith, or non-belief, may also be under pressure as they, too, come to terms with their own inner conflicts in the environment of crisis and tragedy. Responders must be professional but not totally detached. They must allow the people affected to feel comfortable enough to express honestly their faith in or anger against God. It is important in this scenario that the responders are aware of the importance of being a good listener, as many feel an initial embarrassment in talking about matters of faith. It may be the responder who will hear of conflicts in belief, as the person affected may not feel able to share such thoughts with either family or religious advisors. Platitudes such as 'It's God's will' slip easily into conversations. Responders should be extremely careful that their words and actions encourage people to go on sharing such thoughts with them. They may be able to encourage people to seek help from their own faith community. Such encouragement must be seen as responders co-working, rather than as rejection on the part of the responder.

In our multiracial society, responders must be sensitive to various religious and ethnic practices (Table 10.1). Their future bereavement reaction may be significantly affected by the way in which such rituals have been carried out. The responders should acquaint themselves with such practices as quickly as possible. Where possible, responders should be sought from the same ethnic origins as those seeking help. The nature of death, and the belief or non-belief in an afterlife, will have a significant effect on how the bereaved person perceives their situation.

Table 10.1: Key factors for various faiths

Religion	Key factors to be considered
Anglican	Faith in the resurrection of Jesus Christ and life after death. Deceased may be taken to the church some days prior to the funeral. Funeral service usually takes place in a church with further prayers of committal at the graveside. Hymns and prayers reflect the Christian faith. Service is adapted in the case of cremation.
Roman Catholic	Faith in the resurrection of Jesus Christ and life after death following an interim state of purgatory. Last rites are always offered at the time of death. This is very important to Roman Catholics and must be considered in the case of disasters. The funeral director may be asked to place religious medals or ribbons on the deceased. A rosary (beads associated with prayer) may be placed in the hands of the deceased. Funeral service consists of (1) bringing to the church, (2) requiem mass, (3) the final commendation and farewell, (4) the burial/cremation. The Roman Catholic church now accepts cremation.
Free Church, Baptist, Methodist, Presbyterian, United Reformed	All these denominations are Christian in their belief in a life after death. Services are usually held in church and there is a variety of forms of worship. Ministers have more flexibility in the order of service than the Anglicans or Roman Catholics. Services in the home of the deceased are permitted. This is common practice in the case of the Scottish Presbyterians.
Salvation Army	Their strong Christian belief is translated into practical care for others in need, as well as being the focus for their worship. The Salvationists are organised like an Army for Christ and take 'military' titles. Their centres are called Citadels.

contd.../

Table 10.1: contd.../

Religion	Key factors to be considered
Atheist or agnostic	By definition, an atheist is a person who does not believe in the existence of God, while the agnostic neither believes nor disbelieves. No service is held, and atheist families usually prefer cremation. The essence of any funeral remains the same – a dignified farewell to the deceased. The family may design their own form of words.
Jewish funerals – Orthodox	Belief in a Heaven but not in Jesus Christ. The synagogue makes all the arrangements and carries out some of the funeral director's duties. Cremation is not accepted. Burial must take place before the second sunset after death. Rabbi organises and controls the service.
Jewish funerals – Non-Orthodox	Service similar to the Orthodox rites, but more liberal and cremation is acceptable.
Reformed Jew	At all Jewish ceremonies, all males should have their heads covered throughout proceedings.
Greek Orthodox	Belief in a life after death. Funeral services tend to be longer with a private service being held for the family prior to the church service.
Jehovah's Witness	This sect hopes to be one of the few who are to be saved when the end of the world is at hand. They do not recognise any leader other than the supreme God. The discourse at the funeral service is taken by one of the committee of the local Kingdom Hall.
Quaker (Friends)	The Religious Society of Friends believes in an afterlife but their basic approach to life and death is one of quiet peace and love. They have no ministers. The funeral service will be similar to other meetings they hold and predominantly one of silent meditation. Cremation or burial is acceptable.
Muslim (Moslem)	Muslims favour burial. They believe that Mohammedan or death is the end of the present Islamic life to be followed by life hereafter. They believe that all men are called to be God's servants, where God controls their will, and that death is a temporary separation from the loved one who will be brought back to life on the day of judgement. They venerate the Koran, which they believe contains the eternal word of God. Muslim religious law demands daily prayers, recitation of the Koran, fasting, giving alms and the duty to make a pilgrimage to Mecca at least once in a lifetime and to bury the dead according to their rites. Muslims believe that the soul remains in the body for some time after death, and that the body remains conscious of pain. Muslims of the same sex carry out their own ritual washing of the dead. They are urged to bury their dead without delay within 24 hours. The relatives play a major role in all funeral rites. The simple coffin may be passed from person to person at shoulder height. Mourners usually fill in the grave themselves.

contd.../

Table 10.1: contd.../

Religion	Key factors to be considered
Chinese	Chinese relatives need to visit the site of the disaster or accident in order to carry out some religious ceremonies at the scene of the death. After attending a Chinese funeral or memorial service, it is necessary to walk with a group of people, to allow the evil spirits to dissipate, before returning to work.
Hindu	Hindus favour cremation. Hindus believe in reincarnation as the person survives to be born again. The bereaved can therefore have no thought of reunions in an afterlife. The ashes of the deceased should be scattered into a river, preferably a holy river, such as the Ganges. The rivers flow into the ocean and merge in this symbol of the divine. Suttee, the cremation of the widow on her husband's burial pyre, is now illegal. Some castes and ethnic groups have their own practices and customs.
Buddhist	Buddhists favour cremation. Buddhists also have the ethos of reincarnation incorporated into their belief of an after-life. Their ultimate aim is 'Nirvana', or becoming one with the Divine.

The media

The role of the media is to inform and entertain. This dual purpose can easily be identified in the written word of newspapers, the spoken word of radio and the visual presentation of television. At the time of a disaster, responsible media can assist in the response by issuing important information to the public quickly. The Charter of the British Broadcasting Corporation (BBC) enshrines its raison d'être in the words 'to inform, educate and entertain'. There are commercial factors to be considered, overtly or covertly, in all media activities.

Traumatic events make news. There will be media reporting of some personal disasters as well as major ones. The way in which such events have been reported has evoked some fierce controversy over the last few years. The 'best' stories are in fact the worst stories in terms of human pain and tragedy. Reporters have sought to report the facts of the event, depict the horror and seek to promote debate on the cause of the incident.

Relatives and those involved in recent major disasters have reported intolerable intrusion by some members of the press. It is appreciated that employment in the media depends on getting news material. This is particularly pertinent for freelance journalists or photographers who, having gained the information or photographs, must sell them to the larger consortiums or agencies. However, intrusions into privacy, where there is deep emotional pain, cause additional distress to very vulnerable people at a critical time. Photographs of bodies being removed from wreckage or, as in the case of the Hillsborough football stadium, being crushed against the perimeter fence, are particularly distressing. These are not just scenes of anonymous persons, they are someone's husband, son, mother or friend. These scenes may 'haunt' people for years to come.

In reporting such events, the media have been accused of being intrusive to those involved. Such intrusions have been justified on the grounds of the need to tell the truth, to depict the full horror of the event. On arrival at John F. Kennedy Airport, a woman was told that the daughter she had come to meet had been killed in the Pan Am jet explosion over Lockerbie. She collapsed in hysteria on the floor. As people sought to comfort her, flashing cameras and TV lights surrounded them as the media attempted feverishly to record the event. These pictures were transmitted all over the world. The woman has made repeated attempts to prevent the continued use of these pictures, but without success. She described in a recent interview on television that she recalls nothing of this event and feels that her personal privacy has been violated. The editor who permitted the use of the pictures feels that these scenes caught the true horror for relatives in such an incident. He feels that he was doing a service in reporting the authentic scenes of grief to the world. Such pictures could, he argues, deter someone from contemplating such an act of terrorism in the future. Here is the kernel of any debate on the role of the media.

The media must seek information. Being first with the facts or with the pictures can increase sales and viewing figures. This need to be first can result in intrusive reporting by some of the media. Hospital accident and emergency departments, under pressure with the arrival of victims, also have to cope with the media clamouring for information and pictures. Distraught relatives arriving at a hospital may have to run the gauntlet of cameras and microphones.

Public concern at such intrusions has created much debate. While there is no specific law in Great Britain to ensure a right to privacy, a citizen has the right to complain to several of the media's own regulatory bodies. The National Newspaper Code of Practice has five points:

1. **Respect for privacy**: intrusion into private lives, in particular those not in the public eye, will have public interest justification.
2. **Opportunity for reply**: a fair opportunity for reply will be given when reasonably called for.

3. **Prompt corrections**: mistakes will be corrected promptly and with appropriate prominence.
4. **Conduct of journalists**: subject only to the existence of an overriding public interest, information for publication will be obtained by straightforward means. Similarly, newspapers will not authorise payment to criminals to enable them to profit from crime.
5. **Race, colour**: irrelevant references to race, colour and religion will be avoided.

The editors of all the national newspapers have endorsed this declaration. The new comprehensive editorial guidelines issued to all programme makers throughout the BBC enshrine similar principles. The BBC guidelines recognise the problems of reporting personal or major disasters. The guidelines state that reporters should not pursue victims or relatives unduly. If an approach is rejected, the reporter should not persist, even though another news organisation may have been accommodated. Agreement is needed for all interviews, which should be carried out with consideration and in as private a place as possible. Tearful scenes of distress should be kept to a minimum.

Some members of the press have agreed to a voluntary system of pooling information and pictures. This can mean that one television and one newspaper crew, who later share the material with their colleagues, record the visit of a VIP to survivors. It should, however, be remembered that some events attract media attention from abroad and from freelance reporters who do not feel bound by these guidelines.

The media may also fulfil the role of investigator in terms of the cause of the incident. Amid the horror, grief and destruction, they can seek to initiate debate on who was responsible. In many recent incidents, the media have been involved in prematurely 'scapegoating' individuals or companies as those responsible. Such investigative journalism can pre-empt public opinion to such an extent that witnesses' accounts can be influenced in any official inquiry or inquest.

The effect of media attention on the bereaved can influence their long-term grieving process. The media may intrude into their privacy and use the material gained to label the persons concerned. The bereaved can, in shock, make allegations or comments that they may later wish to retract or amend, but the media may repeat such material later. The person concerned may feel 'locked' in the distraught relative role and unable to progress in their rehabilitation and return to normality. The forgiving relative who makes a statement at the time of the event may also feel locked in this response. They, too, may need to have space to be angry and condemning as part of the natural grieving process. The public image may have helped other people affected to cope with their feelings. The bereaved may be forced to live out their public role because they feel responsible for others at a time when it is difficult to be responsible even for themselves.

Media reports often identify heroes. These heroes may be victims who die or who are injured, bystanders or responders. The mantle of hero may surround a person who has never been exposed to such attention before. Such people often speak of 'only doing their duty to others'. The description of a deceased person as a hero can help the bereaved have 'good' feelings about the dead person. If the person died helping others, in some cases the relatives may gain comfort from the fact that others lived as a result of their loss. The survivor who is identified as a hero can, however, be trapped by this label. They may feel unable to have a normal reaction to the abnormal events because 'the strong don't cry'. The hero or heroine may gain satisfaction and comfort from their acts because they helped save 10 people, but there is often a feeling of guilt that more could have been saved. They may be haunted by the screams of the 11th victim who slipped from the saving grip to their death. The reporting of such feelings may be painful for a society who would rather live with details of positive results. Such reports can also increase the sense of failure and guilt in those who feel they could have done more for others. Insensitive reporting can enshrine disturbing inner thoughts that may affect emotional rehabilitation for some of those involved.

The recent developments in mobile phone technology meant that, during the traumatic evacuation of the bombed London tube train (2005), a passenger was able to show the terrible scenes by the use of his mobile phone video facility. The BBC was later criticised for transmitting these images of such intimate personal distress. The video shots were the first confirmation for the police of the exact time that the explosion occurred, and this confirms the coordinated nature of the multi-site attack. Many people involved in traumatic events report how destructive the repeated use of associated news material can be in their emotional recovery process. The amateur video taken at the scene of the Enniskillen bomb may be used whenever any discussion takes place on Semtex explosions or terrorism. The scene of the Herald of Free Enterprise lying on its side in the Channel is frequently used in any discussion of the event or on marine safety. There is repeated use of the class photograph of the children and their teacher at Dunblane when any incident concerning a school occurs. The use of this type of material is often unannounced and can cause great distress to those involved by its unexpected portrayal at unexpected times.

Some people interviewed report that they suffer reoccurrence of their feelings of fear, smells of the event, nausea or associated sweating when they see these scenes transmitted.

Cooperation with the media on the part of those affected who choose to cooperate can provide them with a means of expressing their feelings. Such expressions may be therapeutic as a vehicle for their anger. The desire to warn others of the dangers of certain activities can help some relatives. The distraught father of a daughter killed by a drunken driver may feel that he can use the media to enable his grief to make others think about how they can avoid another similar tragedy. Parents of a child who has died as a result of solvent abuse may want media coverage to help deter other children from exposing themselves to this risk. In these situations, the media can be viewed positively and are also seen in the role of responsible communicators.

It should be noted that the repeated use of news items on major disasters at the time of anniversaries or litigation connected with compensation could be hurtful to those who are coping with a personal disaster. They can resent the apparent public sympathy directed towards certain bereaved or injured people. Some speak of this adding to their sense of societal isolation and rejection.

The media can be used in a positive way by the caring agencies. In pre-planning for the response to disasters, the role of the media should be considered. Spokespersons should be identified to cooperate with the press. Such proactive cooperation with the media should include prearranged press conferences, as frequently as necessary. Caring agencies can utilise the press network to give essential information such as helpline numbers, legal advice and how the support services can be accessed. The media can also be used to aid society's awareness of the possible psychosocial effects on those involved.

I believe that responsible reporting of the types and degree of emotional reaction that may be experienced, not only by the victims and their relatives but also by the responders, has aided the recognition of such needs. Recognition of these needs has prompted much of the work currently being undertaken to ensure that 'people provision' is a feature of any disaster planning.

In an age when our world is influenced and fashioned by mass media, the responder should advise the people involved on the role of the media in relation to the event. They should warn the persons affected that the media may approach them and that it may be desirable to elicit the help of a spokesperson. The responder should advise that any phone caller might be from the media. If a family is made known to the public through the media, they may be the subjects of 'crank calls' from undesirable people. Media coverage of compensation claims often brings 'begging' letters. The media coverage of a funeral can be viewed in both a positive and a negative way by the relatives. It may help them to realise that their loss is of local or national concern. The absence of such coverage may be perceived as rejection and cause comparison to be made with other incidents deemed to be similar. The media spotlight may return with equal intensity at times of memorial services, inquests, inquiries, compensation cases and anniversaries.

The disaster or memorial fund

When society learns of a disaster, people usually want to help by giving financial aid to those affected. This can occur following a personal or major disaster. Prominent local or national figures are usually asked to become involved as trustees of such funds. The sending of money can begin very quickly after the event and is yet another situation where order needs to be established from chaos. Some offers of help may be totally inappropriate in the disaster situation. People may send clothes, children's toys or medicines, which may not be appropriate, and the 'relief' sent could add to the problems of those organising the relief on the site.

The setting up of a fund should be announced as soon as possible. The criteria for allocating such funds need to be established at the same time. Various legal requirements exist to guide trustees and ensure that the wishes of contributors are met. The needs of those affected will vary, and any criteria for allocation must recognise this variety. Three methods exist for the distribution of the funds:

1. Some funds have made allocation of monies to all affected, irrespective of need. This method presumes that the disaster is such that 'all' those affected are known.
2. Means testing has been undertaken by some funds for those who apply for help. This necessitates form filling and the investigation of personal financial circumstances. The investigation can require those applying for help to declare all sources of help that they are receiving.
3. Some funds have made an initial payment to those directly affected. This is then followed by an invitation for applications to be made by anyone affected. Those who have received the initial payment can also make an application.

The timing of the distribution of funds needs to be sensitively handled. Immediate hardship may exist. Compensation payments often take some time to settle and people may become financially distressed in the interim period.

Trustees bear a heavy responsibility in their role as receiver and distributor of such funds. They will receive many genuine applications and also some fraudulent claims. They will be dealing with people who are in both practical and psychological chaos. Their methods of vetting should not add to this chaos. Some funds have been severely criticised for their insensitivity in dealing with distressed people. The nature of need is very subjective and the trustees must maintain objectivity. Money can never replace the losses that have been endured, but it is society's way of expressing their support.

Newsletters

Following some major disasters, a newsletter has proved to be a very valid method of providing support to those affected. Initial issues usually contain information on support services. It is often very helpful if normal stress reactions are discussed in the newsletter. Self-help groups of those affected often produce and circulate such newsletters. Information on legal matters and dates of the inquiry are important and can be circulated through this medium. The newsletters can become a vehicle for people's anger at the person or persons whom they perceive to be responsible for causing the disaster. The newsletters can also become part of a pressure group to force changes in work practices, design of aircraft, buildings, etc. that are seen as having the potential for further death or injury.

The date to stop the publication may be as important as the decision to start: 'It was to become for many the only acceptable place to share a feeling, to divulge a problem, to ask a question. Here, at least, the audience would understand. Here there was no stigma ...' (Stewart, 1988). The decision to cease publication three years after the tragedy was a difficult one, yet people felt they had to move on and cease to be 'disaster victims'. A publication produced by children and young people bereaved by the Hillsborough football tragedy proved an invaluable vehicle for expressing their thoughts through writing and artwork.

The helpline

The police quickly establish information lines for people concerned to contact for news. Relatives all report that these lines are quickly overloaded. This can add frustration to their distress. A helpline, as its name suggests, is a designated telephone line, which is established following major disasters. The helpline does not replace the police line to the casualty bureau, but it can aid the police by dealing with some of the numerous calls that are received. It may have many lines and many uses. When the decision is made to establish such a link, there will need to be responders ready to operate the service. As it is likely to be a 24-hour service, the responders should have a clear understanding of their role and its parameters. The helpline can also be used to access information, and can later become part of the supportive network to those affected. Calling people back can establish the credibility of the caller as the press often use such lines to gain information.

Table 10.2 illustrates use of a helpline in the UK when a major incident occurs.

From this table of the probable usage of the system, it can be clearly seen that there is a need to have lines that are designated for incoming or outgoing calls only.

Procedure for those operating the system

Immediate post-crisis period

- Responders should be given as much basic information about the situation as possible to share with the callers.
- A system should be devised to update responders as regularly as possible. Factual information must be accurate. It is the responsibility of the police to notify where there has been the loss of a life. Hospitals issue information on the injured. Rumour and unverified information should never be discussed.

Table 10.2: Uses of a helpline

Inward calls	Outward calls
The general public seeking information.	Returning calls to earlier callers as information becomes available.
Relatives of those involved needing help.	Calls to nearby hospitals.
Helping agencies offering assistance.	Calls to police casualty.
Official information sources.	Calls to summon extra assistance.
Crank calls.	

- A caller should be asked their telephone number at the very beginning of the call, and details of the call recorded systematically. It may be necessary to speak to the caller later.
- All offers of help should be recorded as they may be useful later.
- Long conversations should be avoided but sympathetic structured conversations are most beneficial.
- Where callers are very distressed, they should never be dismissed from the call without asking them if they would like a responder to contact them later.
- Telephone numbers of other helping agencies or religious establishments should be available to the caller.
- Crank calls should also be recorded but dealt with firmly.

The use of a helpline should be part of pre-planning in the emergency plan. The staff should be supervised by a management structure that will have a responsibility for issuing information to the responders and organising rotas and appropriate rest periods. Clerical help may be needed to collate the types of help offered. The flood of calls received in the initial stages may dwindle after a few days.

Short-term post-crisis period

When the initial crisis is over, the helpline can fulfil a vital role in providing support. Those suffering a reaction to the event may feel that it is an acceptable way to access help. They may feel that they can use it anonymously to talk to someone who will understand their feelings. Responders should be able to use good listening skills and may feel it is appropriate to advise callers of other support mechanisms that exist. Responders should offer to refer callers to another organisation if they request it. We sometimes underestimate the courage it has taken to make the first call.

Long-term post-crisis period

The decision to close the helpline must receive the same publicity as the opening of the line. Alternative sources of help should be made known. An answerphone may need to be used for a period of time. The helpline number may be incorporated into any ongoing support that is organised. The telephone link remains advantageous to some of those affected as help can be sought anonymously.

The planning process

Planning for a disaster means that planning has to take place for an event that it is hoped will never happen. This fact can give a sense of unreality to the discussions. The recent legislation following terrorist attacks has increased the urgency to plan. The strategic planning, as detailed in the 2004 Civil Contingency Act, can be viewed on two levels. Macro-planning has been described as a shield covering large areas or continents. When we consider the concept of such shielding, it can gain reality if we remember how a shield is actually designed. The shield has a surface which faces out. This could describe 'macro-' planning. The shield also has a surface facing inwards towards the holder. This side could represent micro-planning in organisations or in local areas. The surfaces are different but complementary to each other if the shield is to fulfil the function for which it was designed. Planning should be a participative process for all those involved as this will aid authenticity and ownership. The provision of support for the psychosocial needs of those affected should be central to all planning. Following an incident, the emergency plans should be re-evaluated and any changes seen as necessary implemented.

Conclusion

The need for responders and responding organisations to be prepared in the event of an emergency or a disaster is vital. The psychosocial needs created will be comprehensive and complex and will change over time. Cooperation and collaborative working between systems is not achieved at the time of the incident but is the result of the work carried out in the pre-planning stage. Responders, and the systems within which they work, must never become complacent in their level of preparedness or skills.

ELEVEN

Responders: research into the impact of their work

Just as the awareness of the psychosocial needs of those directly affected in emergencies and disasters has increased, so there has been a similar increase in relation to the impact on responders. Over the years, there has been an expectation that the professional training and experience of responders will immunise them against any negative reactions. Being professional has historically been believed to have shielded the professional from becoming 'over-involved' in the human aspects of their work. However, we all know of many highly qualified professionals who have left their profession because the impact of being a responder broke through their 'shield' and resulted in 'compassion fatigue', the term used by Figley (1988).

Even though it appears that disasters are becoming more frequent, it must be remembered that few professionals will have experience of dealing with them. Their training has given them a code of practice, and they may have coped with the results of many traumatic incidents, but it is unlikely that they have had to cope with so many dead or injured at one time. One house fire may result in loss of life and property, but having to cope with the results of a bomb or crashed aircraft, where many people are affected, will stress even the most experienced and professional responder.

The numbers of responders who could be affected can also be seen in terms of a pebble in a pool of water; responders can become 'secondary victims'. As such, their needs need to be recognised by management and provision must be made to meet these needs.

Michael Stewart of the Centre for Crisis Counselling describes the reaction of responders as a 'mirror of pain' in relation to the pain they observe or attempt to alleviate. During the training of the Piper Outreach team of social workers in Aberdeen, Stewart found that: 'Staff were mourning the potential loss of their own families. They were experiencing a "mirroring" reaction, a sudden awareness of fragile vulnerability in their own lives' 1989, p 11). The fact that at times of emergency or disaster so many people expect responders to cope, to know how to act, and to be able to bring order from the physical and emotional chaos places extreme pressures on the responders (see the secondary traumatic stress model described in Chapter 4, pp 67-71).

The impact of trauma work on responders has been a special interest of mine throughout my professional life and became the subject of my doctoral research. From a personal context, I found that the more I studied the subject the greater my understanding and ability to cope with my own stress levels. I based the research on the hypothesis that, if we could introduce training to alert responders to psychosocial reactions that may arise as a result of the work, such training would ameliorate or prevent compassion fatigue.

I embarked on the research after my experience of responding to the Kegworth crash (1989) (see case studies 7 and 14 at pp 23 and 75). This research was the first large-scale analysis of the psychosocial reactions of responders to their work in the aftermath of two major incidents. While responding to Kegworth, we worked long hours and had to cope with the intense emotional stress involved. It was eight months later that I needed to seek the support of a psychologist colleague to help me 'keep going', to make sense of my reactions and to learn how one traumatic experience can link to previous reactions to other incidents. This positive experience of being helped in a confidential and acceptable way formed the basis for the formation of Staffcare some years later.

The research into the reactions of the responders involved in the aftermath of Kegworth had commenced when the terrorist bombing took place on the Shankill Road in Belfast in 1993. Involvement in this response provided me with the opportunity to extend the research into the reactions of the same professional groups of staff and to implement a comparative study. The outcomes of the study had implications for policy and practice, and formed the basis of a modular training programme specifically designed for those who have to face trauma in their work environment (see Chapter Twelve).

The needs of responders were identified in an empirical study of four groups of professional staff involved as responders in the aftermath of the two major incidents identified. The four groups of staff chosen for the research, both in England and Northern Ireland, were social workers, ambulance personnel, accident and emergency nurses and clergy. The samples were matched, in terms of profession and rank wherever it was possible.

The methodology employed was a literature review and a postal questionnaire circulated to the Kegworth sample in 1991 and to the Shankill sample in 1995. The questionnaire included a section that was based on Roger's and Nesshoever's (1987) validated assessment tool on coping strategies. The results of the questionnaires were analysed and used in semi-structured interviews with a selected sample. The results from both incidents were compared to highlight the impact of the work on responders working with those experiencing the aftermath of a single incident trauma and those experiencing multiple incident traumatisations.

In the literature studied, those affected were primarily seen as those who had been injured or bereaved. It was Raphael (1986) who described the responders as 'third level victims' when she noted that they too were traumatised by the work that they undertook. While it is accepted that, after the loss of a close relative or friend, the traumatic circumstances may result in reactions which can be classed as Acute Stress Reaction (ASR) or Post-Traumatic Stress Disorder (PTSD), I believe that the psychosocial impact on the professional and personal lives of responders mirrors similar reactions. The impact may be to a lesser degree and the time involved may be less, but research would support the view that the trauma experience will produce similar negative outcomes for these tertiary 'victims'. For the injured or for friends or relatives, there may be a time when their exposure to acute trauma ceases, but for those who are constantly exposed to trauma, as part of their work role, the aspect of serial traumatisation must be acknowledged.

While reactions outlined in the psychobiological model (see Chapter Four) contribute to initial survival in a threatening environment, in the longer term they may give rise to more persistent neurobiological responses that can become maladaptive and affect future reactions to similar stimuli. This phenomenon could have serious implications for those involved in work situations that require them to be re-exposed to similar situations.

Setting the research in context

Research was integrated into the major incident plans held by a variety of organisations. It was noted that few of them had planned for systems to provide psychosocial support to responders. To set the research in context, a description of the incidents follows using a few examples of practice that highlight the range of stressful tasks with which multi-disciplinary responders are faced (see case study 6, p 19).

From the time of the Kegworth crash, helping agencies, including social workers, clergy, airline staff and voluntary organisations were involved at Heathrow and Aldergrove Airports to support distressed relatives. Social workers from the Leicester emergency team were called to the Thistle Hotel, which was situated on the East Midlands Airport site, to meet relatives and work in collaboration with the airline staff and police to accomplish the distressing task of identification of the dead. Clergy and some members from voluntary organisations were also involved. The reception centres established in each of the hospitals where the injured were being treated were to prove a vital focal point during the initial stressful days. The location of the incident challenged many organisations to collaborate across geographical and administrative boundaries.

The relatives from Northern Ireland were flown to East Midlands Airport early the following morning. Relatives of the injured were transported to the hospitals. The remaining relatives were taken to the Thistle Hotel, where they were told that it was likely that their relatives were dead. Each of these family groups was then linked to a designated policeman and social worker to help them through the identification procedures.

All the tasks undertaken by professional responders and volunteers required an adaptation of their previous training to cope with the multiple unfamiliar demands of the victim population. Visits to the crash site were organised from the hotel for the bereaved, people with minor injuries and the relatives of the more seriously injured. As they stood near the twisted wreckage, the only sounds that could be heard were muffled sobs. Someone had displayed great sensitivity and had arranged for the salvage work to be halted. Police and army personnel stood in silence forming an informal guard of honour; they too shared in the sorrow felt by so many.

Arrangements had to be made for a special flight to transfer the bodies of the Northern Ireland residents and their relatives home. One young man became very distressed and approached me with a piece of paper that bore the number 6A. He insisted that he sat on the same seat number as his mother had travelled on her last fateful journey. While it was difficult to organise, arrangements were made, discreetly, to facilitate this request.

Later that night, I joined a small group of responders standing outside in the dark and watched the plane take off. A discussion on shared reactions followed and one of the policemen recalled how he had coped by working 'on automatic pilot' as he handled the remains of the bodies in the mortuary. He had felt the stress building up as the forensic processes progressed and numbered corpses became named people with family members who identified and mourned them. He had coped with the help of his colleagues and the escape of alcohol. Now, he realised the full psychosocial impact of the work he had carried out. He felt able to share his reaction with fellow responders, but unable to seek support within his own organisation as he feared that his reaction would be assessed as 'lack of moral fibre', incompetence or weakness, which would jeopardise any future promotion prospects.

These examples identify some of the multiple new tasks that were undertaken by the responders. The response provided by the responders based in the East Midlands area was time-limited, with the longer-term response being provided elsewhere. It was the first experience of a major incident for the majority of the responders. It was also unlikely that they would have to utilise such skills on a regular basis. As the stress of such work became evident at an early stage, responders supported each other. Some responders were given encouragement to seek professional support, some were told of professional support but not encouraged to avail themselves of it, while in many cases their needs were neither recognised nor dealt with.

On 23 October 1993, a terrorist bomb exploded at lunchtime in the busy shopping area of the Shankill Road in Northern Ireland. The Irish Republican Army (IRA, a paramilitary group) placed a bomb in a fish shop. The location was chosen because it was thought that a meeting of the Ulster Defence Association (UDA, a loyalist paramilitary group) would be taking place in the office above the fish shop. The meeting was not taking place and when, without warning, the bomb exploded it killed 10 people and injured some 52 others. The scene was chaotic as passers-by and emergency services dug in the rubble with their bare hands. The injured were taken to the nearby hospitals. The identification of the dead was a very protracted process due to the nature of their crush injuries, and also it was difficult to establish who had been in the area at the time. Responders were involved at the scene, in the hospitals and at the mortuary.

When some of the social workers arrived at the mortuary to support families through the identification process, the senior police officer explained that one of the police officers sent to the mortuary to assist in the identifications had discovered that his uncle and cousin were among those killed. He had identified them and then made several frantic phone calls to relatives before he could establish that the body of a child was not that of another relative. This direct linkage of roles as both a responder and a relative was not an uncommon experience in the history of responding to traumatic incidents in Northern Ireland over the years.

It was suggested that support would not be needed for the family of one of the bombers who had been blown up while placing the bomb. The social workers involved had to remind those in charge of the identification process that they were there for the bereaved, irrespective of how they had been bereaved. The family later chose not to attend the mortuary as identification had been established through scientific methods. This situation illustrates the personal dilemma for the responders who had to deliver a professional service regardless of the circumstances of the disaster. They also had to cope with continuing to work in the midst of the community tensions that followed, and to remain ready to respond quickly if another incident occurred.

Support was offered at the ambulance depot to the crews on their return from the scene; there was an unnatural silence as weary crews climbed down from their vehicles. Some of the crews began the initial cleaning of the vehicles in case another call came. The occupational health consultant and I helped to serve fish and chips that had been donated by the local shop. Some of the responders needed to talk and some wanted to eat in silence. Some of the comments demonstrated not only the depth of reactions experienced but the way that one incident could stimulate previous painful reactions. These responders had to cope with their reactions to this incident in the knowledge that it was likely that they would have to deal with another incident almost immediately.

There was a high degree of anger and fear within the community and talk of retaliation emerged at an early stage. Three days later, UDA gunmen rushed into a council cleansing department depot and killed two workers; many of the other 23 were injured. Within the week, a gunman burst into the 'Rising Star' bar in Greysteel, outside Londonderry and shot eight people dead; 19 others were seriously injured.

Responders involved in the response to these incidents were traumatised by the tasks, but they also had the additional pressure of community tension. For many of those involved, their response was treated as 'just another incident'. The nature of the accumulative psychological impact of serial traumatisation was explored in the research.

The Shankill incident was different from the Kegworth incident in several significant ways. The Kegworth incident was a unique accident, caused by the failure of technical systems and human error. The Shankill Road bombing was a deliberate act of murder designed to affect local people within their own community. This incident was not an isolated occurrence; it followed the pattern of others that the responders involved had responded to, and they were acutely aware that further responses would be required in the near future.

Organisation of the study

The choice of methods to be utilised in the research was determined by a critical review of the literature and knowledge gained through practice in the field. Of particular note was the paucity of information about guidelines on training for staff who might be involved in traumatic response work. The literature review identified that organisations were becoming more aware that increased sickness absence levels, early retirements and poor morale appeared to result from working with trauma (Duckworth, 1986).

The survey questionnaire was designed in two sections. Section one sought information on background data of the respondent, information on their involvement at the time of the incident, their perceived reactions at the time of the incident and the impact of such reactions on their personal and professional lives. The questionnaire was not designed to establish the presence of PTSD. Questions were asked about their previous training experience in relation to the tasks that they performed at the time of the incident. Section two involved the Coping to Care (CTC) questionnaire that was adapted from a validated assessment tool on coping styles (Roger and Nesshoever, 1987). The need to consider individual coping styles had emerged as a main theme in the literature, and as a key issue that would need to be addressed in the design of the training programme. Roger's instrument was constructed on the assumption that we cannot always change what happens to us, but we can alter our perceptions of such events by understanding our normal coping skills and developing the positive aspects of such behaviours.

Following an initial evaluation of the postal questionnaires, a semi-structured interview schedule was prepared. Responders to the postal survey had been asked if they were willing to be interviewed, and the interview samples were selected and matched from these responses. The sampling relationship for the two groups is shown in Table 11.1.

The decision to use a postal survey was based on the need to elicit information from a large number of responders who were geographically separated. The time delay between the incidents and contact being made with potential responders brought increased difficulties in response rates similar to those identified by Reid and Boore (1987). Staff had moved posts and, due to the large number of staff who volunteered extra support at the time of the crisis, official records sometimes only recorded those who were officially on duty. Because of the nature of information being researched, both quantitative and qualitative methods were used. Kane (1995) described the use of a variety of research methods to illuminate the one subject as triangulation.

The use of semi-structured interviews allowed the development of the themes identified at the survey stage; this was seen as important given the sensitive nature of the information being gathered. Throughout the research process, care was exercised to protect the confidentiality of the respondents. Each questionnaire was coded to enable the location and professional group to be identified. Responders to the questionnaire were asked to signify their consent to selection for interview. I carried out all the interviews, and the fact that I had been actively involved with both incidents appeared to help establish my credibility with the responders when they were discussing their reactions to their work.

One of the recognised limitations of the research was that some of the questions asked of the respondents were concerned with traumatic incidents in the past, and uncontrolled variables, such as further life experiences or other traumatic events, may have had a causal effect on their attitudes, thoughts and behaviours. As the researcher, I noted that when responders were recalling painful memories of their work, the memories were still very acute and did not appear to have been dimmed by the passage of time. Respondents gave a positive reaction to the nature of the research and the fact that the proposed training programme would assist responders in the future. Many of the respondents had been involved in previous research which had centred on the needs of the primary victims only, and they recorded that they felt their needs had been ignored. When undertaking the interviews, I identified support resources that were available to each of the responders if they required such support as a result of any re-stimulation of negative reactions prompted by the interview.

The results from the questionnaires and the interviews were analysed in relation to the impact of the work on the responders' subsequent functioning in their home and work environments. The findings were used as the basis for the design of a modular training programme. The results obtained from the validated coping styles assessment tool (Roger and Nesshoever, 1987) were used in a limited way to allow respondents to make judgements about their present ability to manage their psychological reactions to their work. These results were also incorporated into the design of the training programme.

Table 11.1: Sampling relationship for the two groups

	Questionnaires distributed	Questionnaires returned	Percentage returned	Number who refused further contact	Number interviewed	Percentage interviewed
Kegworth						
Ambulance	85	35	41.2	14 (40.0%)	17	48.6
Social workers	76	35	46.0	9 (25.7%)	18	51.4
A+E nurses	44	28	63.6	6 (21.4%)	15	53.6
Clergy	17	6	35.3	0 (0.0%)	4	66.7
	222	104	46.8	29 (27.0%)	54	51.9
Shankill						
Ambulance	27	6	22.2	3 (50.0%)	3	50.0
Social workers	28	19	67.8	6 (31.0%)	10	52.6
A+E nurses	22	6	27.3	2 (33.3%)	4	66.7
Clergy	12	5	41.7	2 (40.0%)	3	60.0
	89	36	40.4	13 (36.1%)	20	55.5

Summary of the results of the survey questionnaires and of the interviews

A comparison of the results from the interviews with responders to the Kegworth incident with those from the Shankill Road incident indicates some significant differences which identified areas that needed to be addressed in the proposed training modules.

All responders were from professional organisations and had received professional training. There were no significant differences in the demographic profile of the responders. The results from the Kegworth sample identified that they had never had to deal with so many casualties or been required to activate major incident plans before. In the Shankill sample, 100% of the social workers and of the ambulance personnel had experience of major incidents. Eighty per cent of the nurses and 90% of the clergy had been involved before. Those involved in the Shankill response recorded a 50% longer involvement with the victims than those from Kegworth. Sixty-seven per cent of the Shankill responders felt that they were trained to fulfil the tasks they were required to undertake, while the proportion from Kegworth was only 36%. A complex range of responses to the questions concerned with physical and psychological reactions reveal some interesting areas for comparison.

The findings detailed in Table 11.2 illustrate the extent to which the respondents in the Shankill sample appear to exhibit higher levels of distress/impact than their counterparts in the Kegworth sample, as identified in 15 key areas. In relation to general eating patterns, there was no discernible difference between the two sample groups. Neither groups reported any use of sleeping tablets. However, there were differences between the two groups in the area of intrusive thoughts (18% more in the Shankill than in the Kegworth group).

In 9 of the remaining 10 key areas, the Shankill group reported higher scores than their Kegworth counterparts. For example, some 52.9% of the Shankill respondents reported feeling depressed as against 33.5% of the Kegworth respondents. In the areas of intrusive dreams and effect on sleeping patterns, Shankill respondents reported 43.8% and 54.3% respectively, compared with 17.8% and 27.7% among the Kegworth respondents.

In the questions concerning the effect on family, colleagues, friends, work performance and ability to concentrate, the Shankill sample scored consistently higher, presumably as they were exposed to frequent traumatic incidents in Northern Ireland. Only 15.8% of the Kegworth sample had used the support offered by their organisations, while 57.7% of the Shankill sample recorded that they had done so.

The responses to the question concerning physical and mental health status again reflected a more negative perception about the disaster

Table 11.2: Physical and psychological reactions of responders dealing with traumatic events

		Area of distress					
		Kegworth		Shankill		Group total	
		Count	Total %	Count	Total %	Count	Total %
Abnormal tiredness/lack of energy	Yes	30	30.0	22	62.9	52	38.5
	No	70	70.0	13	37.1	83	61.5
Anxious	Yes	38	37.6	20	62.5	58	43.6
	No	63	62.4	12	37.5	75	56.4
Depressed	Yes	24	23.5	18	52.9	42	30.9
	No	78	76.5	16	47.1	94	69.1
Irritable	Yes	25	24.8	22	62.9	47	34.6
	No	76	75.2	13	37.1	89	65.4
Intrusive thoughts	Yes	41	40.2	18	58.1	59	44.4
	No	61	59.8	13	41.9	74	55.6
Intrusive dreams	Yes	18	17.8	14	43.8	32	24.1
	No	83	82.2	18	56.3	101	75.9
Overeating	Yes	5	6.8	2	8.3	7	7.1
	No	69	93.2	22	91.7	91	92.9
Undereating	Yes	9	11.1	7	29.2	16	15.2
	No	72	88.9	17	70.8	89	84.8
Change in intake of alcohol	Yes	8	8.1	10	30.3	18	13.6
	No	91	91.9	23	69.7	114	86.4
Change in level of smoking	Yes	8	8.5	6	18.8	14	11.1
	No	86	91.5	26	81.3	112	88.9
Change in sleep patterns	Yes	28	27.7	19	54.3	47	34.6
	No	73	72.3	16	45.7	89	65.4
Start using sleeping tablets	No	100	100.0	33	100.0	133	100.0
Increased use of sleeping tablets	No	99	100.0	33	100.0	132	100.0
Avoid scene of disaster in similar situation	Yes	5	5.1	3	8.8	8	6.1
	No	93	94.9	31	91.2	124	93.9

among the Shankill sample. Only 16.9% of the Kegworth sample felt their mental health had been affected, whereas 57.1% from the Shankill sample thought it had. In sharp contrast to the negative impacts recorded was the high percentage of responders who recorded the positive impact of the work, a fact that is often overlooked in much of the previous research in this area.

In the section concerned with training, 88.1% of the Kegworth sample and 75.0% of the Shankill sample had not received training on stress management during their initial professional training. Both samples indicated levels of dissatisfaction (60%) with training for psychological responses to disasters. The range of qualitative comments, which emerged from the question about training in coping with psychological reactions, indicated that both sets of responders felt that further education on psychological reactions and coping styles was necessary.

In the semi-structured interviews, the social workers from Kegworth and the Shankill area all referred to having to adapt their basic training to meet the needs of those involved in the trauma. Of all the groups surveyed, they seemed to view their prior training as the most appropriate to the tasks they were asked to undertake. They were, however, overwhelmed and stressed by the wide range of tasks that had to be undertaken. There was general dissatisfaction with management's lack of understanding of the work, which meant that there was no provision made, within the existing caseloads, to accommodate the disaster work. This lack of understanding had also contributed to the difficulties experienced by some of the staff on their return to normal work after the initial response had been provided. The majority of the social workers recorded a general level of satisfaction with the work they had done.

In the results from the interviews, the ambulance personnel from both samples felt that they needed training on the normal psychological reactions that could be expected and how to cope with such reactions. Most of the ambulance training that existed was concerned with skills and techniques; they wanted training that linked the psychological impact to the tasks. All the ambulance personnel recognised that disaster work was stressful, but they also linked such stress to their everyday experiences. The nature of their everyday work prompted the suggestion that stress management training should be integrated into all types of training in the service.

Among the accident and emergency nurses, there was a general feeling of dissatisfaction that their emotional needs had largely remained unrecognised. Where support was made available, the nurses felt guilty if they admitted that they had used it. There was a culture that trained nurses would also be expected to act within a professional approach, which included emotional control at all times. Management appeared to feel that 'business as usual' was the best policy.

For the clergy involved in England, the disaster was a unique event. Many of the rituals and their ways of coping simply evolved as a matter of necessity. The clergy involved in the aftermath of the Shankill Road incident were already involved in repeated trauma work. While this appeared to aid their understanding of pastoral care needed, it had resulted in physical and emotional weariness. For them there was no end to their involvement – they continued to live and deal with their traumatised communities. On the subject of their training needs, all the clergy wanted multidisciplinary training as an aid to inter-agency involvement and role understanding for the future.

To sum up the reactions of the responders, it is perhaps appropriate to record a few examples of the comments made.

The Kegworth responders:

'I talked to my friend who works in another hospital. You couldn't tell the family what you really saw and had to deal with, it was too upsetting.'

'My marriage broke down one year later, my husband said that I never came home from Kegworth.'

'My congregation encouraged me to travel to Belfast to attend her funeral. She had become very special to all of us who got to know her in hospital. Her husband had coped with so much through all the anxiety, the joy of the recovery of the baby and then the death. I will never forget this family.'

'My husband pulled me through; as usual he just listened if I wanted to talk.'

'Having seen the dead children, I went home and just wanted to hug my own.'

'Having seen relatives writing their farewells on the cards attached to the bunches of flowers to be left at the scene, I went home and told my family how much I loved them then and everyday – I don't want to wait to tell them when they are dead, today is the day.'

The Shankill responders:

'It was frightening as the crowd pulled us from the vehicle and pushed us towards the injured and dying.'

'It seemed so unreal, the chaos; we just got on with our job.'

'I went for a drink with some of the lads in the pub that night when we got finished. Some people wanted to buy us drinks as they said we had done a great job. It didn't feel like that. We were thinking about the ones we could not save.'

'There was chaos, noise and screaming. Yet some people stood stunned and silent, they had seen it all before.'

'They taught us the skills but no one prepared us for the feelings you get inside when you have to use those skills.'

'It reminded me of the bombings in the 1970s. It made me feel sick.'

All the respondents recorded that they would welcome pre-crisis training provided on a multidisciplinary basis, which included training on post-trauma reactions and how to cope with them. Such training would have to be culturally sensitive to the different organisational cultures involved, and be provided by experienced trainers who would incorporate the experience of some practitioners into their presentations.

The emphasis of this research was not on the post-traumatic symptoms but on the impact of the experience on the ability of the responders to function in their work and social environments. While this research was based on two major incidents, the knowledge gained is perceived to be transferable to other staff who have to cope with smaller traumatic incidents in their work environments.

TWELVE

Modular training programme for responders

The outcome of my research has been the development of a modular training programme for responders. As indicated in Chapter Eleven, research suggested that the psychosocial impact experienced by responders was significant and that care should be taken not only to recognise such impact but to seek ways to minimise the risks. Exposure to highly stressful work for a prolonged period often leads to physical and emotional exhaustion (see Table 12.1).

Stress Inoculation Training (SIT) was described by Meichenbaum (1994). He envisaged its use with responders in a pre-crisis period. He noted that Weisaeth (1994) used SIT in a preventative way when he was preparing United Nations soldiers to perform peacekeeping roles, when they had to change their offensive-type training to meet the humanitarian needs of traumatised populations. Miller and Birnbaum (1988) found that, where there was a disparity between the requirements of the stressful situation and the cognitive and social skills of the individual, the greater the negative impact that was experienced.

Miller (1959) found that effective education was a key in learning behaviour which could reduce fear of danger. He concluded that learning can affect visceral responses. People can be taught to become aware of those stimuli which trigger defensive reactions, and to develop coping strategies. The timing of such training was seen as an important consideration for organisation. Ellison and Geny (1979) in their work with police officers urged that training for the prevention and minimisation of stress should begin at recruitment level before police officers are exposed to traumatic stressors associated with their work. Their research identified the need for pre-exposure training and suggested that such training is integral to all training and service delivery. Dyregrov and Mitchell (1993) found a decrease in measured stress among paramedics three months after stress awareness training had been received. As they described it:

> Our own experience has demonstrated that stress education programs for emergency personnel have enhanced their

Table 12.1: Impact of secondary traumatic stress on professional functioning

Performance of job tasks	Morale	Interpersonal	Behavioural
Decrease in quality	Decrease in confidence	Withdrawal from colleagues	Absenteeism
Decrease in quantity	Loss of interest	Impatience	Exhaustion
Low motivation	Dissatisfaction	Decrease in quality of relationship	Faulty judgement
Avoidance of job tasks	Negative attitude	Poor communication	Irritability
Increase in mistakes	Apathy	Subsumption of own needs	Tardiness
Setting perfectionist standards	Demoralisation	Staff conflicts	Irresponsibility
Obsession about details	Lack of appreciation		Overwork
	Detachment		Frequent job changes
	Feelings of incompleteness		

Source: Yassen (1995, p 191)

sense of self-confidence in their ability to cope successfully with distressing events … and partially desensitized emergency personnel to the sights, sounds and experience of the emergency scene so that they were less distressed by those stimuli. (Dyregrov and Mitchell, 1993, p 908)

They note that emergency personnel who received training displayed more understanding of stress reactions. This understanding resulted in a greater sense of personal control. These personnel also sought help earlier because of their ability to recognise symptoms of traumatic stress reaction in themselves or in others. Training, of course, must be tailored to the needs of the responders and must be presented in an appropriate format, building on the experience of responding to real-life traumatic situations. Some organisations resist such training, perceiving it as expensive and unnecessary as 'disasters' rarely happen. As a result of the literature reviewed for my research, I would argue that enhancing knowledge and skills in this area can also enhance responders' everyday practice with the many people who experience traumatic incidents in their lives such as domestic violence, child abuse and the devastation to the livelihood of farmers that can result from an outbreak of foot and mouth disease.

Research findings in relation to training

A postal questionnaire survey was used to elicit demographic information, experience in relation to pre-crisis training and the psychosocial impact of the work in both the Kegworth and Shankill samples. Many of the responders felt that their training had been about specific skills and lacked any insights into the psychosocial impact of such work on them. Many of the responders involved commented on the perceived expectation, by their organisations, that they could cope because they were professionally trained.

However, 82% of the Kegworth responders and 71% of the Shankill ones described the tasks which they undertook as 'not normal duties'. Forty-seven per cent of the Kegworth sample and 30% of the Shankill one recorded that they were not trained to fulfil the tasks that they had to perform at the time of the disaster. Results from the questionnaire concerning training showed that 88.1% of the Kegworth sample and 75.0% of the Shankill one had no guidance on stress management in their initial training.

A summary of the key results from the interviews revealed that responders felt that management did not understand the work, and that this had resulted in inadequate and some inappropriate management. The social workers from Kegworth and the Shankill area all referred to the need to adapt basic training to meet the demands of those involved in these disasters. They felt that such adaptation had benefited their general practice in other types of traumatic situations, such as crisis situations associated with mental health cases. There was general dissatisfaction with management for their lack of understanding of the work, which meant that little provision had been made within existing caseloads to accommodate the trauma work. This lack of understanding had also contributed to the difficulties encountered by some of the staff on their return to normal work after the initial response had been provided. The majority of social workers recorded their general level of satisfaction with the work they had done. They felt that the trauma situation had demanded sound social work practice and skills of counselling that they were not always able to utilise in their current everyday practice. The provision of any pre-crisis trauma training was seen as crucial not only to the quality of the response provided but also to the well-being of the responders.

The ambulance personnel from both Kegworth and the Shankill area valued the use of live exercises, but felt that they needed training on the normal psychosocial reactions that could be expected and how to cope with such reactions. Most of the paramedic training that existed was about skills and techniques; they wanted training that linked the 'feeling' impact to the tasks. Ambulance personnel, especially those from the Shankill sample, recognised that disaster work was stressful, but they also linked such stress to their everyday experiences. The nature of their everyday work prompted the suggestion that stress management training should be integrated into all types of training within the service.

Among the accident and emergency nurses, there was a general feeling of dissatisfaction in the way that their psychosocial needs had largely remained unrecognised. Where support was made available, the nurses felt guilty if they admitted that they had used it. There was a culture that expected trained nurses to act professionally and maintain emotional control at all times. Management appeared to feel that a policy of 'business as usual' was the appropriate panacea for any reactions that might be experienced.

The clergy had been trained to support people through illness or bereavement, but recorded that they had received little training in coping with their own reactions to trauma work. They requested that any training provided in the future should be delivered in a multi-agency setting. They felt that this training would not only enhance their skills but also promote collaborative working through a greater understanding of each other's role.

The term 'stress management' was used in this research to focus the thoughts of the responder on understanding work–related stress. Such training usually identifies the factors that cause stress, and how stress can be recognised in oneself and in others. This type of training increases the participant's awareness of the factors in the work environment which can impact on them. Understanding Post–Traumatic Stress Disorder (PTSD) is also necessary for those involved in long-term work. Issues such as these should be included in initial training to prepare staff to deal with the reality of stress in the workplace.

The results of my research indicated that there is a major need for training in all aspects of trauma work. We live in an age of increasing litigation against organisations that provide care that is perceived by users as inadequate. Perhaps an economic argument could act as justification for organisations to take these aspects of training more seriously. It is my belief that training associated with providing a caring response to situations of major trauma should gain more acceptance as 'mainstream' training. Organisations might be more responsive to such training programmes if the transferability of the skills involved was made more apparent.

Outline of the modular training programme which prepares people to cope with traumatic stress in the workplace

The outline for a modular training programme is based on the issues identified in the research. There is a core module linking to a series of other specialist modules (see Figure 12.1). While these modules are designed to meet the needs of the sample groups in the research, they can be adapted for a wider use with a range of professional and voluntary organisations. The time needed for the modules is approximately half a day per module but with flexibility the programme can be used to meet the specific needs of any group of staff or organisation. The module for managers can be adapted to last two hours if it forms part of other training programmes. If an organisation was providing an induction programme for friends or relatives of newly recruited personnel, the module designed for them could be reduced to an hour's duration and incorporated into the overall programme.

The overall aim of the training programme is to provide participants with the knowledge and understanding of post-trauma reactions that will help them to cope with trauma in the workplace. When delivering

Figure 12.1: The core module

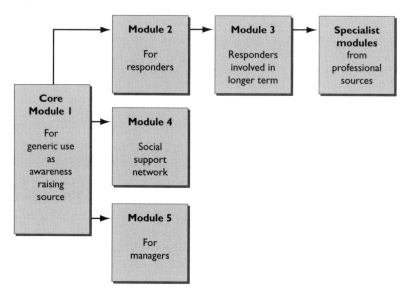

this training, Staffcare now incorporates the two CISM programmes accredited by the International Critical Incident Stress Foundation into longer courses. This enables the knowledge base to be updated in the light of international research. In practice, I have found that this modular programme can be adapted to address sensitive issues in a way that is culturally acceptable in a global arena. Modules have been delivered to embassy staff in Bangkok involved in post-tsunami relief work, to healthcare professionals in Belarus who deal with mothers following the birth of a baby with disabilities and to staff working with adult survivors of institutional child abuse in Ireland.

Module 1 – the core module

The objectives of this module are to:

- understand the different types of traumatic incidents that may occur;
- raise awareness on the psychosocial reactions of people to trauma;
- understand the tasks that will be required when providing a caring response;
- promote the understanding of the psychological impact of such work on responders and to highlight the importance of the support provided; and

- link the understanding of issues discussed to major incidents or other smaller traumatic incidents that may occur in the work environment of the participants.

The modular approach allows a variety of methods to be used which all reflect the findings of the research and the needs of responders and organisations. This module has the potential for generic use within a wide range of work situations. It also allows such training to be seen in the wider context of trauma training within other professional and voluntary sector training programmes.

Module 2 – for responders

The research indicated that responders lacked knowledge of the type of tasks with which they might be involved. Kegworth social workers found the trauma work demanded a proactive approach to a population who would not normally form part of their caseloads but who had been rendered vulnerable by a shared unique experience. Traditional professional boundaries were blurred and these led to some inter-agency and inter-disciplinary conflicts. Where there was a lack of role clarity, the stress on responders increased. The lack of prior knowledge added to their stress especially when managers also lacked knowledge of the demands of the situation. Social workers in Northern Ireland had more experience on the nature of traumatic incidents, but they felt that they needed more training in how such work could impact on their personal and professional lives.

This module is designed to identify the tasks required in the initial stages of the response. It includes information on the practical needs of those involved and advice on strategies for meeting such needs. Examples would be drawn from recent traumatic incidents. A speaker who had personal 'hands on experience' of providing such a response could enhance such teaching. Information on the services to be provided would be underpinned by the theoretical models involved in understanding the psychosocial implications of trauma for both responders and those seeking help. The training also links disaster work to responding to the more 'everyday' disasters that occur in people's lives. This link allows participants to appreciate the value of transferring their trauma-oriented response skills to their normal duties and the traumas that can underpin their practice.

Module 3 – for responders involved in longer-term care

Responders from all the groups who took part in the research identified their need for a greater understanding of the long-term implications for psychological morbidity. Responders in the Shankill sample recognised that many of those affected and the responders had been exposed to previous traumatic incidents. In their work, they had to deal with psychosocial reactions to the Shankill bombing which often provoked memories of previous traumatic incidents that may not have been resolved. The majority of the responders had difficulty in separating their Shankill experience from the series of previous responses. Their reactions provided evidence of the impact of serial traumatisation. This evidence suggests that policy and practice relating to professional groups who are subjected to repeated trauma work need to consider the serial effect. It was the experience of many responders that, while attention may have been given to their needs following a major high-profile incident, little cognisance was given to the accumulative effect of continuous stressful situations. This issue has implications for the support available to such staff and the need for organisations to consider the attitudinal culture of their workplace.

Module 3 builds on the previous module but includes training on meeting the long-term needs of those involved. The module includes an aspect of assessment that aids the responder to recognise the symptom severity indicators that mean that a trauma reaction will need medical or psychiatric intervention. Elements of trauma counselling are introduced to promote good practice. Information is supplied on factors that may alter the course of normal psychological processing such as inquests, an inquiry or an anniversary. The teaching in this module is again underpinned by teaching on the implications of the impact of such work on the responder.

Specialist modules

These modules are designed to build on the previous modules but to supply the participants with further professional training in relation to traumatic reactions. These modules should be provided from professional sources. It is envisaged that these modules could focus on such subjects as:

- Bereavement Counselling;
- Cognitive Behavioural Therapy (CBT);
- Eye Movement Desensitisation and Reprocessing (EMDR); and

- Critical Incident Stress Management (CISM) (accredited by the International Critical Incident Stress Foundation), which includes skills training in a range of crisis intervention techniques.

While other courses may deal with these subjects in generic practice, it was felt that there was a need to focus on trauma work. As was reported by many of the nurses, their generic training had failed to equip them for trauma work. Clergy found that working with traumatic death was very different from their usual bereavement work. All staff reported that the traumatic nature of the work added to their stress and their own reactions of vulnerability.

Module 4 – for social support networks

Throughout the research, the wider implications of trauma reactions on the families of those involved were indicated. Responders spoke of their difficulties in sharing knowledge of their work and their reactions to it within close relationships. Many referred to the fact that they felt they needed to protect their family members. Their effort to protect was often interpreted as emotional withdrawal from those who wished to help and to support. Unnecessary frictions were reported at a time when sensitive support would have been valued. From an organisational point of view, the significant relatives or friends can be the most appropriate screening mechanism for staff who may have become less competent at work as a result of unrecognised trauma reactions. A shared knowledge of how the work can impact on relationships, which promotes a more supportive environment for staff and for organisations, could develop a sense of partnership. Organisations would be viewed as caring by both staff and their family members, and this surely would contribute to the general well-being of the staff involved. Responders who feel valued appear more capable of providing quality support to others.

This module is specifically designed for family members or significant friends of those responders who are exposed to trauma as part of their work. It would be envisaged that this module could be used in the pre-crisis situation as part of an induction programme for new employees to such services as the ambulance service, fire brigade or police. The module could also be used in post-trauma situations.

Module 5 – for managers

The comments on lack of managerial understanding came from all the staff groups. Trauma work was often given to already busy staff without the managers fully understanding the type of work or time involved. Many comments were received that managers were insensitive to the impact of such work on the responders. The impact needed to be addressed to facilitate future work performance. In discussion with several of the managers involved, they agreed that they too needed training in trauma awareness to avoid causing additional stress to staff which could impede other areas of their practice.

Any response to trauma requires the managers to understand the range of tasks that may be required. They also need to be aware of the impact which such work will have on responders. The need for caution in the selection of responders will be outlined in the module. Training needs of staff will be discussed and issues such as workload management and supervision will be highlighted. This module also addresses such subjects as performance guilt, implications of over-involvement and problems of reintegration back into normal work patterns.

Reflection on issues of training, organisational attitudes and support to staff inherent in the research and identified throughout this book, finds resonance with individual and group users of Staffcare. Most organisations appear to work on the principle that 'it will never happen here'. Many staff using Staffcare for support identified organisations which fail to recognise staff needs and where any concerns are met with attitudes reminiscent of the 'lack of moral fibre' debates of the early 19th century.

Litigation cases have reminded organisations that they have a 'duty to care' under health and safety and European legislation which requires a 'safe working environment including a stress free work base'. The implications of not doing this are manifold and can be argued on both a humanitarian and economic basis. Staff who feel unprepared to face trauma in their workplace will suffer stress that will reflect on their personal and professional lives. Legislation requires that staff exposed to hazardous substances must be appropriately trained and must wear protective clothing. The impact of trauma situations and the stress of working with traumatised people has also been recognised, yet staff are rarely protected by the provision of pre-training or post-incident psychological support. I believe it is essential to increase the understanding of key managers with regard to the hazards of such work in terms of pre-planning and pre-training for staff. Where such provision exists, the staff concerned, and indeed their organisations, will benefit because the training will reflect on to all areas of practice through the quality of care they can provide to others.

Conclusion

Research to date appears to have reflected the medical model which identified the negative side of the symptoms of distress that may be experienced by responders. My research focused on the implications of reactions in the professional and social context of the real world of the responders. Training was viewed as a means of ameliorating some of the stress reported. The most significant feature of my research was the dedication of the responders interviewed and their desire for more training that would enhance the quality of future responses. Responders felt that, although the work had been demanding, it had enhanced their lives as human beings and as professionals:

> Generally the literature has focused on pathological adjustment and testifies to the severity and chronicity of distress often experienced by survivors of traumatic incidents. But there are often positive psychological reactions following trauma such as increased ability to appreciate life and show more compassion toward others. (Joseph et al, 1993, pp 501-3)

THIRTEEN

The challenge of bringing order from chaos

In the final chapter of the second edition of this book, published in 1998, when addressing the subject of 'the challenges of bringing order from chaos', I quoted the words of Tony Austin in his book on the Aberfan disaster of 1966: 'Dedicated to the hope that the lessons will not only be appreciated but applied.' In this final chapter of the third edition, being published seven years later, I will reflect on these words. Have we applied the lessons that we have learned over the years?

My first introduction to trauma was as a child listening to the news reports about the capsize of the car ferry, the Princess Victoria, when high seas burst open her stern doors en route from Stranraer in Scotland to Larne in Northern Ireland. It happened on a stormy Saturday in January 1953. I remembered a very rough crossing on the same ferry the previous summer, when returning from a glorious family holiday. The ferry was etched in my memory by my first and hopefully last experience of severe seasickness. On that trip, we stood watching the waves breaking over the stern doors, as my father believed that fresh air was the best treatment for seasickness. The loss of the Princess Victoria was not just a news report to me. I thought that could have happened when we were on board. The Donaghadee Lifeboat, which aided in the rescue, was the lifeboat into which we had been allowed to clamber and play when it was on the quayside being painted. My parents knew some of the people lost on the ship and attended several of the funerals. We were taken to the seaside village of Donaghadee to make a donation to the lifeboat funds. We gazed in wonder at the smallness of the craft that had played such a heroic role rushing through the mountainous waves. Her paintwork bore some of the scars of that night as she lay in the safety of the tiny harbour, now surrounded by a placid blue sea. My father shook hands with some of the crew members who were standing on the quayside and congratulated them on their heroic work. We were told to shake hands as my father spoke of their true bravery in the service of others. As a child, I remember noting the firmness of the grip in the handshakes and thinking of what the grip of the same hands must have meant to people being plucked from the sea. I watched as sadness became etched on the rugged face of a crew member as his eyes looked out to sea. In response to my father's words of appreciation, he said quietly 'Thank you sir, but I wish we could have saved more.' At that moment of silence, we all looked towards the scene of the disaster, far out to sea towards the horizon. Was it only the bitter wind that had caused his eyes to fill with tears? This was my first lesson in the reality of responding to tragedy. I was to hear the words that lifeboat man said repeated so many times by so many responders over the years that have followed.

While working on this third edition, I have been struck by the new vocabulary of trauma that has emerged. As I have reflected on the issue of vocabulary, I feel that some of the words capture the new developments in research and practice, which we must embrace if we are to apply the lessons learned from the past and face the challenge of 'bringing order from chaos' in our current and future circumstances.

On Christmas Day 2004, few of us knew the word tsunami; yet, within 24 hours, that word was to crash into our vocabularies and into our minds with a force reminiscent of the wave itself. Through the media coverage we could see and hear the human distress from all the countries affected by so much destruction. We learned of sudden impact and the horror experienced as the tsunami pounded on to coastlines of tranquillity. The loss of life and destruction to people's lives through injury was incomprehensible as the statistics rose. Some of those statistics were to become real people for me when I was honoured to be seconded to the Red Cross to aid the work in Thailand. I have many memories from that work – my apprehension on arrival, the intensity of the work in the hospitals and in the embassy, and the overarching aura of sadness and loss that pervaded all aspects of life. My memory is also of the quiet dignity of the Thai people who were struggling to resume their lives and return their devastated coastal region to the holiday paradise that would once again ensure their economic stability. I also recall the courage of the British citizens in the hospitals who had to cope with both injuries and bereavement. In Thailand, I also experienced the dark side of such tragedies as we learned of instances of the exploitation of vulnerable people. It was noted that the sex trade was the first industry to fully recover and I heard of the trafficking of some tsunami orphans, referred to as 'freebies' by the evil entrepreneurs. These were surely examples of person-made disasters making a natural disaster worse. In these days of the need for evidence-based indicators, it was with some amusement that I noted several weeks later that one of the indicators that life was returning to normal in the waters around Thailand was a report that the pirates had returned to their usual work of preying on ships. From a professional perspective, the crisis interventions identified in this book, and used to promote rebuilding in people's lives, proved to be valid in post-tsunami situations. Environmental and economic factors will take many years to rebuild. The young Thai woman who lost her husband and her family of three children typifies rebuilding in the lives of those I worked with. In an interview, which she gave to a newspaper shortly after the tragedy, she stated that as she was the only one left she had felt like 'walking into the sea to join them'. At a recent meeting, she gave me a copy of the memorial book that had been distributed at the cremations and in this she says, 'You have all been so kind and may not realise that you have somehow lifted up my spirit. I have found comfort in your condolences and have begun to see the light at the end of the tunnel. I am looking forward to the day that I come out of it.' She described how she 'still weeps inside' but, with incredible courage, is trying to refocus her life as she feels the family would have wanted her to do. She has commenced training to convert her university lecturing qualification to a qualification to enable her to teach children. The rituals required by her Buddhist faith have been completed, she has turned away from the sea and is walking to the future. She is rebuilding from the chaos of 'loss' to a new 'order' for her future life. These thoughts on rebuilding were used to design the cover for this book: the progression from the darkness of traumatic incidents through the confusion of colour representing the chaos that follows, to the restoration of a new order bringing the yellow of hope for the future.

In this book I have replaced the word 'victim' with the more acceptable term 'those affected by the incident'. I welcome this change of term in more recent research and reports. I have long advocated that the use of the word 'victim' denoted a high degree of helplessness and dependency on others. While this may be true in the initial chaos following an incident, I feel that it has also encouraged responders to see themselves as 'benefactors' and people who could put things right for victims. We could be in danger of adopting a somewhat paternalistic attitude to our work. Such a philosophy often brought great comfort to the victims and a sense of satisfaction to the responders, but it could also lay a dangerous seed of dependency within a relationship. The newer term reminds us that we are responding to the unique needs of 'people affected by a unique situation'. They are people who, on the whole, were in control of their lives until something traumatic happened and their normal ways of coping have been temporarily disabled. Their cognitive processing has been altered by an overload of information to process. Responders need to help them in such a way that they do not 'take over their lives' but do all they can to support and assist, and to minimise any additional loss of life, or further physical or psychological injury, until their cognitive equilibrium returns.

As we reflect on all the traumatic incidents discussed in this book, this lesson may have been appreciated, but I believe that it is a lesson that has not always been applied. Eagerness to help and the desire to be involved has predominated with some individuals and organisations. I have witnessed overzealous professionals and untrained volunteers rushing to a scene to help without any assessment of need or indeed any assessment of their skills in relation to a particular situation. Some voluntary organisations, perhaps anxious to satisfy committee members, feel that their organisation must be seen as an essential responder at the impact time, when in fact their skills and expertise may be more appropriately utilised later on in the response. This attitude can lead to inter-organisational jealousy that hinders collaborative working at the expense of a coordinated response for those most personally affected.

I have witnessed responders (and indeed I have recognised this in myself) who display an overpowering sense of possessiveness towards their 'victim' or 'victim' family. This is where supervision and management skills are essential if responders and the people affected are to gain most from the relationship. I believe that this is best achieved by pre-training and pre-planning which increase collaboration and integrated working. I note with some cynicism those professionals who experience an overwhelming desire to be at every scene to enhance their curricula vitae. I have also strong feelings about the paramount need for ethical controls on research in such circumstances. The people affected and their needs must remain central to the responses offered. Pop bands have groupies who follow their idols around wherever they go in order to indulge their need for constant contact and self-gratification from their idols. I have met 'trauma groupies' who appear to have a similar need and who can become a second disaster for the people most affected.

The physical and psychological effects of any traumatic incident are complex and comprehensive. Whether the incident is described as personal or major, the after-effects can appropriately be likened to the ripples which result from the dropping of a pebble into a pool of water. The extent of the rings of reaction, radiating out from the centre, is difficult to assess in terms of intensity or timing. These factors mean that planning to provide psychosocial support to those affected requires responders and systems to be coordinated and integrated. Plans must be clearly defined yet flexible enough to respond to the unique demands of the particular traumatic incident. The tasks of recovery and rehabilitation may be overwhelming but they will never be accomplished unless those affected, and those who are responders, begin to work on the response by breaking it into steps of manageable size.

Ann Kaiser Stearns (1989), in her book *Coming back*, identifies those who come through crisis and rebuild their lives as 'triumphant survivors'. These are responders as well as the people affected by emergencies and disasters, and who develop survival strategies. They deal with the pain they may experience in small segments; they go forward and reinvest in life. They are those who face the pain, resist staying in a state of helplessness and know how to balance independence with the ability to rely on others when necessary. In my professional life, I have been privileged to know many 'triumphant survivors' from situations of crisis. They are those who have regained order from their emotional chaos.

Seven years ago, we knew of terrorism but, since then, we have added the words 'global terrorism' to our vocabularies. We have had to learn through the advent of global attacks that what happens in one country can have an effect on other societies. Following such incidents as 9/11, and the bombing of the embassy in Africa and tourist locations in Bali, there has been a reawakening of interest in emergency planning, and new legislation to enable appropriate equipment and training to be made available. Governments appear to be collaborating more in the support of each other and the sharing of intelligence matters. Local Resilience Teams have been established to assess local risk and prepare for any emergency or disaster in their own areas. As a result of my contract to provide training for the International Christian Maritime Association, I took part in a tutorial given by Professor Lars Wiesreich of Oslo University to promote an understanding of the human implications of a terrorist attack in international waters. He described three types of terrorism. First, 'concrete' – this is a high-profile attack that has a beginning and an end such as 9/11, Bali, Madrid or 7/7; such incidents attract media attention and propaganda for the terrorists. The second type is 'silent', such as a biological attack by possible contamination of a water supply. He described how this type of incident activity presented the least personal risk to the terrorists. The targets are indiscriminate, creating a lot of anxiety for the total population, especially for mothers who fear for the health of the present and future generations. The third type of attack is that of 'threat'. Professor Wiesreich described the insidious spread of the anxiety that is created. There is potential for a high level of fear fuelled by the imagination and the power of propaganda. He reminded us that new types of terrorism created new challenges to those of us in the caring professions.

The toll of bloodshed and the indiscriminate taking of life continue unabated with incident lists of locations of such atrocities growing daily. The use of suicide bombers reminds us of those whose zeal for their own philosophy or political view means that they are prepared to die for their cause, and who are also particularly hard to identify within society.

The suicide bombers incidents in London had the core elements identified in other disasters: both personal and major chaos caused by the impact and in the initial rescue period; chaos in the information gathering and in the convergence of helpers, people affected and the media; chaos in the psychological reaction of those injured or bereaved. Order came when the various emergency plans began to work and some structure was established. The organisations which were unused to working together found that collaboration and coordination were necessary across geographical, professional and organisational boundaries. Order came when the people affected felt that they could adapt their coping mechanisms to meet the challenge of the crisis. Life was changed for them all. Their experiences had to be integrated into their psychological chaos to bring an order with which they could face the future.

Disasters, whether caused by natural phenomenon, by technical problems or by a person, also bring opportunities on a personal and organisational level, opportunities to analyse what has been done and what could have been done better, and opportunities to plan for any future response with the knowledge gained. The threats and stress of disaster can be turned into opportunities for growth.

This book has been about the processes involved in helping people bring such order out of their own emotional chaos. It has been about the responders. Many of the responders I have interviewed, and those with whom I have worked, and who have been involved in crisis situations, find that the experience alters their everyday practice. The skills needed for disaster responses can be transferred to those they meet in other settings who are dealing with emergencies or crisis in their own lives. They develop the desire to ensure that good practice methods are maintained. Even after many years of responding to civil disturbance in Northern Ireland, it was the post-Kegworth experience (1989) that prompted the development of a network of Crisis Support Teams to be ready to respond to disasters of all kinds in our community. Through these teams learning from such responses, their practice was shared with others and used to change practice. The personal experience of the stress of providing such responses led to the establishing of

Staffcare, the organisation that provides support to organisations and their staff who face stress in their personal or professional lives.

I was teaching members of the North London Incident Support Team in the headquarters of the London Resilience Team when the attacks on 7 July 2005 started. A colleague came into the lecture theatre to tell us that our theoretical learning might have to be turned in practice as a result of the attacks. Contacts were quickly made with families and colleagues, and plans made for continuing the training until we were advised that it was safe to leave the building. Many of the team had to walk miles to get home because of the lack of transport. I stayed on in the centre to provide some support to the team who were managing the response to the attack. We continued our training the next day out of the centre of London. I saw how the well-rehearsed plan swung into action and the professional approach to the crisis that was put into action over the next week. The centre was established to assist family members, and plans progressed for the temporary mortuary to be established within an army base.

At the invitation of the team, I was taken to see the areas prepared for the family and friends who would attend the mortuary to view the bodies of their loved ones. All the technical areas were hidden from their sight and care had been taken to minimise the noise on site and to shield families from the media. Members of Disaster Action, an organisation established by and for survivors and relatives from disasters, had been consulted and their ideas, many of which were a response to bad experiences in the past, had been incorporated into the design. The emphasis had been to create an environment that treated people with dignity and respect. Care had been taken to provide sensitively furnished areas to wait in prior to viewing the body. Having experienced the full viewing process, the families had access to a garden area, still under cover, where they could sit or walk among the flowering plants. A great sense of calm had been created with subdued lighting and the provision of garden benches. Plants of lavender were mingled with many pots of the plant called 'Peace'. As I sat in the 'peace' of that garden area and thought about the many disaster sites with which I had been involved, the memories came rushing back. I remembered the words of Tony Austin and his desire that lessons would not only be appreciated but also applied. The lessons learned from the past had been applied to improve the facilities for the relatives involved in the mortuary in London. I believe that in all our practice we, as responders, must keep learning from the past in order to improve our ability to respond in the future.

Bibliography

Adamson, L.Y., Seligram, M.E.P. and Teasdale, J.D. (1978) 'Learned helplessness in humans: critique and reformulation', *Journal of Abnormal Psychology*, vol 87, pp 47-94.

Alexander, D.A. (1990) 'Psychological intervention for victims and helpers after disaster', *British Journal of General Practice*, vol 40, pp 345-48.

Alexander, D.A. and Wells, A. (1991) 'Reactions of police officers to body handling after a major disaster. A before and after comparison', *British Journal of Psychiatry*, vol 15, pp 547-55.

American Psychiatric Association (APA) (1952) *Diagnostic and statistical manual of mental disorders*, Washington, DC: APA.

APA (1968) *Diagnostic and statistical manual of mental disorders (DSM-II)*, 2nd edition, Washington, DC: APA.

APA (1978) *Diagnostic and statistical manual of mental disorders*, 2nd edition, Washington, DC: APA.

APA (1980) *Diagnostic and statistical manual of mental disorders (DSM-III)*, 3rd edition, Washington, DC: APA.

APA (1987) *Diagnostic and statistical manual of mental disorders (DSM-III-R)*, 3rd edition reviewed, Washington, DC: APA.

APA (1994) *Diagnostic and statistical manual of mental disorders (DSM-IV)*, 4th edition, Washington, DC: APA.

Austin, T. (1967) *Aberfan: The story of a disaster*, London: Hutchinson & Co.

Babbington, A. (1997) *Shellshock. A history of the changing attitudes to war neurosis*, London: Leo Cooper.

Barker, P. (1995) *The ghost road,* (Winner of 1995 Booker prize) Part of a trilogy of books: *Regeneration, Eye in the door* (winner of 1993 *Guardian* fiction prize), London: Penguin.

Battye, L. (1974) 'The Chatterley syndrome', in D. Boswell and J. Wingrove (eds) *The handicapped in the community*, London: Tavistock.

Berne, E. (1961) *Transactional analysis in psychotherapy*, London: Souvenir Press.

Berne, E. (1964) *Games people play*, NY: Grove Press.

Bernstein, N.R. (1976) *Emotional care of the facially burned and disfigured*, Boston, MA: Little, Brown & Co.

Berren, M., Beigel, A. and Barker, G. (1982) 'A typology for the classification of disaster: implications for intervention', *Community Mental Health Journal*, vol 18, no 2, summer, p 27.

Berren, M., Beigel, A. and Ghertner, F. (1980) 'Theoretical and conceptual questions', in D. Black, M. Newman, J. Harris-Hendrick and G. Mesey (eds) (1997) *Psychological trauma – A developmental approach*, London: Gaskell Royal College of Psychiatrists.

Beveridge, A. (1996) 'On the origins of post-traumatic stress disorder', in D. Black, M. Newman, J. Harris-Hendrick and G. Mesey (eds) (1997) *Psychological trauma – A developmental approach*, London: Gaskell Royal College of Psychiatrists.

Biestek, F.P. (1934) *The casework relationship*, Chicago, IL: Loyola University Press.

Bisson, J. and Deahl, M.P. (1994) 'Psychological debriefing and prevention of post-traumatic stress: more research is needed', *British Journal of Psychiatry*, vol 165, pp 717-20.

Bisson, J., McFarlane, A.C. and Rose, S. (2000) 'Psychological debriefing', in E.B. Foa, T.M. Keane and M.J. Friedman (eds) *Effective treatments for PTSD*, London: The Guildford Press.

Bisson, J., Jenkins, P.L., Alexander, J. and Bannister, C. (1997) 'Randomised controlled trial of psychological debriefing for victims of acute burn trauma', *British Journal of Psychiatry*, vol 171, pp 78-81.

Black, D. (1985a) 'Children and disaster', *Bereavement Care*, vol 4, no 3, winter, p 8.

Black, D. (1985b) 'Widowed parents' circle', *Bereavement Care*, vol 4, no 2, summer.

Black, D., Newman, M., Harris-Hendrick, J. and Mesey, G (eds) (1997) *Psychological trauma – A developmental approach*, London: Gaskell Royal College of Psychiatrists.

Bluebond-Langer, M. (1978) *The private worlds of dying children*, Princeton, NJ: Princeton University Press.

Bomam, B. (1982) *The Vietnam veteran as a disaster*, London: Tavistock.

Boscarino, J., Adams, R. and Figley, C. (2005) 'A prospective cohort study of the effectiveness of employer-sponsored crisis interventions after a major disaster', *International Journal of Emergency Medicine*, vol 7, no 1, pp 9-22I.

Bowlby, J. (1979) *The making and breaking of affectionate bonds*, London: Tavistock.

BPS (British Psychological Society) Professional Practice Board Working Party (2002) *Psychological debriefing*, Leicester, UK: BPS.

Braddon, R.L. (1968) *The crisis reaction to the spinal injury*, Athens, OH: Ohio University Press.

Brammer, L.M. and Shostrum, E.C. (1997) *Therapeutic psychology*, 3rd edn, Englewood Cliffs: Prentice Hall.

Brooke, R. (1990) *An introduction to disaster theory for social work*, University of East Anglia SW: Monographs N83.

Bryant, G. (1989) 'Sudden death in infancy', *Children and Society*, vol 3, no 2, p 21.

Burton, L. (ed) (1974) *Care of the child facing death*, London: Routledge and Kegan Paul.

Cantor, P. (1977) *Understanding in a child's world*, New York, NY: McGraw Hill.

Capewell, E. (1996) in Mead (ed) *Journeys of discovery: Creative learninig from disaster*, London: National Institute for Social Work.

Caplan, G. (1968) *An approach to community mental health*, New York, NY: Guinne Statton.

Cathcart, F. (1988) 'Seeing the body after death', in D. Black, M. Newman, J. Harris-Hendrick and G. Mesey (eds) (1997) *Psychological trauma – A developmental approach*, London: Gaskell Royal College of Psychiatrists.

Civil Contingencies Secretariat (2005) 'Responding to emergencies', (report available at www.ukresilience.info/contingencies/support.htm).

Corey, G.F. (1991) *Theory and practice of counselling psychotherapy*, Belmont, CA: Brooks Cole.

Coulston, T.T. (1896) *Clinical lectures on mental diseases*, London: Oliver and Boyd, and in D. Black, M. Newman, J. Harris-Hendrick and G. Mesey (eds) (1997) *Psychological trauma – A developmental approach*, London: Gaskell Royal College of Psychiatrists.

Daly, R.J. (1983) 'Samuel Pepys and post-traumatic stress disorder', *British Journal of Psychiatry*, vol 143.

Deahl, M.P., Gillham, A.B., Thomas, J., Searle, M. and Srinivasan, M. (1994) 'Psychological sequelae following the gulf war', *British Journal of Psychiatry*, vol 164, pp 60-5.

Duckworth, D.H. (1986) 'Psychological problems arising from disaster work', *Stress Medicine*, vol 2, pp 315-23.

Dyregrov, A. (1989) 'Caring for helpers in disaster situations: psychological debriefing', *Disaster Management*, vol 2, pp 25-30.

Dyregrov, A. (1998) 'The role of family dynamics in PTSD', presented at the 28th Congress, *European Association for Behavioural and Cognitive Therapies*, Cork, Ireland, 8-12 September.

Dyregrov, A. (2003a) 'Early intervention', paper presented at the Australian Critical Incident Stress Association Conference, Melbourne, September.

Dyregrov, A. (2003b) *Psychological debriefing*, Ellicott City, MD: Chevron Publishing Corporation.

Dyregrov, A. and Mitchell, J.T. (1993) 'Traumatic stress in disaster works and emergency personnel, prevention and intervention', in J.P.Wilson, and B. Raphael (eds) *International handbook of traumatic stress syndromes*, New York, NY: Plenum Press.

Ellison, K.W. and Geny, P. (1979) 'Police officer as burned out samaritan', *FBI Law Enforcement Bulletin*, vol 47, no 3, pp 1-7, in J. Wilson and B. Raphael (eds) (1993) *International handbook of traumatic stress syndromes*, New York, NY: Plenum Press.

Emmerick, A.P., Kamphuis, J.H., Hulsbosch, A.M. and Emmelkamp, P.M.G. (2002) 'Single session debriefing after psychological trauma: a meta analysis', *The Lancet*, vol 360, p 7 (www.thelancet.com).

Erichsen, J. (1882) *On concussion of the spine: nervous shock and other obscure injuries of the nervous system in their clinical and medico-legal aspects*, London: Longman, Green and Co., and in D. Black, M. Newman, J. Harris-Hendrick and G. Mesey (eds) (1997) *Psychological trauma – A developmental approach*, London: Gaskell Royal College of Psychiatrists.

Everly, G. and Mitchell, J.T. (1997, 2000) *Manual of critical stress debriefs*, Ellicot City, MD: Chevron Publishing Corporation.

Everly, G. and Mitchell, J. (1999) *Critical incident stress management CISM: A new era and standard of care in crisis intervention*, 2nd edn, Ellicott City, MD: Chevron Publishing Corporation.

Everly, G. and Mitchell, J.T. (2001) *Critical incident stress debriefing*, Ellicott City, MD: Chevron Publishing Corporation.

Everly, G., Flannery, R.B. and Eyler, V.A. (2002) 'Critical incident stress management (CISM): a statistical review of the literature', *Psychiatric Quarterly*, vol 73, no 3.

Fields, H.L. and Bisson, J.M. (1988) *Pain modulation: Progress in brain research*, 77, Amsterdam: Elsevier, and in D. Black, M. Newman, J. Harris-Hendrick and G. Mesey (eds) (1997) *Psychological trauma – A developmental approach*, London: Gaskell Royal College of Psychiatrists.

Figley, C. (ed) (1978) *Stress disorders among Vietnam veterans, theory, research and treatment*, New York, NY: Brunner/Mazel.

Figley, C.R. (1988) 'Post traumatic family therapy', in F. Ochberg (ed.) *Post traumatic therapy and victims of violence*, New York: NY: Brunner/Mazel.

Figley, C.R. (1993a) 'Compassion stress and the family therapist', *Family Therapy News*, February, pp 1-8.

Figley, C.R. (1993b) 'Trauma and its wake', *Traumatic Stress Theory, Research and Intervention*, vol 2, New York, NY: Brunner/Mazel.

Figley, C.R. (1995) *Compassion fatigue – coping with secondary stress disorder in those who treat the traumatised*, in Psychosocial Stress Series, New York, NY: Brunner/Mazel.

Figley, C.R. (2005) 'Trauma and its wake – the study and treatment of post-traumatic stress disorders', *International Journal of Emergency Mental Health*, vol 7, no 1, winter, pp 398-451.

Flannery, R.B.Jr (1998) *The assaulted staff action program (ASAP): Coping with the psychological aftermath of violence*, Ellicott City, MD: Chevron Publishing Corporation.

Foa, E.B. and Rothbaum, B.O. (1989) 'Behavioural psychotherapy for post traumatic stress disorder', *International Review Psychiatry*, vol 1, pp 219-26, quoted in A.Y. Shalev, S. Freedman and T. Peri (1996) 'Treatment of post traumatic stress disorder: a review', *Psychosomatic Medicine*, vol 58, pp 165-82.

Frank, E. and Stewart, B.D. (1984) 'Depressive symptoms in rape victims', *Journal of Effective Disorders*, vol 1, pp 269-77.

Frazer, M. (1973) *Children in conflict*, London: Gaskell Royal College of Psychiatrists, presented by Dr Kellner at the Inaugural Conference, Warburg, September 1989.

Frenenczi, S. (1931, 1933) 'Child analysis in the analysis of adults', in (1955) *Further contributions to the problems and methods of psychoanalysis*, London: Hogarth Press, pp 126-42, and in D. Black, M. Newman, J. Harris-Hendrick and G. Mesey (eds) (1997) *Psychological trauma – A developmental approach*, London: Gaskell Royal College of Psychiatrists.

Freud, E. (ed) (1961) *Letters of Sigmund Freud*, New York, NY: Basic Books.

Freud, S. (1912) *The dynamics of the transference*, standard edn, London: Hogarth Press, pp 1-64.

Gibson, M. (1991) *Order from chaos – Responding to traumatic events*, Birmingham: Venture Press.

Gold, S.D., Marx, B.P., Soler-Baillo, J.M. and Sloan, D.M. (2004) 'Is life stress more traumatic than traumatic stress?' *Journal of Anxiety Disorders*, June, downloaded via hospital medical library 2/10/04.

Goodall, G.E. (1975) 'Rehabilitation: family involvement in hospital', *Rehabilitation Medicine*, NY: American Journals.

Green, B.L., Wilson, J.P. and Lindy, J.D. (1985) 'Conceptualising post traumatic stress disorder: a psychosocial framework', in C.R. Figley (ed) *Trauma and its wake: The study and treatment of post traumatic stress disorder*, New York, NY: Brunner/Mazel.

Grey, R. (1989) 'Adolescents experiencing the death of a parent', *Bereavement Care*, vol 8, no 2, p 9.

Hawley, D.R. and Dehann L. (1996) 'Toward a family definition of family resilience: integrating lifespan and family perspective', *Family Process*, vol 35, pp 283-98.

Healy, D. (1993) *Images of trauma, from hysteria to post traumatic stress disorder*, London: Faber, and in D. Black, M. Newman, J. Harris-Hendrick and G. Mesey (eds) (1997) *Psychological trauma – A developmental approach*, London: Gaskell Royal College of Psychiatrists.

Hembree, E.A. and Foa, E.B. (2000) 'Post-traumatic stress disorder, psychological factors and psychosocial interventions', *Journal of Clinical Psychiatry*, vol 61 (supp 17), pp 33-9.

Herman, J.L. (1992) 'Complex PTSD', *Journal of Traumatic Stress*, vol 5, pp 377-92.

Herman, J.L. (1992) *Trauma and recovery*, New York, NY: Basic Books.

HMSO (Her Majesty's Stationery Office) (1991) *Disasters – Planning for a caring response*, report of the Disasters Working Party, London: HMSO.

HMSO (2004) *NICE guidance – post traumatic stress disorder draft*, November, London: HMSO.

Hobbs and Adshead (1996) 'Preventive psychological intervention for road crash victims', in M. Mitchell (ed) (1997) *The aftermath of road accidents: Psychological, social and legal perspectives*, London: Routledge.

Hodgkinson, P.E. and Stewart, M. (1991) *Coping with catastrophe: A handbook of disaster management*, London: Routledge.

Hopper, E. (1991) 'Encapsulation as a defence against the fear of annihilation', *International Journal of Psychoanalysis*, vol 72, pp 602-24, and in D. Black, M. Newman, J. Harris-Hendrick and G. Mesey (eds) (1997) *Psychological trauma – A developmental approach*, London: Gaskell Royal College of Psychiatrists.

Horowitz, M.J. (1973) 'Phase-orientated treatment of stress response syndromes', *American Journal of Psychotherapy*, vol 27, pp 506-15.

Horowitz, M.J. (1974) 'Stress response syndromes: character style and dynamic psychotherapy', *Archives of General Psychiatry*, vol 31, pp 768-81.

Horowitz, M.J. (1976) *Stress response syndromes*, NY: Aronson.

Horowitz, M.J. (1986a) 'Stress response syndromes: a review of post traumatic and adjustment disorder', *Hospital and Community Psychiatry*, vol 37, pp 241-9.

Horowitz, M.J. (1986b) *Stress response syndromes*, 2nd edn, New York, NY: Jason Aronson.

Horowitz, M.J. (1990) 'Post traumatic stress disorder: psychotherapy', in A.S. Belleck and M. Herson (eds) *A handbook of comparative treatments for adult disorder*, Chichester: Wiley, pp 289-301.

Humphries, C. and Carr, A. (2001) 'The short-term effectiveness of critical incident stress debriefing', *The Irish Journal of Psychology*, vol 22, nos 3-4, pp 188-97.

Hytten, K. and Hassle, A. (1989) 'Fire fighters: a study of stress and coping', *Acta Psychiatrica Scandinavica*, vol 80 (supp 355), p 97.

Janoff-Bulman, R. (1992) *Shattered assumptions: Towards a new psychology of trauma*, New York, NY: Free Press.

Jones, J.C. and Barlow, D.H. (1990) 'The aetiology of post traumatic stress disorder', *Clinical Psychology Review*, vol 10, pp 299-328.

Joseph, S.A., Brevin, C.R. and Yule, W. (1991) 'Causal attribution and psychiatric symptoms in the survivors of the Herald of Free Enterprise disaster', *British Journal of Psychiatry*, vol 159, pp 542-46.

Joseph, S.A., Yule, W. and Williams, R. (1993) 'Post traumatic stress: attributional aspects', *Journal of Traumatic Stress*, vol 6, pp 501-3.

Kane, E. (1995) *Doing your research, how to do basic descriptive research in the social sciences and humanities*, London: Marion Boyers Publishers Ltd.

Kardiner, A. (1941) *The traumatic neurosis of war*, New York, NY: Hoeber.

Kastenbaun, R. (1977) 'The kingdom where creatures die', *Journal of Clinical Psychology*, vol 101, p 141.

Keane, T.M., Caddell, J.M. and Taylor K.L. (1986) *The Mississippi scale*, Boston, MA: Virginia Medical Centre.

Keane, T.M., Fairbank, J.A. and Caddell, J.M. (1985) 'A behavioural approach to assessing and treating post traumatic stress disorder in Vietnam veterans', in C. Figley (ed) *Trauma and its wake: The study and treatment of post traumatic stress disorder*, New York, NY: Brunner/Mazel, pp 257-94.

Kearney, M. (1996) *Mortally wounded*, Dublin: Marino Books.

Kenardy, J.A. and Carr, V.J. (2000) 'Debriefing post-disaster – follow up after a major earthquake', in B. Raphael and J.P. Wilson (eds) *Psychological debriefing – theory, practice and evidence*, Cambridge: Cambridge University Press.

Kubler-Ross, E. (1969) *On death and dying*, London: Tavistock.

Lahad, M. and Cohen, A. (1988) *Community stress prevention*, Israel: Department of Education, Community Stress Prevention Unit.

Langer, S. (1967) *Mind: An essay on human feeling*, Baltimore, MD: Johns Hopkins Press, and in D. Black, M. Newman, J. Harris-Hendrick and G. Mesey (eds) (1997) *Psychological trauma – A developmental approach*, London: Gaskell Royal College of Psychiatrists.

Lavan and MacManamly (2003) *A review of critical incident stress management in the emergency services in Ireland*, Dublin: Social Science Research Centre, University College.

Lazare, A. (1979) 'Unresolved grief', in A. Lazare (ed) *Outpatients psychiatry: Diagnosis and treatment*, Baltimore, MD: Williams and Wilkins.

Lee, C., Slade, P. and Lygo, V. (1996) 'The influence of psychological debriefing on emotional adaptations in females following early miscarriage', *British Journal of Medical Psychology*, vol 69, pp 47-58.

Lewis, C.S. (1966) *A grief observed*, London: Faber.

Lifton, R.J. (1967) *Death in life: Survivors of Hiroshima*, New York, NY: Random House.

Lifton, R.J. (1968) 'Observation on Hiroshima survivors', in H. Krystal (ed) *Massive psychic trauma*, New York, NY: International Universities Press, pp 168-203.

Lifton, R.J. (1973) *Home from the war*, New York, NY: Simon and Schuster.

Lifton, R.J. (1993) 'From Hiroshima to the Nazi doctors: an evolution of psycho-formative approaches to understanding traumatic stress syndromes', in J.P. Wilson and B. Raphael, (eds) *International handbook of traumatic stress syndromes*, New York, NY: Plenum, pp 11-23.

Lindemann, E. (1944) 'The symptomatology and management of acute grief', *American Journal of Psychiatry*, vol 101, p 141.

Lyons, H.A. (1972) 'Depressive illness and aggression in Belfast', *British Medical Journal*, vol 1, pp 342-5.

MacLean, D. and Gould, S. (1988) *The helping process*, London: Croom Helm.

Martin, P. (2002) *Counting sheep: The science and pleasures of sleep and dreams*, London: Harper Collins.

Maslow, A. (1954) *Motivation and personality*, New York, NY: Harper and Row.

Mayou, R.A., Ehlers, A. and Hobbs, M. (2000) 'Psychological debriefing for road traffic accident victims', *British Journal of Psychiatry*, vol 176, pp 589-93.

McFarlane, A.C. (1987) 'Life events and psychiatric disorder: the role of a natural disaster', *British Journal of Psychiatry*, vol 151, pp 362-7.

McIvor, R. (1997) 'Physiological and biological mechanisms', in D. Black, M. Newman, J. Harris-Hendrick and G. Mesey (eds) *Psychological trauma – A developmental approach*, London: Gaskell Royal College of Psychiatrists.

Meichenbaum, D. (1985) *Stress inoculation training*, New York, NY: Pergamon.

Meichenbaum, D. (1994) *Mourning process*, Philadephia, PA: The Charles Press.

Mesey, G. and Robbins, I. (2001) 'Usefulness and validity of post-traumatic stress disorder as a psychiatric category', *British Medical Journal*, vol 323, 8 September, pp 561-3.

Miller, N.E. (1959) 'Liberalization of basic S-R concepts: extensions to conflict behaviour, motivation and social learning', in S Koch (ed) *Psychology: A study of science*, vol 2, New York, NY: McGann-Hill.

Miller, S.M. and Birnbaum, A. (1988) 'Putting the life back into "life events": towards a cognitive social learning analysis of the coping process', in S. Fisher and J. Reason (eds) *Handbook of life stress, cognition and health*, NY: Wiley.

Mitchell, J.T. (1983) 'When disaster strikes – the critical incident stress debriefing process', *Journal of Emergency Medical Services*, Baltimore, vol 8, no 1, January, pp 36-9.

Mitchell, M. (ed) (1997) *The aftermath of road accidents: Psychological, social and legal perspectives*, London: Routledge.

Mitchell, M., Stevenson, K. and Poole, D. (2000) 'Managing post incident reactions in the police service', prepared by the police research unit and the occupational health unit for the Health and Safety Executive.

Mowrer, O.H. (1947) 'On the dual nature of learning: a reinterpretation of "conditioning" and "problem solving"', *Howard Educational Review*, vol 17, pp 102-48, and in D. Black, M. Newman, J. Harris-Hendrick and G. Mesey (eds) (1997) *Psychological trauma – A developmental approach*, London: Gaskell Royal College of Psychiatrists.

Murgatroyd, S. and Woolfe, K. (1982) *Coping with crisis: Understanding and helping people in need*, London: Harper and Row.

Myers (1989) 'Mental health and disaster, preventive approaches to intervention', in R. Gist and B. Lubin (eds) *Psychological aspects of disaster*, NY: Wiley.

National Institute for Health and Clinical Excellence (NICE) (2005) *National guidelines for the treatment of post traumatic stress disorder*, London: NICE.

National Institute for Social Work (1996) *Journeys of discovery: Creative learning from disasters*, London: National Institute for Social Work.

Newburn, M. (1993) *Making a difference? Social work after Hillsborough*, London: National Institute for Social Work.

Nutt, D., Davidson J.R.T. and Zohar, J. (2000) *Post-traumatic stress disorder diagnosis, management and treatment*, London: Martin Dunitz.

Orner, R.J., Avery, A. and Boddy, C. (1997) 'Status and development of critical incident stress management services in the United Kingdom national health service and other emergency services combined', *Occupational Medicine*, vol 47, no 4, pp 203-9.

Parad, H. and Lindemann, E. (1968) 'A study of crisis orientated planned short term interventions, Part II', *Scientific Consultations*, vol 49, pp 418-26.

Parkes, C.M. (1986) *Bereavement: Studies of grief in adult life*, London: Penguin.

Parkes, C.M. (1972, 1996) *Bereavement: Studies of grief in adult life*, London: Tavistock/Routledge, Harmondsworth: Pelican and New York, NY: International Universities Press.

Parkes, C.M. and Weiss, R.S. (1983), *Recovery from bereavement*, New York, NY: Basic Books.

Parkes, C.M., Laungani, P. and Young. B. (1997, 2003) *Death and bereavement across cultures*, Hove: Brunner/Routledge.

Parkinson, F. (2001) 'Debriefing and research', *Counselling and Psychotherapy Research*, vol 1, no 3, pp 177-80.

Perlman, H. (1957) *Social casework*, Chicago, IL: University of Chicago.

Peterson, K.C., Prout, K. and Schwarz, R.A. (1991) 'New theoretical dimensions of PTSD', in D. Black, M. Newman, J. Harris-Hendrick and G. Mesey (eds) (1997) *Psychological trauma – A developmental approach*, London: Gaskell Royal College of Psychiatrists.

Pitman, R.K., Lasko, N.B. and Orr, S.P. (1993) 'Psycho-physiological assessment of post traumatic stress disorder imagery in World War II and Korean combat veterans', *Journal of Abnormal Psychology*, vol 102, pp 152-9.

Prigerson, H.G., Jacobs, S.C., Roesnneck, R.A. and Maciejewski, P.K. (1999) 'Criteria for traumatic grief and PTSD', *The British Journal of Psychiatry*, vol 174, no 6, pp 560-61.

Rachman, S.J. (1980) 'Emotional processing behaviour research and therapy,' *The Behaviour Therapist*, vol 18, pp 51-60.

Raphael, B. (1984) *Anatomy of bereavement*, New York, NY: Basic Books.

Raphael, B. (1986) *When disaster strikes – Handbook for caring professions*, London: Hutchinson.

Raphael, B., Meldrum, L. and McFarlane, A.C. (1995) 'Does debriefing after psychological trauma work?' *British Medical Journal*, vol 310, pp 1479-80.

Raphael, B., Singh, B., Bradbury, L. and Lambert, F. (1983-84) 'Who helps the helpers? The effects of disaster on the rescue workers', *Omega*, vol 14, no 1, pp 9-20.

Reid, N.G. and Boore, V.R.P (1987) 'Research methods and statistics in healthcare', in D. Black, M. Newman, J. Harris-Hendrick and G. Mesey (eds) (1997) *Psychological trauma – A developmental approach*, London: Gaskell Royal College of Psychiatrists.

Resick, P.A. (2001) *Stress and trauma*, Hove: Psychology Press (Taylor and Francis Group).

Robinson, R. (2003) 'Psychological debriefing: a closer look at the facts', *Critical Incident Stress Management Foundation Australia newsletter*, special edn, October.

Robinson, R. and Mitchell, J.T. (1993) 'Evaluation of psychological debriefing', *Journal of Traumatic Stress*, vol 6, no 3, pp 367-82.

Roger, D. (1988) 'The role of emotional control in human stress responses', British Psychological Society annual conference, Leeds.

Roger, D. and Jameson, J. (1988) 'Individual differences delayed heart-rate recovery following stress: the role of extraversion and emotional control', *Personality and Individual Differences*, vol 9, no 4, pp 721-6.

Roger, D. and Morris, J. (1991) 'The internal structure of the EPQ scales', *Personality and Individual Differences*, vol 10, pp 845-53.

Roger, D. and Najarian, B. (1989) 'The construction and validation of a new scale for emotional control', *Personality and Individual Differences*, vol 10, pp 845-53.

Roger, D. and Nesshoever, M. (1987) 'The construction and preliminary validation of a scale for measuring emotional control', *Personality and Individual Differences*, vol 8, pp 527-34.

Rose, S. (2000) 'Evidence-based practice will affect the way we work', *Counselling*, vol 12, no 2, March, p 11

Rose, S. and Bisson, J. (1989) 'Brief early psychological interventions following trauma: a systematic review of literature', *Journal of Traumatic Stress*, vol 4, pp 697-710.

Rose, S., Berwin, C.R., Andrews, B. and Kirk, M. (1999) 'A randomised controlled trial of individual psychological debriefing for victims of violent crime', *Psychological Medicine*, vol 29, pp 793-9.

Rose, S., Bisson, J. and Wessely, S. (2002) 'Psychological debriefing for preventing post traumatic stress disorder (PTSD) (Cochrane Review)', in *The Cochrane Library*, issue 4.

Rosenblatt, P.C., Walsh, R.P. and Jackson, D.A. (2003) *Grief and mourning in cross cultural perspective*, Washington, DC: HRAF Press.

Ross, R.J., Ball, W.A. and Sullivan, K.A. (1989) 'Sleep disturbances as the hallmark of post traumatic stress disorder', *American Journal of Psychiatry*, vol 146, and in D. Black, M. Newman, J. Harris-Hendrick and G. Mesey (eds) (1997) *Psychological trauma – A developmental approach*, London: Gaskell Royal College of Psychiatrists.

Scheppe, K.L. and Bart, P. (1983) 'Through women's eyes: defining dander in the wake of sexual assault', *Journal of Social Issues*, vol 39, pp 63-81.

Seligman, M.E.P. (1995a) 'The effectiveness of psychotherapy: the consumer reports study', *American Psychologist*, vol 50, no 12, pp 965-74, December.

Seligman, M.E.P. (1995b) *Helplessness: On depression, development and death*, San Francisco, CA: M.H. Freeman.

Shakespeare, W. (1598) *Collection of plays*, Oxford: Heinemann Education Publishers.

Shakespeare, W. (1972) *Henry VI*, Part 1, Act 2, Scene II, Oxford: Oxford University Press.

Shapiro, F. (1989) 'Efficacy of the eye movement desensitisation procedure in the treatment of traumatic memories', *Journal of Traumatic Stress Studies*, vol 2, pp 199-223.

Shoor, M. and Speed, M. (1963) *Death, delinquency and the mourning process*, Philadelphia, PA: The Charles Press.

Short, P. (1979) 'Victims and helpers', in R.I Heathcode and B.G Thorn (eds) *Natural hazards in Australia*, Canberra: Australian Academy of Science.

Silverman, D. (ed) (1998) *Qualitative research, theory, method and practice*, London: Sage Publications.

Smallwood, J. (2004) *Psychological care in the aftermath of trauma*, Report prepared for the Area Psychological Group, NHS Ayrshire and Arran.

Snaith, R.P. and Zigmone, A.S. (1983) 'The hospital anxiety and depression scale', *Acta Psychiatrica*, Scandinavia, vol 67, pp 361-70.

Solomon, S.D. (1985) 'Enhancing social support for disaster victims', in B. Sowder (ed) *Disasters and mental health: Selected contemporary perspectives*, DHHS Publications, no 14-8521, Washington, DC: US Government Printing Office, pp 107-21.

Solomon, S.D., Gerrity, E.T. and Muff, A.M. (1993) 'Efficacy of treatments of post-traumatic stress disorder: an empirical review', *JAMA*, vol 268, no 5, pp 633-8.

Staudachel, K. (1987) 'Natural disasters', in J.P. Wilson and B. Raphael (eds) (1993) *International handbook of traumatic stress syndromes*, New York, NY: Plenum Press, Part IV, pp 750-60.

Stearns, A.K. (1989) *Coming back*, London: Methuen.

Stephens, C. (1996) 'Debriefing, social support and PTSD in the New Zealand police: testing a multidimensional model of organisational traumatic stress'. *The Australasian Journal of Disaster and Trauma Studies*, New Zealand: Massey University.

Sterweis, D. (1984) 'Traumatic stress experienced by children and adolescents', in J.P. Wilson and B. Raphael (eds) (1993) *International handbook of traumatic stress syndromes*, New York, NY: Plenum Press, Part V, pp 820-4.

Stewart, M. (1988) 'Survivors who must turn tragedy into opportunity', *Social Work Today*, 11 August.

Stewart, M. (1989) 'Mirrors of pain', *Community Care*, 2 February.

Stroebe, M.S. and Schut, H.A.W. (1999) 'The dual model of coping with bereavement: rationale and description', *Death Studies*, vol 23, pp 197-224.

Stroebe, M.S., Stroebe, W. and Haussan, R. (eds) (1993) *Handbook of bereavement, theory, research and intervention*, Cambridge: Cambridge University Press.

Taylor, A.J.W. and Frazer A.G. (1980) 'Interim report of the stress effects on the recovery teams after Mt Erebus disaster', *New Zealand Medical Journal*, vol 91, pp 311-2.

Taylor, A.J.W. and Frazer, A.G. (1982) 'The stress of post disaster body handling and victim identification work', *Journal of Human Stress*, vol 8, pp 4-12.

Tehrani, N. (2004) *Trauma in the workplace: Concepts, assessment and interventions*, Hove and New York, NY: Brunner-Routledge.

Turnbull, G.J. (1997) 'Classification', in D. Black, M. Newman, J. Harris-Hendrick and G. Mesey (eds) *Psychological trauma – A developmental approach*, London: Gaskell Royal College of Psychiatrists, p 19.

Ursano, R. (2002) 'Post traumatic stress disorder', *The New England Journal of Medicine*, vol 346, no 2, pp 130-3.

Van der Kolk, B.A. McFarlane, A.C. and Weisaeth, L. (1996) *Traumatic stress: the effects of overwhelming experience on mind, body and society*, NY, Guildford Press.

Velsen, C.V. (1997) 'Theoretical Models of PTSD: psychoanalytical modes', in D. Black, M. Newman, J. Harris-Hendrick and G. Mesey (eds) *Psychological trauma – A developmental approach*, London: Gaskell Royal College of Psychiatrists.

Wainwright, D. and Calnan, M. (2002) 'Work stress: the making of a modern epidemic', *British Medical Journal*, vol 325, p 1307.

Waite, T. (1994) *Taken on trust*, London: Hodder and Stoughton.

Weisaeth, L. (1994) 'Preventing after-effects of disaster trauma: the information and support centre', *Prehospital Disaster Med* (2004), Jan-May, vol 19, no 1, pp 86-9.

Weisaeth, L. (2002) 'The European history of psychotraumatology', *Journal of Traumatic Stress*, vol 15, no 6, pp 443-52.

Wessely, S. and Deahl, M. (2003) 'Psychological debriefing is a waste of time', *British Journal of Psychiatry*, vol 183, pp 12-14.

Wessely, S., Rose, S. and Bisson, J. (1998) 'A systematic review of brief psychological interventions ("debriefing") for treatment of immediate trauma related symptoms and prevention of post traumatic stress disorder', *Cochrane Review* in the Cochrane Library, Issue 2 Oxford, Software.

Whitham and Newburn (1991) *Coping with tragedy: managing the response to two disasters*, Nottinghamshire County Council.

WHO (World Health Organisation) (1978) *Mental disorders: Glossary and guide to their classification in accordance with the ninth revision of the International classification of diseases* (ICD-9), Geneva: WHO.

Wilson, J.P. (speaker) (1983) 'New theoretical dimensions of PTSD (cassette recording)', Dayton, OH: Serco Marketing and Human Resource Initiative, reported in K.C. Peterson, K. Prout and R.A. Schwarz, (1991) *Post traumatic stress disorder − a clinician's guide*, New York, NY: Plenum Press.

Wilson, J.P. and Krauss, G.E. (1985) 'Predicting post traumatic stress disorder among vietnam veterans', in W.E. Kelly (ed) *Post traumatic stress disorder and the war veteran patient*, pp 102-47, New York, NY: Brunner/Mazel.

Winnicott, D.W. (1974) 'Fear of breakdown', *International review of psychoanalysis*, vol 1, and in D. Black, M. Newman, J. Harris-Hendrick and G. Mesey (eds) (1997) *Psychological trauma − A developmental approach*, London: Gaskell Royal College of Psychiatrists, pp 103-7.

Wolfe, J. (1990) 'Women veterans', in *Updates and trends*, NCP clinical newsletter 1, pp 9-10.

Worden, J.W. (1988, 1991) *Grief counselling and grief therapy*, London and New York, NY: Routledge.

Yassen, J. (1995) 'Preventing secondary traumatic stress disorder in compassion fatigue', in C. Figley (ed) *Compassion fatigue: Coping with secondary stress disorder in those who treat the traumatised*, Brunner/Mazel Psychosocial Stress Series, New York, NY: Brunner/Mazel.

Yule, W. (1990) 'The effects of disasters on children', *Bereavement Care*, Cruse, spring.

Yule, W. (2000) *Post traumatic stress disorders: Concepts and therapy*, 2nd edn, Chichester: Wiley.

Yule, W. and Williams, R.M. (1990) 'Post traumatic stress reactions in children', *Journal of Traumatic Stress*, vol 3, no 2, pp 279-95.

Yule, W. and Gold, A. (1993) *Wise before the event: Coping with crises in schools*, London: Calouste Gulbenkian Foundation.

Zuckerman, M. and Spielberger, C.D. (eds) (1976) *Emotions and anxiety*, New York, NY: Wiley, and in J. Wilson, and B. Raphael (eds) (1993) *International handbook of traumatic stress syndromes*, New York, NY: Plenum Press.

Appendix

List of case studies

Case study 1   Death of a golfer
Case study 2   Road traffic accident involving death of a child
Case study 3   Home accident
Case study 4   Hillsborough football stadium tragedy (1989)
Case study 5   Bank raid
Case study 6   Piper Alpha oil rig
Case study 7   The Kegworth air crash (1989)
Case study 8   9/11
Case study 9   Enniskillen bomb (1987) and Omagh bomb (1998)
Case study 10 Hostage-taking to achieve funding for terrorist organisations
Case study 11 Hungerford and Dunblane
Case study 12 Lockerbie
Case study 13 Bomb victim – reactions recalled
Case study 14 Kegworth air disaster – care of relatives in hospital
Case study 15 Rehabilitation following an industrial accident
Case study 16 Survivor syndrome following an air crash
Case study 17 Mother with severe burns injuries following terrorist attack
Case study 18 Aberfan
Case study 19 Strategic planning – Dunblane
Case study 20 Multi-agency working following bomb blast in Belfast

Index